I0453912

The Room
on the Right

The Room on the Right

A Memoir of Despair, Hope, and Reckoning in the Face of Abuse, Trauma, and PTSD

Lawrence Mieczkowski, MD

GFB

Copyright © 2025 by Lawrence Mieczkowski, MD

All rights reserved.

No part of this book may be reproduced, or stored in a retrieval system, or transmitted in any form or by any means, electronic, mechanical, photocopying, recording, or otherwise, without express written permission of the publisher.

Some names and identifying details have been changed to protect the privacy of individuals.

Published by GFB™, Seattle
www.girlfridayproductions.com

Produced by Girl Friday Productions

Design: Paul Barrett
Production editorial: Alyssa Brillinger
Project management: Abi Pollokoff

Image credits: cover © Adobe Stock/Dolores Harvey; Adobe Stock/Олег Мальшаков; Adobe Stock/bongkarn

ISBN (hardcover): 978-1-964721-70-5
ISBN (paperback): 978-1-964721-71-2
ISBN (ebook): 978-1-964721-72-9

Library of Congress Control Number: 2024927515

First edition

For the millions of children, teenagers, and adults who have experienced trauma and abuse.

May this book help in some way.

CONTENT WARNING

Be advised that this memoir contains explicit details of abuse, depression, PTSD, suicidal thoughts, and other content, which some readers may find disturbing.

CHAPTER 1

Crossing the Threshold

When I was seven years old and said my bedtime prayers of five Hail Marys and five Our Fathers, I always silently added another prayer: "Please, God, let me die in my sleep and take me to heaven. In your name, amen." When I woke up every morning, I questioned why God had not answered my prayer. Bizarre as it may seem, I envied those children who had cancer, with their sad stories shared on telethons, knowing that most of them would pass away soon. I always thought how unlucky I was to have the parents I did and to live in our house at 815 Pekruhn Court in Polish Hill, a working-class neighborhood in Steubenville, Ohio.

To the outsider, there was nothing ominous about the appearance of our home. It looked like other houses in our neighborhood, a two-story wood-frame dwelling constructed in the early 1900s, similar in design to thousands of buildings in the downtown section of the city, providing shelter for the families of the men who walked to work in the nearby steel mills or coal mine. The exterior of the property was well maintained by my father; the concrete surrounding our home was swept and hosed off daily in warm weather; the front porch always had flower boxes filled with marigolds, violets, and other annuals in the summer; and the white wooden structure with green trim was repainted every other year. On the inside, however, our home was dimly lit, dirty, cluttered with my mother's stuff that she refused to give away or throw out, and overcrowded with small living spaces: a kitchen, dining room, and living room on the first floor and three small bedrooms and a tiny bathroom on the second floor for two adults and seven children. Like other inner-city homes, a concrete sidewalk served as our front yard with only a tiny patch of grass in the back, barely large enough to hang clothes out to dry on sunny days and to plant tomato and green onion seedlings for fresh vegetables in the summer.

In our household, I was the youngest of the seven children born to Stanley and Eleanore Mieczkowski. My mother was forty-two years old and my father was forty-four in 1956 when I was born, their ages not being unusual in large Catholic families at the time. Within a year of my birth, my oldest sister, Joanne, married and moved into a small second-floor apartment in the large five-unit building next to our house that my uncle John had built and owned.

Oddly, considering my parents were Catholic, the seven of us were spaced three years apart, unlike other families in which children came one year after another. Because there was a twenty-year age difference between Joanne, my oldest sister, and me, she was often mistaken for my mother when we were together at a social gathering or the swimming pool. My parents likely never considered that having seven children so spread apart would have a major impact in the dynamics of our household, since there were essentially two generations of siblings living under one roof. Since she lived next door,

Joanne was always around, as if she never really moved out. She, Patricia, and Stas were the three oldest. The connections and attitudes among them were similar to my middle-aged parents, quite different from the world Bob, Mary Ellen, and I knew. My brother Tom, being the middle child of the seven, crossed over both groups.

Everyone in the neighborhood was raised Catholic, with Saint Stanislaus Church, a massive cathedral-like structure just a stone's throw from our front porch, looming large over us, both literally and culturally, with the Felician Sisters ensuring we knew our catechism as well as our ABCs.

Yet, there were horrible things that occurred in our house that caused me to prefer death over life. Hidden behind the well-maintained facade was a life few of my friends saw or had to deal with in their own homes. I had been neglected, unloved, underfed, and physically battered by my parents. When the abuse started, I was a four-year-old child and small for my age, likely a result of inadequate nutrition. Both parents towered over me like giants. Nearly everything I did was wrong in my mother's eyes, and her preferred method of punishment was hitting me with a wooden spoon that she kept in a kitchen drawer. My two oldest sisters also physically disciplined me when I did something wrong, one time by my sister Patricia for simply leaving a dirty cereal bowl in the kitchen sink.

As a young child, I did all sorts of things that triggered my mother's wrath. One of the most vivid memories I have of being punished occurred when I was around four years old. My father was at work, and my mother might have been outside hanging the laundry to dry. (We didn't have a clothes dryer at the time.) My older siblings were in school, and I was alone in the house when I drew on the living room wallpaper with crayons, filling in the printed swirls on the paper with assorted colors, trying to stay within the lines, just like I would have done in a coloring book.

When my mother discovered what I had done, she grabbed my little arm with one hand and dragged me behind her from the living room to the kitchen. Still holding on to me, she pulled the twelve-inch wooden spoon from the drawer. Pleading with her not to hit me, I said that I was sorry. "Please let me go. Don't hit me. I promise I'll never do it again. I promise." Being terrified, I started crying before the first strike of the spoon. She beat me on my upper back, shoulders, and arms, screaming, "Don't you ever color on the wall again!"

One strike, then another, then another, and I would cry and beg her to stop and let me go. I covered my face and head with my arms and hands as best I could at my early age. She yelled, "You're supposed to know better" as she hit me with the spoon. How was I supposed to know better as a young child? It felt like she was beating me for hours, even though it may have gone on for only seconds before her rage subsided or I was able to break free of her grip.

My mother hit me if I spilled milk from the carton onto the kitchen floor, got muddy playing in the nearby creek, or was noisy like all kids. With the slightest irritation, she'd lose her temper and would grab me by the arm and drag me to the kitchen so she could get the spoon. One of the longest punishments came after I snuck a nickel from her change purse to buy a popsicle from Mr. Softee one evening in summer after she had said that I didn't deserve to get a treat.

Yet, the duration of a punishment didn't always correlate to the severity of the offense but often seemed more related to the mood she was in at the time. Perhaps she was reeling after a beating from my father and she transferred her pain and anger down to me. Maybe that was why she didn't hit me as much when my father was away on a fishing weekend. On rare occasions she'd let my misbehavior go, which always shocked me.

Each time she hit me, I cried from the emotional hurt as

much as the physical pain from the beatings. Why did she not see me as a child worthy of love? How could she treat me this way? Wanting to strike back at her, I retaliated in the only way that I could as a four-year-old boy: I screamed at her, "I hate you! I hate you! I wish you weren't my mother." Often, after such an encounter, I ran up the stairs and curled up under a blanket on the bed, sobbing into my pillow, secretly wanting her to come upstairs to comfort me after she'd struck me, saying that she was sorry for what she did, and to tell me she loved me. My wish never came true. When my older siblings were in the house, they did nothing to stop her. I felt completely alone and thought I must be a terrible kid to warrant such a severe beating.

My father was also physically abusive to me at an early age. He didn't use the wooden spoon; instead, his usual method of violence directed my way was a backhanded slap to my face when I did something that triggered his short temper. He hated it when I dripped coffee on the floor as I carried my cup over from the counter to the table. Although I tried hard not to, the cups were big for my little hands, and they were hard to hold. He'd yell at me, "You do this all the time. I've told you a hundred times to not fill the cup to the brim." Thwack. A backhand slap to my face. Neither he nor my mother ever poured the coffee into my cup so that I wouldn't get burned or added the milk for me so that I might not drop the heavy container, making a mess. I didn't intentionally spill the coffee just to get slapped by my father. You might be thinking, why did they even let me drink coffee for breakfast when I was that young? Couldn't tell you.

My mother often deferred punishment to my father, threatening, "Wait till your old man gets home." The anticipation of the upcoming beating from him was punishment by itself, knowing that he would unfasten his leather belt from his pants and whip me on my butt and the back of my legs for whatever crime I had committed. On these occasions, since the abuse was always worse when he was drunk on returning home, if I saw him staggering up the street, I took off to hide in the hills for hours, often missing dinner.

Even at that age, I physically resisted the punishment by pulling away or squirming enough to break free of my mother's hold while she was striking me with the spoon or when my father hit me with his belt. I would run through the house, exit through the front door, and then hide in the nearby woods for a while, hoping that my mother might calm down and soften the inevitable punishment when I returned home, if I was lucky.

Our house had a shotgun-style layout. From front to back there was the concrete porch, living room, dining room, and then the kitchen, all in a row. The entrance to the living room from the porch had two doors, an inner storm door and an outer aluminum screen door, which had a pane of glass in the lower section and a removable screen in the top. Except for the winter months, the storm door was always wide open to allow fresh air into the house since we didn't have air-conditioning. The screen door latch didn't work well, so you had to deliberately pull on the door handle to firmly latch the door. Well, no one did that. My family members were used to simply pushing on the screen door frame or the lower window to nudge the door open.

It was another day when I got in trouble for something that I can't recall. My mother grabbed my arm as she opened the drawer to get the spoon for another beating. Squirming out of her hold, I broke free and took off, hoping that I could make it into the woods above our street to hide again without her seeing me. Through the kitchen and then the small dining room, I ran, my little heart pounding with fear. She was only three or four steps behind me, screaming, "You're really going to get it when I catch you." Just a few more feet until I was safe, and then I streaked through the living room and, as I normally did, pushed on the middle of the pane of glass to pop open the door. But the screen door didn't give; someone had pulled it tightly and latched it shut. With my arms outstretched I hit the windowpane, shattered the glass, and flew through a jagged portal, in a flying position almost like I was Superman, and unbelievably landed safely on my hands and knees beyond the glass shards now lying scattered on the concrete porch. Unlike today's safety glass, the windowpane hadn't broken up into hundreds of small pebble-like pieces. I quickly looked back at the razor-sharp splintered triangles of glass still tightly bound in the aluminum frame and saw the hole that I had created by bursting through the middle.

The flight instinct kicked in as I quickly got up, jumped down the steps, and started running. I knew they would look for me in the woods, so instead I went up our street and then took a right just past the apartment building next to our house and scooted up the two flights of wooden stairs and hid in a corner of the porch where no one could see me. I crouched down, shivering in fear. I had never been so terrified, so afraid of what would happen to me, so afraid of being punished. What terrible thing could I have done at such an early age to justify that kind of pursuit? On top of being beaten by my mother for whatever I did, I knew that I would also face a severe beating from my father with his belt for breaking the glass. The thought that I might have cut myself and was bleeding didn't really cross my mind until I had sat there silently listening to the frantic cries of my mother, my sister Mary Ellen, and my oldest sister, Joanne, pleading for me to come out and to stop hiding. I'm sure they thought that I couldn't have gone through a glass window without being cut.

After what seemed to be hours, I heard Mary Ellen calling for me. She was at the bottom of the stairs leading up to Joanne's apartment but couldn't see me. She heard me crying and climbed up the flight of steps to my hiding place. She was relieved that I wasn't bleeding anywhere and called out to the others that she had found me. I don't recall what happened next, whether I was punished or not. I know for certain that I wasn't hugged and comforted. I would've remembered that. You'd think that this entire traumatic and horrifying experience would've steered my parents to ease up on the severity of the physical punishments they used. It didn't.

As a child, I lived in a state of constant fear and sadness since physical abuse from my parents was almost a daily occurrence. The emotional neglect was also too much to cope with. If dying was the way to end the abuse from my parents, then so be it. I just wanted the pain to end and figured no one would really miss me since I already had been told repeatedly for years by my parents, as well as my two oldest sisters, Joanne and Patricia, and my oldest brother, Stas, how much of a pest and burden I was. None of them realized or cared how much the physical abuse and belittling affected me as a child, contributing to the emotional abuse I suffered for years. I hated them as much as a seven-year-old child could.

When I was a bit older, I began hoping that my father would die, even thinking about doing something to him. The conscious thoughts were accompanied by recurring dreams in which others suspected that I had in fact killed him and buried his body in the hills above our home. I would have to make it look like an accident, perhaps hiding behind a rack of jackets on the landing of the cellar stairs and then tripping him so that he would tumble down the steps and land on the concrete basement floor.

My inner rage was just below the surface. The anger I felt toward my parents and the way they treated me became part of who I was. No one questioned why a straight-A student always got a C in conduct and didn't accept authority or take corrections well. My anger would find its way to the surface in fistfights with other boys in the neighborhood when I was in second or third grade, contradicting the nuns on Catholic doctrine, which resulted in punishments with the school's leather strap, in fights with high school classmates, or on the high school football field when I stood up to a belligerent coach and got into a physical altercation with him. Later, as a physician lecturing across the country, I never hesitated to call out an arrogant physician on their rude behavior, to the dismay of the pharmaceutical representatives in the room.

My own death wish almost became real when I was nine or ten. It wasn't until I was in counseling that I considered my reckless behavior in that context. Climbing trees was one of my favorite activities that I could do alone, which I continued doing even after falling from a high perch on a pine tree and landing on my butt uninjured. I ignored the danger of riding sleds down steep snow-covered streets into oncoming traffic. I ignored the risk when my friends and I walked two miles from our neighborhood to cross a railroad bridge spanning the broad Ohio River to fish for catfish and carp in a pond on the West Virginia side. Early in the summer of 1968, when I was twelve years old, a cousin my age was playing in the street when he was run over by a car driven by a fourteen-year-old boy. I wasn't there to see him get hit when the teenager lost control, pinning my cousin under the front of the car, resulting in a broken pelvis and a compound fracture of his thigh bone. He could have died from those serious injuries. No one ever knew my secret wish that it had been me who had gotten run over and maybe would have died.

My mother's physical battering became less frequent when I was about ten years old. It wasn't because she had a divine revelation that the near-daily physical abuse was wrong; rather, I was physically bigger and stronger and began to defend myself. The anger that I had suppressed for years started to surface. I easily wrestled the spoon out of my mother's hand, although she might still try to slap me with her hand. She began to have a look of resignation on her face, acknowledging to herself that she was losing the war with me, perhaps thinking, *What's the point? Larry's just going to grab it from me.*

As for my father, he still occasionally slapped me on the face when the moment presented itself, until I challenged him after he hit me with the back of his hand when I was thirteen or fourteen. This time, his action unleashed years of buried rage that I had held in. I glared and challenged him, "Go ahead. Hit me on the other side." My anger was boiling over as I turned my face, and he then slapped the other side even harder. There were no tears rolling down my face as I openly confronted him, now face to face, almost spitting at him in fury, "That's the last time you'll ever hit me. I swear to God that I'll kill you if you touch me again," and I walked away. I meant it in the moment, and he knew it. He never touched me again. The years of physical abuse from my parents had only made me more willful and angrier. And I made sure it stopped.

By that age, I was able to get away from the confines of our house, spending hours in the hills next to where we lived, playing baseball, football, or basketball—anything that would minimize my interactions with my parents. I ignored my mother's discouraging words and attempts to restrict my activities away from home, such as playing organized football and baseball or signing up for the Boy Scouts. During my high school and college years, I was learning how to pack my past abuse into boxes that I taped shut and stacked in the basement of my mind, not to be opened with anyone.

However, two days after my college graduation, a ticking time bomb exploded at 2:30 in the morning, blasting open the doorway to my past and ripping through the sealed boxes. Within days my life changed. Whatever inner peace I had was gone, replaced by fear and anxiety. Everyone and everything posed a danger, just as it had been when I was a child. Afterward, I was constantly hypervigilant when walking in a mall or a grocery store and was terrified to go out at night for any reason, even just to the grocery store. Recurring nightmares of being chased or threatened interrupted my sleep nightly.

The darkness of depression, the anxiety, and the turmoil in my head started slowly to emerge in my late twenties and worsened over the next decade. In 1985, my wife, daughter, and I moved back to Cincinnati, where I had gone to medical school, after I completed my three-year internal medicine residency in Pittsburgh. We bought our first home in the well-to-do Hyde Park area of Cincinnati and after seven years moved to the village of Wyoming (Ohio). Although my depression worsened throughout my thirties, I was good at hiding it, but by the time I was in my early forties, suicide seemed to be the only way to end the constant turmoil in my head. I didn't understand then how the trauma of my past was the trigger to a host of dark and threatening emotions.

After the Columbine massacre on April 20, 1999, my depression, hypervigilance, periodic thoughts of suicide, nightmares, and intrusive daytime thoughts became more persistent and intense. Watching the videos of these monsters dressed in black, stalking classmates and going from person to person killing one after another, made me sick to my stomach and was a trigger for my memories. I wanted to walk away from the TV but found myself morbidly drawn to the newsclips shown on every network. The Columbine shootings took me back to when I was a ten-year-old watching the newsclips of the Vietnam War, afraid that my brother Tom, who was in the army, would be shipped overseas and killed. Black body bags containing dead soldiers—one after another—were lifted into helicopters and taken away from the battlefields where they had been alive only an hour before. The shootings also unearthed that terror I faced in the early-morning hours of May 17, 1978, after my college graduation, bringing back the fear of what could have happened to me and my sleeping parents that night.

The fear and daily intrusive thoughts affected my work as a physician in private practice, making it difficult to concentrate while seeing twenty to thirty patients daily. As the months progressed, I fell deeper into the dark hole of depression and fear. It was no longer just strangers that I feared. I began to see danger in the faces of people I had known for decades—they had become people to fear. I couldn't put these feelings aside. As it became more obvious that something was wrong with me, my friends at work expressed their concerns over my depression and their worries that I might end my life. I ignored their words, brushing them away with my own: "I'm fine. You don't need to worry about me." After nearly a year of cajoling from them and outbursts with my family, I finally agreed that I needed help. In 2001 I reached out to my primary care physician for a referral to a psychiatrist, providing vague details of my past and how I was feeling. When I called the psychiatrist's office to schedule the appointment, the receptionist told me that he kept his own calendar and would call me himself. When he called back later that day, my receptionist interrupted me in the exam room, saying, "There's a Dr. Kirkendoll on the line." I said, "Tell him I will be right there." I apologized for the interruption to my patient and went to my private office, closed the door, and picked up the phone, saying, "Hello, this is Larry Mieczkowski."

"Hi. This is Dr. Dan Kirkendoll. I'm returning your phone call. How can I help you?"

I nervously introduced myself, told him what I did as a physician, and shared the key reasons for my phone call— the trauma of dealing with my older brother Tom, who had schizophrenia, my abusive childhood, and my worsening depression. He listened patiently and agreed to take me on as a new patient. I mentioned my concern about the impact on my medical license of seeing a psychiatrist. He reassured me that I need not worry about it; he had numerous patients who were physicians. I was very relieved, since this concern had been part of my reluctance to seek help over the past years. I was self-employed and couldn't work if my medical license was suspended because of my depression. I felt safe talking to him unlike so many others who weren't. He sounded like a caring physician, and I was glad that I had found him. Yet, when he hung up, the feeling that I was a failure came roaring back, as I again was ashamed that I had not been strong enough to deal with my issues on my own.

On the appointment day, my patient schedule was cut short so I could leave my office early to avoid the Cincinnati traffic on the hour-long drive to his office in Mount Lookout, a lovely suburban neighborhood. It was next to the Hyde Park neighborhood where my wife, Beth, and I and our two children had lived for seven years. As I approached the Edwards Road exit off I-71, my anxiety worsened while my stomach ached. I passed Busken's Bakery, which I frequented years ago to get my daily cup of coffee and zucchini muffin for my long drive to my office in Kettering. I drove past the country club that I had hoped to be able to join, through Hyde Park, and down to Mount Lookout. As I slowly approached the square at the center of the neighborhood, looking for parking, my apprehension and anxiety levels were overwhelming. I wasn't sure that I could do this.

I had arrived early, too early to sit in the waiting room for thirty minutes, so I parked and began walking around the square. The area was familiar to me because my family and I frequented Zips, a popular pub there well known for their hamburgers and skinny fries. The kids just loved eating there. I choked up as those memories surfaced of happier times when my children were young, weekends were unscheduled, and life just felt easier.

Eventually I walked up the steps and entered the office building, a converted old home. The dimly lit waiting room was empty and had enough seats for eight people, and various end tables topped with magazines. I immediately heard the white noise machine in the corner, there I presumed to muffle not only conversations but also the sounds of crying. Since the receptionist had left for the day, the registration material with my name on it was on a clipboard left at the check-in window. At exactly 4:30 p.m., I heard an upstairs door open, footsteps, then creaking of the old wood stairs. A man stopped on the landing, looked over with kind eyes, and said, "Hello. I'm Dr. Kirkendoll."

He was somewhat older than me with gray hair and a gray beard and wasn't threatening, as other men often were. His kind face conveyed an appearance of caring and that he could understand my pain. "Hi, I'm Larry Mieczkowski. I go by Mitch."

With his hands and eyes, he motioned that his office was on the second floor. As we reached the upstairs landing, he said, "It's the room on the right." Since his office was located on the hill side of the house rather than the street side, it was quiet, without the sounds of traffic or of people walking by conversing. Although there were two windows, there wasn't much natural light because of the angle of the steep, treed hillside just three feet away. He had two well-worn brocade cloth chairs positioned along one wall facing each other, with his desk and diplomas against the other wall and hooks for jackets on the wall next to the door.

As we entered the room, he gestured that I should take the first chair, nearer the door, as he sat opposite me. I liked his mannerisms and style, and judging from his age, he had done this thousands of times. His certificates and awards were hanging on the walls. Besides graduating from the University of Cincinnati College of Medicine as I had, he was the recipient of three Golden Apple Awards from the medical school for his volunteer teaching services. It was impressive that he had earned one of the most prestigious accolades given to a medical school faculty member, reassuring me that I was seeing the right person.

The digital clock on his desk was positioned at an angle for him to monitor the time, just as I had two clocks in my exam rooms. Between our two chairs was a small glass table that contained a single box of tissues. We settled into our chairs, he crossed his legs, and he looked at me thoughtfully. Very deliberately and gently he asked, "Are you ready for this?"

Where do I start? How are we going to clean up this mess? I wasn't confident I could manage the sharp and traumatic pieces of my past now scattered in my brain. Hesitantly, I answered, "I'm not sure. This is going to be painful."

Over and over in the days after first scheduling this appointment, I had questioned how I might begin. He and I had not talked about his methods when we spoke on the phone. In this first session, Dr. Dan emphasized that I would set the pace for my counseling. Frankly, I was hoping he would take the reins, since I wanted this to be over as soon as possible. He reluctantly agreed to see me twice a week but cautioned that it might be too much.

"You need to have time between sessions to process and heal before the next session. You need to realize that the healing process takes time, often three or four years."

Years! I wasn't prepared to hear that. I was overwhelmed, dismayed, and confused that the treatment was going to take much longer than anticipated. I was exhausted from the depression, the nightmares, the constant fear, and my unhappy marriage. How was I going to deal with all of this? Every part of me was in a tornado of chaos and unhappiness.

I replied sarcastically, "Three years! You have three appointments to fix me." Time both stood still and flew by as I noticed Dr. Dan glance at the clock.

It's already twenty minutes into the fifty-five-minute session! What? I'm running out of time! How am I going to get through all this? I haven't even started! I need to talk to him about my older brother Tom and his schizophrenia and what happened to me after college graduation.

I panicked, wanting to say everything all at once. *I don't know how to do this. I can't do this.* I found myself wondering what he thought of me. *Is he judging me as countless others have done?* "Hey, Polack!" *The sneers of my older siblings.* "You'll never get into medical school."

My mouth was dry, my heart was racing, and I needed to escape from this place and run into the safety and comfort of the woods of my childhood above our street, like I had done so many times as a kid.

I don't recall what exactly triggered it—perhaps the sense of panic I was feeling then—but a memory from my childhood started flooding back. Dr. Dan saw that I had gone somewhere and was lost in my thoughts.

"What's going on?"

Somehow, I found the strength to begin talking about a part of my life that I had never shared with anyone. "I was five years old. It was an early evening in winter and already dark outside. My father had gone back to the nearby PRCU club, one of three private drinking clubs frequented by patrons of Polish American descent, after dinner, and he was unusually late coming back home, which meant that he had been drinking beer and shots of vodka for more than two hours. I knew that once again hell would break loose on his return. My mother had locked both the front and back doors to prevent him from coming in, knowing that he wouldn't have his keys with him. She had done this before on occasion, and all it did was pour gasoline on the fire. Usually, she would stay in the living room as he stumbled into the house. He was always so drunk that he barely made it up the stairs to pass out in his bed.

"This particular night, my older sister Mary Ellen and I were under the dining room table, crying, and I can't remember where my older brother Bob was. Neither of my two oldest brothers, Tom and Stas, were in the house; maybe they were at high school basketball practice. I pleaded with my mother to unlock the door, knowing it would only frustrate him more. When he realized my mother had locked him out again, he began pounding on the wooden door frame, shouting, 'Open this goddamn door, Eleanore! Open the door or I'm going to break the fucking window!'

"I cowered under the table, crying even harder, shivering in fear, pleading, 'Stop it, please stop it! Mom, please open the door. Just let him go upstairs to bed.' I wanted to run, to be anywhere else but under that table, but I had no place to go. My mother shouted at us, 'Don't you kids open the door!' She yelled at my father through the locked door, 'Go back to your beer joint and your whores! You drunk! I am going to call the police if you break the window!'

"My father pounded harder, and he was yelling, 'Larry, Mary Ellen, open the goddamn door or I'll whip you with my belt! Open this goddamn door!' Previous times when my mother had locked the door, my father whipped me with his leather belt afterward for not letting him in. I was always placed in the middle of my parents, and I was just a child. Turning to Mary Ellen, I asked, 'What should we do?' My parents went back and forth like this for what seemed like an eternity. Suddenly, the glass of the window in the kitchen door shattered, and my father reached inside and unlocked the door. I was terrified as he lumbered into the kitchen and in a rage grabbed my mother by her hair, and then my memory ends."

As the images of that horrific night faded, I mentally

returned to Dr. Kirkendoll's office, my heart pounding. I had been back under that table, reliving the experience as if it had happened yesterday. For the first time, face to face with another human being, I had openly described the hell I had lived through repeatedly as a small child. But this was just one incident; there was so much more that had happened.

Exhausted and drained, I felt my eyes well up with tears that then rolled down my face as I started sobbing with body-wrenching heaves and loud cries, letting out the pain I had bottled up all these years. Dr. Dan reached over and handed me a wad of tissues, leaned on the edge of his chair, and waited patiently for me to compose myself. As I dried my eyes and my breathing slowed, I glanced at the clock and saw that it was 5:25 p.m., time for the session to end. I stood up, tossed the wadded tearstained tissues into the trash basket located behind Dr. Dan, grabbed fresh ones, and reached for my jacket on the coat hook behind me. My session was over. We were both standing when he looked at me with understanding and empathy for my pain. "I'll see you next time," he said gently.

CHAPTER 2

The Aftermath

Dabbing at my wet cheeks, I walked down the stairs into the empty waiting room, relieved that no one would see me crying. When I got into my car, I sat there for a long time—exhausted but relieved that I had finally opened up to a counselor. The tears continued as I sobbed, remembering my abusive childhood, the beatings, and emotional pain. Although I'd found someone to walk alongside me through the memories as they emerged, I knew that I would be alone on the journey back to find them.

What have I done? How am I going to handle this?

While I was sitting in my car, other memories from my past surfaced. Running through the windowpane. Shards of glass everywhere. Everyone screaming, yelling, and calling my name. "Larry! Larry! Larry! Where are you?" Images of crying and yelling as I was lifted out of the bathtub. What did this mean? My brain was tossing me back and forth. Childhood visions, then current arguments with my wife. My recent outbursts of anger directed at my staff, patients, and my wife. My anger as a child. *Stop it! Stop it! Leave me alone,* I shouted in my head. But I couldn't stop it. I was there, back home in Steubenville, not in Cincinnati. This breakdown went on for at least ten minutes. I knew that I had just opened the Pandora's box of my life.

Slowly returning to the reality of the present, I gathered myself, pulled out of the parking spot, and began the twenty-minute drive across town to my home in Wyoming, a lovely upper-class village just north of Cincinnati. By the time I was close to home and took the exit off I-75, I was more composed.

As I drove north on Springfield Pike, there was a sharp transition from the gritty, aging business district of Hartwell Village to the well-kept lawns and lush oak trees in Wyoming. Multicolored Victorian houses with gables and large front porches lined the street. Our three-story home was one of the oldest in the village, having been built before the Civil War. Since it was spring, our lavender rhododendrons were in full bloom, as were the five white dogwood trees. Despite the house demanding so much of my time and money, I loved living in a historical home and the comfort it afforded.

After parking my car in our detached garage that had once been the site of a horse stable, I opened the screen door in the back of the house, said hello to my son, who was on the computer (as always) in my office, then walked into the kitchen. I heard my daughter practicing her violin for an upcoming high school orchestra concert. She heard me come in and yelled out, "Hello, Dad!"

My wife then came down from the bedroom to the kitchen. I had gone back and forth with her over the past months about seeing a counselor because of my worsening mood and my short fuse with her and the kids.

It was pizza night, so nothing was cooking on the stove. My wife and I exchanged our perfunctory welcome kiss before she asked me, "How did the session go?" I had prepared my-self for her questions about the visit, having gone through the script in my head two or three times on the drive home. But I wasn't prepared to tell her yet that I wanted out of our mar-riage. I needed Dr. Dan's help in sorting through my feelings and how to deal with splitting up on top of everything else I was wrestling with in my head.

I didn't waver in replying. "I liked him. He seems like a genuinely nice guy, and I think he'll be a good fit for me."

"When are you going to see him again?"

"We agreed on twice-a-week visits for now and will see how that goes. I'm seeing him this Friday."

"Do you want to talk about anything?"

I replied, "Not really. I'm exhausted and hungry." Shifting the discussion away from me, I asked, "Where are we getting the pizza from tonight?" I thought we were out of earshot from my son, but he yelled out, "LaRosa's." Both of my teenage children knew that I was seeing a counselor for my childhood issues, so I wasn't worried that he had heard the exchange be-tween their mom and me.

I didn't say much during dinner, which had become the norm for me in recent months. Both of my teenage children, and more so my daughter, the older of the two, were very observant and aware of the ongoing conflict between their mother and me, as well as my worsening depression and short temper. After changing upstairs, I went downstairs again to watch TV, hoping it would distract me. Unfortunately, what-ever show I was watching just droned on in the background as I sat there alone replaying the session with Dr. Dan over and over. Episodes of my mother and father hitting me as a child came flooding back. My father's drinking. No food to eat. My family members belittling me.

At around 10:00 p.m., I headed upstairs, much earlier than my usual 11:30 bedtime, hoping that I would be able to sleep through the night and not wake up from another nightmare at 2:30 a.m.—something I had been doing for months, like an incredibly twisted version of *Groundhog Day*.

As I lay down, curled up like a child, I started crying, unable to put the memories of my childhood back into the box. It was the first of many nights to come when I would quietly weep before sleep, sad and knowing it would likely be another long night with the nightmares waiting for me. That night was no exception as I went through the typical assortment of dreams with my parents chasing me or beating me, but also one of the more terrifying nightmares I had a few times over the years. In the dream, I'm in Vietnam, which is puzzling since I have never served in the armed forces. My squad is walking quietly in single file, spaced three feet from each other, through the rain-soaked tropical forest, stopping every time we heard a branch snap or an animal overhead in the dense forest canopy. We're all drenched in sweat, tired, and thirsty and take cover in an abandoned thatch hut to rest. After only a few minutes, the sound of gunfire erupts in the distance, a hundred yards out, but the thuds of mortars exploding keep getting closer to the hut we're in. Reloading my M16 rifle, I begin shooting at the enemy through the windows, but we're clearly outnumbered as the Vietcong keep pushing into the rice paddy in front of us. Three of my buddies are killed instantly from gunshots to their heads, penetrating their helmets with a distinct metal-on-metal sound as their heads jerk back and blood spurts to the ground. Eventually, all of my men are dead, except me. Frantic, I realize that I'm out of ammunition when the wooden door pops open, and there only six feet away from me is a Vietcong soldier pointing his rifle at my head. Everything is in slow motion at this point in the dream as I hear the click of the trigger. I awoke with a start, realizing that I was still alive in my bed in the darkened bedroom. Looking over to the clock, it was around 2:30 a.m. once again.

CHAPTER 3

Opening the Boxes

For months, during all of these persistent nightmares, I had to drag myself out of bed each morning at 6:00 a.m. to get ready for work, but that paled in comparison to the physical and mental exhaustion I experienced after my first session of therapy. It was exhausting to even shave, shower, and get dressed, requiring a deliberate effort to put my clothes on rather than it simply being a morning routine as it had been in the past. The energy I had to muster in cutting the grass or picking up my dry cleaning seemed herculean, like I was climbing a mountain.

With my takeout coffee from Lookout Joe's in hand, I walked up the concrete steps to Dr. Dan's office and entered the waiting room. The office manager was there that day, so I checked in with her and answered her questions about billing my insurance company. When we were finished, I looked around the room for a chair. This time, there were other people sitting, waiting for their appointments. I immediately noted a young man talking to himself, probably in his late twenties. My warning system kicked in. *Oh no, another person with schizophrenia to deal with.* His behavior immediately brought back memories of my schizophrenic brother, Tom, and his battle with mental illness. Avoiding eye contact with him, I buried my face in a *Newsweek* magazine.

Fortunately, within minutes, I heard the distinctive sounds of Dr. Dan walking down the hallway above and coming down the stairs. When I saw him, he looked over, saying, "Hi, I'm ready. Come on up." Unlike the protocol in my office, in which one of nurses would open the door and call out for a patient by name, Dr. Dan would walk down the stairs and stand on the landing, nodding to me that he was ready, maintaining a strict policy of privacy and confidentiality.

Once in his office, I let out a loud sigh as I sat down in my designated chair and placed my cup of coffee on the small table between us. I'm sure that I looked exhausted, with bags under my eyes and the dark circles of fatigue.

Dr. Dan was patient as I got settled and then started the session. "It looks like you've had a rough couple of days. How are you?"

"I'm tired. With hundreds of memories bouncing around in my head throughout the evening, I wasn't able to relax. Then my sleep was full of dreams, mostly about my parents, but I also had one of the more disturbing recurring nightmares I've had for years, which woke me at 2:30 a.m., like many other nights."

Dr. Dan asked, "What is the dream about?"

After I replayed it for him, I said, "I don't understand. I was never in the army. My older brother Tom, though, got drafted in 1966, although he never got sent overseas to Vietnam. My family always watched the CBS news with Walter Cronkite, which had reports from the battlefields and the sounds of gunfire and mortars exploding in the background. The number of

US men who had died or were wounded in the past week was displayed on a graphic along with the body count of how many enemy soldiers had been killed. I heard firsthand from two of my brother's friends who had served the horrible stories of what happened to them or their friends. One stepped on a land mine that ripped through his abdomen and pelvis, leaving him disabled. Another story was from a marine who survived the attack of twenty thousand enemy soldiers on Khe Sanh. But what does all this have to do with me and my recurring horrible nightmare? This can't be normal."

I wasn't prepared for this. I thought counseling was supposed to help me feel better. He didn't tell me how bad it would be.

Dr. Dan replied, "First of all, no, it's not normal, but it is typical for trauma survivors. It's common to feel worse as you pull up memories from the past, but it works to help you deal with your emotions. I'm sure it was difficult to relive the experience of your father breaking into the house that night."

His face changed as he paused, choosing his words carefully. "Your dream was terrifying. Going back to being a young child hiding under the table made you relive that experience but also opened connections to other fears or trauma you've buried for decades. I'm sure there are hundreds of memories you've kept to yourself, which we will need to talk about, like what happened with your brother, Tom."

I replied, "I get it. But why fighting in the jungle?"

He said, "Trauma is trauma. People could have this type of nightmare after having a car accident. Somehow, your brain pulled your brother's friends' horrible Vietnam War experiences and fears and made them part of your nightmare. Plus, you had watched hundreds of Vietnam news stories on television. The nightmare is not normal but very typical of someone who has lived through trauma or witnessed it. Dozens of patients in my practice have had tremendous trauma and abuse in their past. Their experiences may be different from yours, but their brains react the same."

So, I'm not batshit crazy. Not normal for most people but typical for people who have been traumatized.

He continued, "It's clear you lived through hundreds of traumatizing events. That night your father broke the window must have been terrifying."

I replied, as the image of hiding under the table floated before me, "Yes, it was. I remember that evening well, but other memories aren't as vivid. Is it typical to recall some events and not others?"

Nodding, he said, "Yes, most people block out the kind of trauma you experienced that night and can't remember anything, but you didn't block it out. Was Mary Ellen also abused by your parents?"

"She was. We were the two youngest, very mischievous, stubborn, and willful. I suspect my mother couldn't tolerate our talking back to her or doing things that annoyed her. She had no patience with us and was probably just sick and tired of dealing with young kids at that point in her life since she was forty-two years old when I was born. She seemed to think that beating the unruly behavior out of us would work, just like the nuns in our grade school did with their yardsticks and leather paddle. Have you ever seen the car decal that has the skull and crossbones on it with the words 'The beatings will continue until morale improves'? That's what my life was like."

He asked, "Do you remember any of your older siblings saying something to your parents or standing up to them when you and Mary Ellen were being punished?"

I scoffed as I said, "Really? No. Within a year of my birth, my oldest sister, Joanne, who is twenty years older than me, got married and moved into an apartment next door to us, so she was in my life every day. To my recall, she never defended me or stopped my parents from hitting Mary Ellen and me with a leather strap or a wooden spoon. My sister Patricia, who was three years younger than Joanne, always said that Mary Ellen and I deserved the harsh punishments since we were such terrors. I certainly couldn't turn to the nuns or the priests, since they were part of the systematic abuse I experienced."

Dr. Dan said, "I'm sorry. Often an abused child thinks they must've done something horribly wrong to get punished that way. It's difficult to accept that it wasn't your fault. You didn't deserve this. No child deserves this. You were just a little kid, four or five years old. You know how small a four-year-old is compared to adults."

There was much more I had to get off my chest. I continued, "For a young child, I know it's normal to worry about monsters hiding under the bed or in closets. However, monsters in my life were not fictional creatures hiding under the bed to grab me. Instead, I had real monsters to worry about and to fear: my mother and father, two selfish parents who were supposed to care for me, look out for me, and love me. It never happened. I was just another unwanted child to feed and put up with.

"There are no photographs of me as a baby or a toddler that I have seen. My baptism, first birthday, playing with toys in the bathtub, and dozens of other milestones passed without a photo capturing the event for posterity's sake. One of the oldest photos from my early childhood captured me as a four-year-old posing with my brother Bob and Mary Ellen on Easter Sunday in 1960. My older sister was wearing a new dress and a very pretty flowered straw hat. In contrast, I'm wearing a hand-me-down gray-and-black oversized sport coat and ill-fitting pants with the legs rolled up several times. The flat expression on my face, as well as Bob's, is a huge contrast from the big smile she wore. On my pediatric rotation in medical school, I had seen similar expressions on abused young children during my time spent in an outpatient behavioral disorders clinic.

"As I look back at my life, I've wondered why no one

intervened. Why no one looked at the face of the little boy in the photograph and said, 'Oh my God. We need to help him. Pull him out of the hellhole. Save him.' Not my two oldest sisters, who were then twenty-four and twenty-one years old, not my oldest brother, who was eighteen and in high school, and certainly not the parish priest or nuns.

"Few people talked openly about dysfunctional families in the 1960s. Family life on TV was *Father Knows Best, Leave It to Beaver, My Three Sons*, and *The Doris Day Show*, among others. Everyone had a smile on their face, and none of the parents on the shows ever beat their kids for accidentally spilling a glass of milk. There was always plenty of food on the kitchen tables in the make-believe world of Hollywood. There was no *Oprah* or *Dr. Phil* then to show people what processing emotions was like, although I believe my family would've been a *Jerry Springer* highlight."

This got a laugh out of Dr. Dan as he leaned forward in his chair, signaling that it was time to wrap up the session. It was close to 7:30 p.m. As I stood up to leave, I said, "That's just a glimpse of my childhood growing up in Polish Hill. There's so much more to cover."

CHAPTER 4

Polish Hill

I grew up in Steubenville, Ohio, a small rust belt town on the banks of the Ohio River in the northeastern part of the state, about forty miles west of Pittsburgh. It was once a bustling hub of industry, with steel mills, chemical plants, and paper mills providing thousands of well-paying jobs to area residents for nearly a century. In the towns along the Ohio River from Wheeling to Pittsburgh, high school boys assumed that they would find a good-paying job in the steel mills after graduation. After all, the mills had had been producing steel essential for the country's needs since 1899. No one in the industry forecast South Korea flooding the US market in the late seventies with inexpensive versions of the alloy, causing the loss of hundreds of thousands of jobs across the country.

Away from the steel mills and chemical plants on the river south of town, the downtown section of the city sat on a plateau overlooking the Ohio River. Carved out of the hills west of the downtown was a neighborhood known as Polish Hill, where almost everyone was of Polish American heritage.

Besides being known for its steel industry and the birthplace of Dean Martin, Steubenville was widely known for its organized crime and its control of drugs, gambling, and prostitution. My hometown earned the nickname Little Chicago in the 1940s and 1950s because of its sullied reputation. Widespread corruption was rampant in the judicial system, the sheriff's department, and the local police, and it was common knowledge they were all on the take. As my friends and I would walk past a well-known house of prostitution on our way to a movie in one of the three downtown theaters, we always waved to the ladies in their skimpy lingerie waiting for customers in the front parlor. With smiles on their faces, they always returned the greeting.

A standing joke I used for years to characterize my hometown was that I didn't realize that placing a bet on your favorite team or playing slot machines was illegal until I was twelve years old. Everyone wagered on sports, including local high school contests. If I correctly picked the ten winning teams on a football parlay sheet, I'd get a return of ten dollars for my one-dollar bet from a classmate openly working as a bookie in our high school cafeteria.

Jimmy the Greek started his gambling career in Steubenville and became nationally known. Steubenville's favorite son, Dean Martin, born Dino Crocetti, grew up in the Italian Hill neighborhood, a mile or so south of Polish Hill. He quit high school in tenth grade and was a bookie and card dealer in the local casino joints until he was recognized for his singing talent, met Jerry Lewis, and moved on to enormous success.

Growing up in Steubenville, I didn't have many role models. Sure, Dean Martin and Jimmy the Greek made it big and got out of town. There were two or three professional athletes from the area. Like thousands of other boys, I dreamed of re-placing my idol, Bill Mazeroski, the second baseman with the Pittsburgh Pirates in the 1960s. Danny Abramowicz, a Polish American who also grew up in a downtown neighborhood, was a wide receiver with the New Orleans Saints. But there weren't physicians, lawyers, teachers, or other professionals who I saw as success stories if I studied and worked hard. Most high school girls were enrolled in home economics classes, and what mattered most to boys was playing football, chasing girls, and getting drunk on weekend nights. You didn't have to be a rocket scientist to get a job in the local steel mills after graduation from high school. If your father, brother, or uncle worked in the mill, they knew someone who could make a call and get their son a job. Growing up in Steubenville, I learned that who you knew was more important than what you knew.

In our Polish culture, I joked that the most essential food groups were strong coffee, beer, vodka, and whiskey. Everyone drank coffee, regardless of the time of the day. A shot and a beer at one of the local Polish drinking clubs after a strenu-ous eight-hour shift in one of the steel mills was as routine as brushing your teeth. There were three private (translation: no Blacks allowed) Polish drinking clubs located within two blocks of each other near our house. My father frequented each of them, running up a tab that had to be paid off every payday. Ostensibly two were part of a national organization that supported Polish culture and encouraged participation in activities such as providing college scholarships to children of Polish descent.

In Steubenville, however, they were simply beer joints with little if any redeeming social value. The Polish Roman Catholic Union club, referred to as the PRCU, had a sordid reputation and an alleged brothel on the second floor. It was located in a converted two-story house at the corner of North and Eighth Streets, just a hundred yards from our home. The first floor had the typical long varnished mahogany bar with a dozen stool seats and a handful of tables. The second floor had bedrooms to provide a different service to customers. I put it together in my youth that the second floor of the PRCU was where my father most likely spent his money on time with a prostitute. When I was five or six years old, he often used me as a ruse for his activities, since I have a clear memory of sitting alone on a barstool with my feet dangling above the brass footrail, sipping on a Coke, eating pretzels, and waiting for him to come back to the bar.

Our Polish American Catholic heritage was at the core of our lives growing up in Steubenville. My family home was a block away from the Saint Stanislaus complex consisting of the church, rectory, convent, and grade school. The church was built by Polish immigrants in 1915, on a piece of land carved out of the steepest hillside west of town. Its soaring twin towers were the highest point downtown. The church bells tolling every day at six o'clock served as a call for supper for the children playing in the nearby streets. The bells' somber tones also sounded after every funeral held in the church.

The small elementary school offered classes from grades one through eight, with two grades in each classroom taught by nuns. We were burdened with the Felician Sisters, a local order out of western Pennsylvania who were skilled in not only teaching but equally adept at doling out punishments with leather straps and yardsticks. Since all the nuns seemed to relish giving corporal punishment, I sarcastically questioned later in my life whether a paddling class ("Leather Strap versus Wooden Paddle? Pros and Cons") was mandatory for the entry-level-training nuns in their home convent.

Father Chester Szymanski, our parish pastor, served as the leader of the church as well as the head of the school, with the principal reporting to him. He would hand out quarterly report cards, always adding a sentence or so of encouragement or praise as he went through the list of children alphabetically. For the children who hadn't done well on their grades or had remarks about unruly behavior, he left the disciplinary actions to the school's principal, who accompanied him to every classroom. Although I received all As in the academic subjects, I regularly was reprimanded for the Cs I got in conduct.

Like most boys in my school, I considered entering the priesthood after high school. However, by the age of eight or nine I had already started thinking about becoming a doctor. The Polish community looked on entering the priesthood or being a physician as the two most prestigious careers a boy could aspire to. My early ambition to pursue medicine was undoubtedly influenced by the care and kindness I received from the nurses and doctors on my frequent trips to the emergency room for an assortment of cuts requiring sutures, puncture wounds after stepping on nails while rummaging through old, abandoned homes with my cousins, and a broken arm. Becoming a priest guaranteed passage to heaven. Becoming a doctor was much more difficult but promised a separate way of life. It was an easy decision as the turmoil in my life worsened.

With few exceptions, my friends and I became altar boys. We rotated covering the mandatory daily 8:15 a.m. mass before classes, in addition to serving the three Sunday services. I was devoted to my role in the masses, often complimented by nuns and priests, praise that I never received at home. Being an altar boy back then had other distinct advantages. We all competed for wedding masses, as the two of us would traditionally be given a five-dollar bill to split, a fortune for a kid in the sixties when a candy bar was only a nickel or a dime.

Serving funeral masses was also coveted since we would get out of morning classes, get to ride in a funeral home's black limo to the cemetery for graveside blessings, and then return to the church hall to enjoy a traditional Polish meal prepared for the family and friends. Besides getting out of more classes,

I got to eat as much as I wanted without my mother yelling, "Stop eating like a pig!"

Fortunately, we didn't have any known pedophile priests preying on us back then in grade school. However, Father Szymanski had a distressing habit of popping our earlobes by yanking them suddenly, creating a sound like when you crack your knuckles. Because it was very painful, I never understood why he did this to me and other altar boys. Since I was just a ten-year-old boy and couldn't defend myself, who could I tell to get him to stop? My parents wouldn't do anything. Instead of being a Christlike figure, to me he was just another adult who had repeatedly hurt me, reinforcing the fact that I had to succumb to authority with no voice to stand up for myself. As a child, I didn't accept that nuns and priests had the right to abuse me physically and emotionally just as my parents did without consequence, probably one of the reasons I usually got a C in conduct on my report cards. The abusive actions of the nuns in grade school and Father Szymanski added to my bottled-up inner rage toward figures of authority.

Just about every child in the school was of Polish American heritage, with names as long as mine and tongue-twisting combinations of consonants and vowels. There was barely enough room on the back of our football jerseys to spell out Mieczkowski, Kacszmarek, Stasiulewicz, and other long Polish surnames. My oldest brother, Stanley Jr., was called Mitch; my middle brother, Tom, was T Mitch; and my brother Bob was called B Mitch. I was stuck with Larry, a name I disliked, which prompted me to start going by Mitch around the time I began counseling, one of the early results of finding my voice.

There wasn't a playground in the school lot, and since no one in our neighborhood had backyard swing sets, the hills, the streets, and the downtown stores became our amusement parks. Many shenanigans went on during my youth in the hills and streets of Polish Hill, usually with two of my cousins and my next-door neighbor, Jimmy. Since Polish Hill was three blocks from the downtown, the business district served us well for playing tag in the department store, hiding behind sofas on the fourth floor, or standing amid a rack of dresses in the women's apparel department.

I pulled my "Uncle Babe" (a distant cousin) card two or three times as a kid when cornered by a store manager during one of our escapades. After the manager rounded us up in one place, he asked for our names. When he heard mine, he asked, "Mieczkowski—are you related to Babe Mieczkowski, the policeman?" Although I had never met my older distant cousin, I said, "Yes, sir. That's my uncle Babe." He let me go, and my parents were none the wiser—and I avoided another beating at the hands of my mother.

The gang of us, all eight- and nine-year-olds, loved riding the elevators up to the twelfth floor of the city's tallest office building and exiting quickly before the group of people entering the elevator on their way down to the ground floor could see that we had pressed the buttons for all the eleven other floors. We often snuck into movie theaters through a darkened side exit door opened a crack by one of my paying friends and spent our admission quarters on candy and popcorn.

During the winter months, we were always outside, building forts, having snowball fights, and sledding. With the steep hills above Polish Hill and the number of snow-covered trails, we sledded for hours until our cotton gloves were frozen stiff and then trekked home, dragging our snow-and-ice-covered sleds, exhausted and cold but happy. But my mother was always there to sour the mood.

Since there were no foyers or mudrooms in most houses downtown, unlike the homes on the hilltop or in the suburbs, we usually entered through the cellar door and undressed in the basement. However, if we came in through the kitchen, my mother would scream at us for bringing in the snow and dirt. I always thought, *What's she moaning about, since Mary Ellen, Bob, or I are the ones who scrubbed the floor on our hands and knees instead of her?* I must've heard "Damn you kids" a hundred times in my childhood. Not once did she say, "How was sled riding? Did you have fun? Who else was there? Here, I made you hot chocolate with marshmallows. Let me put your wet clothes in the dryer."

Spring and summer were filled with outdoor activities, usually playing stickball with a sawed-off broom handle in the lot behind the school or a pickup game of baseball on a small, poorly kept baseball field up the hill from a playground called Flats Field. We used broken bats, repaired with screws, nails, and black electrical tape, and played with recovered scuffed-up baseballs lost in the woods around the city's baseball fields. Almost all boys in Polish Hill played every team sport, but since I was usually one of the smallest boys, I had the humiliation of frequently being chosen last for a pickup game.

But I grew and got better in sports, especially in Little League baseball, where I played second base. After one contest when I played very well, the coach awarded me the game ball. It was a big deal to me, my first trophy to keep and proudly display. However, none of my family members were there to witness my performance and congratulate me. I was eleven years old.

Since we rarely went to any actual amusement parks like Kings Island in Cincinnati or Kennywood in Pittsburgh, we created our own daredevil rides. It was a thrill playing on a rope swing hanging on a branch of a massive oak tree at the edge of a deep ravine. Swinging back and forth holding on for dear life, I would shriek with glee, looking down at the creek forty or fifty feet below me. We built our own tree houses and cabins, fished in the Ohio River, played kick-the-can, competed in pickup baseball games, and made up other outside activities like a treasure hunt. Occasionally I got into fights with cousins or friends for petty reasons, which were usually wrestling matches back then rather than an exchange of punches. The neighborhood boys knew better than to mess with my sister Mary Ellen or my cousin Regina, two tomboys in our neighborhood who could make you cry "uncle" in a fight within minutes.

Building a pond in the hills was the most memorable of any of my summertime activities. Two of my cousins, my next-door neighbor, and I were the main instigators in diverting a creek running down a steep ravine to a dam we had dug out of the hillside, spending weeks on the project. We stocked it with fish we caught in the river, built a dock, and used my uncle's portable boat-like concrete mixer as a raft. Eventually, the pond was about three feet in depth, allowing us to also wade in it on the hot, muggy summer days. By midsummer we became bored, the fish died, and the water, as in most ponds, became stagnant.

We had the crazy idea that it would be fun to see what happened if we quickly broke the dam open. We underestimated the potential damage, and the wall of water crashed down the ravine with a force that shocked me and my friends, flooding yards next to the creek at the bottom of the hill, spilled over the three-foot-wide metal drainage pipe, and the wall of water then sped past my home and was finally stopped by the property at the bottom of the street, where the water found its way onto their front porch and flooded their basement. I suffered the usual harsh whipping with a leather belt from my father, swearing I would never do that again. But being an immortal part of the legend of the dam break that day in Polish Hill was worth the punishment I received.

Like most ethnic communities across the country back then, aunts, uncles, married brothers and sisters, and grandparents often lived in the same neighborhood or even on the same street. My mother's family was no different. My grandfather, the patriarch of the Humienny family, lived alone in a small three-room one-story house across the street from us. Communication with him was difficult since he had not learned to speak English and my ability to talk in Polish was limited. Family members would gather in his house at Christmas and Easter and in July to celebrate his birthday.

Since his house was so small and the family was so large, the overflow of my relatives spilled over to our house. People sat on the front porch, in the living room, or in the kitchen. I enjoyed having relatives in our house at these occasions, with the blue haze of cigarette smoke floating in the kitchen, half-empty longneck Iron City Beers sitting on the kitchen table while foursomes played pinochle. I looked forward to these Christmas, Easter, and birthday get-togethers. Not only were they fun times, but they provided a respite from the usual fighting and bickering between my parents and them yelling at us or beating us. No one made fun of me, no one whipped me with a leather belt, no one pounded my back with a wooden spoon. Unlike my three oldest siblings, two of my older cousins talked to me on these occasions, often offering encouragement on my growing academic prowess. "I hear you're doing well in school. What do you want to be when you grow up?" There was a table full of food to eat and soda pop to drink without my mother noticing and yelling the usual "Don't eat like a pig." Each family get-together was a day pass out of prison for me.

Year by year, I learned that Polish people held grudges over minor slights like a birthday card arriving late or gifts not being of equal value among siblings. If my mother had been snubbed by one of her friends, she often didn't allow me to play with the children of that person. Even when I was a child, her conduct didn't make sense to me.

My mother loved to gossip about other women and what they wore to church as she watched them walk down to the parking lot when mass was over. She'd make comments criticizing someone's clothing or physique. "I can't believe she's wearing that dress again" or "She looks so fat." If I was watching TV while she went on, I didn't respond, but I didn't ignore it. Her behavior also made me question what she might be saying about me behind my back. Could I trust my own mother?

The chapter of my father's family is filled with mostly blank pages since there was little interaction with them. I never knew what had caused the rift between my mother and my father's side. My mother had spoken mostly Polish until she went to the public high school, so her English wasn't the best. Maybe my dad's siblings and parents thought my mother wasn't good enough for him to marry. All I knew was that my grandparents, aunts, uncles, and cousins on that side were persona non grata. My mother's anger toward them was always just below the surface. She'd let out a stream of curses and name-calling when I went to visit my paternal grandmother, trying to stop me from going. My Babcia (Polish for grandma) was a petite, white-haired woman who was always welcoming and had cookies and milk when I visited, although I couldn't tell her I wasn't really fond of Fig Newtons. My visits were short, mainly because she also spoke limited English and we didn't have much to talk about since I was a young child. However, I enjoyed my visits and wondered why my mother hated her so much.

On nice days, Babcia and I would sit on the porch swing looking out at the scrapyards and storage bins and chutes of the coal mine just across the street from my grandparents' home. Thousands of eastern European immigrants in the early 1900s dug out the coal with picks and shovels hundreds of feet below the surface, working for maybe a dollar per week while the owners of the mines became millionaires. When I was child, we still had a coal furnace, which did little to take away the chill of an early morning in winter. If we had coal delivered, the truck driver would shovel the coal down a metal chute into the bin under our porch. I remember on occasions joining my father to purchase three or four bushels of coal at the mine itself.

None of my father's siblings lived in Polish Hill. However, three other Mieczkowski households (all second and third cousins) resided near our house. Just with my cousins and other children, there were dozens of kids to play with in my early years. Over time, however, dozens of the families with younger children moved west of the downtown into newer or bigger homes with large grass-covered backyards and majestic oak and maple trees dotted on their property, far removed from the grit and crime downtown. Houses in Polish Hill were sold at a low price to buyers who often did not have the income or interest in maintaining the property. When I was in high school, ransacked empty houses were turned into drug houses. Once rare in our neighborhood, burglaries and muggings became common, adding to my fears and anxieties of walking by myself there. Although my siblings and I tried to persuade them, my parents never considered moving out of Polish Hill.

Families in ethnic neighborhoods are frequently portrayed in a romanticized manner in movies and books, with everyone getting along, helping their neighbors, and sitting around a dinner table covered with plates of food being shared, hugs to go around, joking with each other, husbands and wives getting along.

This was not my reality growing up in Polish Hill. Although I learned how to survive the abuse, the lack of food, the neglect, the daily yelling and screaming, the fear of living in a dangerous neighborhood, and dozens of other threats to my physical and emotional health, there was a cost. I was a damaged child. When I looked back, I questioned how I made it out of Polish Hill.

CHAPTER 5

Fear

With my cup of coffee in hand, I sat down for another session. Dr. Dan said, "How are you doing?"

Instead of denying it, I replied, "Actually, it's been hard for me. Our sessions are opening lots of memories that I had blocked out."

He asked, "So what had bothered you the most?"

"Growing up, I was always petrified that something bad was going to happen to me. I was always afraid of my parents, the nuns, older boys who bullied me, and strangers who might jump me. As a kid, I'd walk an extra ten minutes to avoid certain streets or neighborhoods where I might get jumped. One time, I was walking home alone after a baseball game and three older boys started chasing me when they saw me come out of a small grocery store near the ballfield with a bottle of Coke. Running as fast as I could and looking back every few seconds to check on the distance between us, I was able to pull away from them. After that incident, walking on that section of Seventh Street was too treacherous unless I was with others. Neither my parents nor my older siblings ever dropped me off at the baseball field or picked me up after the games.

"Another time, Jimmy, my next-door neighbor, and I went trick-or-treating in the hilltop neighborhood, with its wealthier families who gave out bigger candy bars. We knew we were in danger when two much older and bigger kids approached us. 'Hey, you two. Come here. We want to talk to you.' As he and I got close to them, they grabbed our bags of candy that we had spent hours collecting on Halloween. There wasn't anything we could do to stop them.

"Then there was the constant fear of being beaten at home. Besides my parents who hit me, I was afraid of my *ciocia*—Polish for aunt—Vandy and my uncle John. My aunt lived on the other end of our U-shaped street. One time, my mom called her on the phone and asked her to come over to our house. I had been accused of throwing a stone and hitting a boy in the face, which wasn't true. After my mother had punished me, my aunt joined in and slapped me repeatedly on my face. 'Tell me the truth and I'll stop.' I'd reply each time, 'I am telling the truth. I didn't throw the stone.' Another slap. At least it was with her open palm, which wasn't as painful as when my dad gave me a backhand. Stubborn and unwilling to confess to something that I hadn't done, I wouldn't give in. Eventually she and my mom stopped hitting me as I held my ground. I couldn't understand why my aunt was allowed to hit me and why my extended family considered her to be a saint. My true feelings about her, the raw anger, and how much I disliked her, have been bottled up for years. You're the only person to whom I've ever revealed my true feelings about her."

Dr. Dan asked, "Was your mother there when she was hitting you repeatedly? She didn't stop your aunt?"

I scoffed as I said, "Hell no. She was standing there, hovering over me like it was a tag team with her and my aunt. My mother never took my side on these kinds of issues, instead always believing that I was guilty. Even when something happened at school, she took the nuns' side."

Dr. Dan asked, "You mentioned that you were afraid of your uncle as well. Why?"

The issues with my uncle John and his ten children could take an entire session, but there wasn't time for that. Explaining, I said, "He was like Dr. Jekyll and Mr. Hyde. When he was sober, he was a good uncle to me and dad to his children, but like my father he would become this horrible person when he drank heavily. If I was playing with my cousins in their house when he came home in a drunken rage in the middle of a Saturday, I hid in a closet along with my cousins. He'd yell for my aunt, and then we would hear her crying. One time, my uncle was punishing my cousin for something he had done. My uncle grabbed him, lifted him off the ground, and pinned him against the wall. Terrified, I took off through the door and went to escape into the hills. That was one of the scariest times in my childhood."

My uncle was a big man, heavily muscled by years of building houses and doing the heavy lifting himself. Unlike Ciocia Vandy, my uncle never hit me, but I thought of my ten cousins and their mother and what they had lived through when he was drunk.

Once again I looked to Dr. Dan for insight, although I knew he couldn't do anything to make those memories go away. But he listened and was sympathetic, commenting, "You've lived through horrible times. I'm sorry." Just hearing those words from another person was healing, since no one in my past had ever expressed remorse at what they had done to me.

I said, "Thanks. Yes, it was horrible. I'll admit, though, that there were times when I did deserve to be punished, but not in the way that my mother tried to teach me a lesson. As a kid, I loved playing with matches and seeing the flame erupt from the head of the old matchsticks. Jimmy, my next-door neighbor, was good at sneaking a box from his house for us to play with since they needed matches to light the gas burners on their stove. We'd light one after another while sitting on a concrete step between our houses where we were hidden from direct view. We would take turns, sometimes arguing, 'Hey, it's my turn.'

"One time my mother caught us, probably by recognizing the distinctive sulfur smell of burning matches wafting into the house from an open kitchen window. In one of her frequent rages, she yelled at both of us, told Jimmy to go home, grabbed the box of matches, and dragged me into the kitchen. She turned on the front burner of the electric stovetop and held my arm tightly like a vise as the coils turned red. I couldn't believe she was going to do what I thought was going to happen. Immediately, I knew the pain of when I burned my finger with a match a few times in the past would be nothing compared to my hand placed onto one of the coils.

"She kept yelling at me that she wanted to teach me a lesson as she pried my little fingers open from my clenched fist, then held my outstretched hand palm down. She slowly lowered it closer and closer to the red-hot coil. My fingers started to tingle, and then the burning sensation spread and got stronger as she held my hand just inches above the glowing loops on the stovetop. My fingers felt like they were on fire. I was screaming at her by then and didn't try to pull away, knowing that I might touch the coil if I did. Hysterical with fear, I begged her, 'Stop it. Stop it. I'll never play with matches again. I promise. Please let me go.' Tears were running down my face as I was certain she was going to place my hand directly on the coil. Finally, she let me go and yelled, 'I hope you've learned your lesson. If I ever catch you again playing with matches, it'll be even worse. Now, get out of here and go upstairs until I tell you that you can come down.' I ran upstairs and threw myself on the bed and cried for what seemed like hours."

This was one of the more difficult memories to discuss. Dr. Dan asked, "Were you OK? Did she burn your fingers?"

I replied, "No, I was lucky."

Dr. Dan said, "You know that there is a line between discipline and abuse, and this was clearly child abuse. There's no question in your mind about that?"

"Yes, I know that, but what I'll never understand is how my mother could do that to me. You have no idea how much I prayed someone would step in and stop my mother from hurting me. Now you can understand why I prayed that I would die in my sleep when I was a kid." Once again, I couldn't control my emotions, and the tears rolled down my cheeks as I reached for the box of tissues.

He paused for a moment for me to compose myself before offering, "I'm sorry." What else could he say?

CHAPTER 6

Hallucinations and Dreams

Dr. Dan was a man of few words, mostly offering brief responses to my questions and keeping his opinions and judgments to himself. He rarely gave specific advice on how to maneuver through the chaos in my life. Instead, he always emphasized that it was my life to live and that I needed to learn from my experiences, whether good or bad. His counseling technique was traditional face-to-face discussions about events and my feelings. As I opened the many boxes of memories with him, there was no need for hypnosis, role-playing, or other techniques, since most of my memories were captured by my brain in crisp Technicolor. However, there was an odd experience from my childhood that I wanted to discuss with him.

I said, "There's a memory from my childhood that has puzzled me throughout my life, but it's hard to describe what happened."

He asked, "What's it about? Take your time."

"For a year or so when I was about five years old, every few weeks, I experienced what I now believe were hallucinations. These visions occurred when I was in bed trying to fall asleep. They weren't dreams, because I was fully aware of my surroundings and could hear the sound of the television downstairs. The experiences never varied and always started out with an ill-defined sense of impending doom coming over me, like someone was going to come into the room and strangle me. Then there would be a gradual onset of this weird sensation in my left arm and left hand, best described as being similar to the buzzing and numbness arising from falling asleep on your arm, but I was flat on my back. Then, like some bizarre magic trick, my small hand would slowly balloon into a much larger one, disconnect from my body, and hover over my face, just inches away. The image continued floating in the air despite shaking my arm to wake it up. Usually, after ten minutes or so, the tingling sensation would begin to recede, and the large hand would fade back to normal while the fear that had run through me drifted away as well. Once this was all over, I would turn over on my side and fall asleep within minutes."

What I had just described definitely caught Dr. Dan's attention. I continued, "As an adult, I knew this couldn't have been real, but as a young child it was frightening and defied any semblance of reality. I wasn't seeing things that were actually there like an illusion. When I became a physician, I questioned whether these experiences were hallucinations and had been caused by migraines, a small seizure, or even something like a benign brain tumor. Do you have any thoughts on this?"

He asked for more information. "Did you discuss this with your mother or see a doctor for it?"

I replied, "No. I've never shared this with anyone else. My mother would have ignored me even if I had told her."

"OK. Were there ever sounds, voices, or unusual smells associated with them?"

"No, just what I described."

He then asked, "And you hadn't hit your head or anything like that?"

Getting impatient, I replied, pushing to get his opinion, "No. So what do you think?"

He put his notepad on the table and said, "I agree with you that these were likely hallucinations and they actually have a specific name, hypnagogic, which is the definition of the state in the brain immediately before sleeping. They are common and not generally considered to be harmful, although they are often seen frequently in individuals with psychiatric disorders."

I interrupted, "But these occurred when I was a young child, not yet in first grade."

He went on, "When they occur in children, they are more likely to be auditory in nature, where the person hears voices commenting on something in their life, rather than visual or tactile in nature. That age was a painful and turbulent time in your life. From your descriptions, you seemed to be living amid a hurricane of abuse and trauma and had no escape. A very disturbing event that you don't remember may also have been the trigger. Were you having other vivid dreams or nightmares around the same time?"

I answered, "Yes, I had what I call a nightmare that began when I was in first or second grade. By then, the hallucination episodes had stopped, replaced by a dream in which I buried a body in the hills and was afraid others would discover the dead man and I would go to jail for the crime. Do you want to hear the CliffsNotes version or the full dream?"

He and I both looked at the time. Thirty minutes remained in the session. He said, "We have time for the complete description, so go ahead."

"Well, the dream played itself out the same way each night I had it, which was at least two or three times a month. It was always a hot, muggy summer day in my hometown. The steel mills and coke plants belched their charcoal-gray exhausts high into the air. The hills above our house were lush and green, and the leaves had not yet started their August wilt from the polluted air. Climbing the path to the top of the hill, I heard the intermittent cawing of the black birds in symphony with the crickets' chirping while the useless breeze caused the constant sound of rustling leaves. I heard an occasional bark of a dog in the distance.

"Sweat started to roll down my back as I frantically climbed the steep path. Unlike the more gently rolling landscape far west of the river, the main hill on the western edge of Polish Hill was a steep climb. Walking paths worn down to the bare dirt over the years crisscrossed the steep hills until they reached Angels' Trail, a concrete walkway climbing the hillside amid the dense trees on each side, serving as the proverbial set of railroad tracks separating the area where the blue-collar families lived from the richer folks who had nicer homes in the LaBelle section of town.

"As I continued to climb the path, which started at the end of our street, I knew exactly where I had buried the body. Every bend and every bare root sticking out of the ground serving as steps up the hillside were emblazoned into my memory from the hundreds of times I had climbed the path to the top. The canopy created by the locust, oak, and maple trees provided shade and cooler air, a welcome relief from the hot sun.

"As I reached the top, the heat and humidity hit me. The tall prairie grass in this leveled-out area was thick. I could taste the dryness of the parched dirt and the foliage as I pushed forward. I saw the burial site about ten feet away and started to get nervous, so I went back to the edge of the hills to ensure that no one had followed me up the trail.

"Since the man had been missing for some time, most people and the police suspected that he had been murdered. Even though I was a child, I had the sense that others suspected that

I had done it but that there must not have been enough evidence to arrest me. As I started to push the stalks of dry grass covering the shallow grave aside with a stick, it was hard to understand why I would've hidden the body so close to where people lived and in an area so accessible. Panicking, I had to bury it somewhere else. The fear of going to prison for the crime was overwhelming.

"I was hoping that no one was watching me as I frantically pushed the dirt aside with my hands. As I started to dig through the soil with a stick, the blue sky above me in the dream would fade to gray, and I would be awakened by a hand shaking my leg, always before the dream ends. I opened my eyes to my mother saying, 'Larry, time to wake up for school.'"

Continuing, I said, "This recurring missing-body dream had always disturbed me, making its way into my sleep for over a year. It's like an episode from the old TV show *The Twilight Zone*."

He said, "You were right, it is incredibly detailed and vivid. Did you worry about this dream the next day?"

"No, it never felt like a real nightmare, unlike those I had with Dracula or Frankenstein in them. As kid, I didn't know who the buried man was or why I was involved at all. It's obvious to me now that it was my father in the dream, but as a child, I didn't make the connection."

He looked at the clock. It was time to end the session. Nodding in agreement, he said, "I'm glad your brain at least protected you by not revealing the dead body of your father in the hastily dug grave. I think that would've made the dream even more disturbing for you."

As I stood up to leave, I said, "It's just so upsetting that I had these dreams when I was a kid instead of visions of swimming or playing baseball." He was silent but nodded again in agreement.

CHAPTER 7

Hiding from My Father

Intrusive thoughts at work, conflict with my wife, persistent fears, bad dreams, and violence-filled nightmares continued. I could cope with these issues at home, but the newsreel of my past life constantly playing in my head affected my professional life. It was difficult to concentrate and stay focused with the awful memories of my childhood distracting me from my interactions with patients. I found myself tearing up prescriptions I had just written because of a mistake I had made, such as an incorrect date of birth or a misspelled name. Nothing was routine anymore.

With so much going on in my brain, I started a journal to capture my feelings and events. Also, since I had always been a visual learner, seeing things on paper made it more real to me than just talking about it. At times, writing about something from the past also triggered other memories I had buried. For example, I never understood why the urine smell in a public restroom in my travels caused uneasiness until I tied it back to the smell in the men's room in a movie theater and the restroom of an ice cream parlor in Steubenville.

In the counseling process, I needed to keep track of time in the sessions and what issues I could cover in fifty minutes, not unlike what I had to do with patients in my own practice. If only fifteen minutes remained in my session with Dr. Dan, I wouldn't mention an issue that couldn't be wrapped up in the remaining time. Having to abruptly end a session with my raw emotions hanging in the air was difficult. There needed to be a transition from talking about the past and returning to the present.

There were so many things that had happened to me. Although the abuse and neglect from my mother was a major part of my troubled past, I didn't hate her like I did my father, nor did I harbor a wish that she would die, the way I felt about my father. There were snippets of memories that involved my father that I had not discussed with Dr. Dan, nor was I sure that I could ever talk about them to anyone. Could I ever reveal that I had to sleep in the same bed as a child with my father along with my brother Bob because my parents wouldn't buy bunk beds so each of us would have our own bed to sleep in? It wasn't unheard of for parents to share their bed with the children, but I was embarrassed that I didn't have my own bed until age eight. Besides, my father snored and always reeked of sweat and vodka. To stay away from him on the bed, I would start out hugging the opposite edge from him. However, my brother Bob would nudge me toward the middle of the bed when he came upstairs to sleep.

Sometimes on a Saturday afternoon when my dad returned from the beer joint, he would take a nap on the living room floor. He would order me to massage his temples when he had a headache, which I found to be disgusting, while my mother would be yelling at me not to do it. He would slap me on the face if I didn't do it. Once again, my parents put me in the middle of them, like I was a pawn in their game of chess.

I felt trapped in the storm and hated my father for all that he had done to me and my family. Waking up early on a Sunday morning, I hoped he had gone to the nine o'clock mass so I wouldn't have to see him at the eleven o'clock service I usually attended. When we happened to be in church at the same time, I never sat with him, unlike my friends who always sat next to their dads at mass. The same avoidance at mass was true with my mother, who always sat in the last pew with her cronies.

One Friday in early spring, I was outside at recess. My first-grade teacher, Sister Presentatia, had let us out to play in front of the school. The older kids took their recess in the playground in the back of the school, which was off-limits to first- and second-grade students.

As we were playing, my father came around the corner of the street. He had been drinking at the Polish club a block away. Before anyone else saw him, I caught a quick glimpse of him in the distance and instantly had waves of fear, disgust, and embarrassment. Since we were out front, he would see me as he walked home. I dreaded hearing, "Hey, Larry, isn't that your dad?" I was sure that no one in the class hated their father as much as I did. I was embarrassed by him and his alcoholism and sad that I had missed out on having a father who loved me and cared for me.

An overwhelming feeling of panic came over me, making me sick to my stomach, accompanied by an urge to run and hide in the woods as I had so many times in my young life to get away from him or my mother. At the risk of being paddled with a yardstick by my teacher if she saw me, I snuck around to the back of the school, where the older children were playing. Peeking around the corner of the building, I was able to see him walk past the school, up the street, and then into our house. I was safe and snuck back to the front of the school and rejoined my classmates without Sister Presentatia being aware of my actions.

Once again, I teared up and tried to contain my emotions as Dr. Dan leaned forward in his chair, signaling that I should wrap it up. I knew that we had run over again on time. When I had to leave in the midst of crying, it was hard to accept that he was not dismissing my concerns like others had done to me in my past. Given the lateness of the session, all Dr. Dan had time to say was "I'm really sorry."

I responded with tears again in my eyes, "I am too," and walked out the room and down the creaking steps.

CHAPTER 8

Respites from the Beast

As a child, I didn't know why I feared and hated my father more than my mother, even though she beat me more frequently for my actions. Whenever he was away from home, I was always less anxious and afraid, relishing his absence. Since he worked the day shift, he had to leave the house by 6:30 to get to the mill on time, which meant he wasn't home before I went to school. Then, once a week, he had dinner with his mother, so that was another two hours we were apart. The longest respite from the beast I called my father occurred every other year when he had six weeks of vacation in the summer because of his seniority. He usually spent the extended time off work visiting my sister Patricia and her family in Berkeley Springs, West Virginia. It was like heaven for me, almost the entire summer with him away. But like all good things that end, he always returned, heralding the resumption of his excessive drinking and abusive behavior, since nothing in him had changed over the six weeks.

There were two occasions when he was in the hospital for months because of his alcohol addiction and I thought for sure he would die and be out of my life. The first occurred when I was about nine years old and he went into the hospital for elective surgery. The next day, he went into alcohol withdrawal, having not forewarned the nurses or surgeon of his excessive intake of a pint or two of vodka every day. The alcohol withdrawal syndrome, commonly known as the DTs (delirium tremens), was often fatal back then. He became disoriented, his speech was incoherent, and because he kept pulling out his IV lines, he had to be restrained and tied to the bed rails. He moved into a more serious phase of the DTs when he started hallucinating, yelling that snakes were crawling over him. When this happened, my mother gloated about his condition, hoping that seeing them all over him might convince my father to stop drinking. Seeing him physically restrained in the bed with leather straps was traumatic as I was just a small child, evoking feelings of empathy for what he was going through. When he made it past the DTs and was slowly recovering, he couldn't feed himself since his arms shook so much. Feeding him at meals became my responsibility when I was there on a visit with my siblings or my mother, but I was terrified to do so after one time when he choked, gagged, and turned blue trying to take a bite of Jell-O from the spoon I was feeding him with. After that incident, I avoided having to feed him and left the room when I heard a dietary services employee wheeling the cart of food trays down the halls. The nurse or someone else in my family could feed him.

After he was discharged, he spent a month recovering at home before returning to work. He was able to refrain from drinking for about six months but then resumed his intake of vodka and beer. Over the next two or three years, his alcohol abuse worsened. When his binge drinking began, he often would return home stumbling and almost having to crawl up the stairs to his bedroom. One evening when I was twelve years old and alone in the house watching TV, I heard the faint cry of my father calling my name from outside. "Larry. Larry. I need help."

I didn't know what to expect as I walked down the cellar stairs and opened the door to the outside. There he was, lying in the dirt, unable to get off the ground after he had fallen. I had never seen him so drunk and was disgusted as he begged me in his slurred and incoherent voice to help him up. I got him through the door, and I don't know how I was able to maneuver him up two flights of stairs to his bedroom. His boots and work uniform were muddied from lying on the ground, so I took them off before rolling my stuporous father into his bed. Within minutes, he passed out and was snoring.

When the others came home, I told them what had happened and said, crying with frustration, that I was done helping him and didn't care what would happen to him this time. He didn't go to work the next day since he was so sick and hungover. Within twenty-four hours, his eyes were yellow from the jaundice of liver damage and he couldn't keep any food down. He was hospitalized that day and quickly went into a coma that lasted for weeks. This time, his kidneys were also shutting down from the liver failure, decreasing his chances of surviving. As he worsened, about ten days into his hospitalization, his doctor advised that the family should come to the hospital and pay our respects, predicting that my father wouldn't make it through the night.

I was staying in Weirton, West Virginia, just across the Ohio River from Steubenville, with my sister Joanne that night. When she got the news about my father's condition, she and her husband, Angelo, dressed quickly to get to the hospital. It was late, probably ten o'clock, and I was lying on the sofa trying to go back to sleep after the phone call had awakened me. Joanne looked over at me and questioned why I was not getting dressed. When I said that I wasn't going with them to the hospital since I didn't care whether he lived or died, she tried to guilt me into going by saying that I would always regret my decision if my father died that night. Many times in the past, I had let her boss me around, but, standing up to her for the first time, I told her again that I wasn't going and rolled over on the sofa.

When they returned from the hospital early the next morning and told me that he had survived the night, I felt only regret that he hadn't died. Throughout the rest of his hospital stay, I kept hoping that his condition would worsen but he ended up making another full recovery. This time, though, he learned his lesson about excessive drinking, staying off vodka and other hard liquors and drinking only an occasional beer.

Once he had recovered from the illness, a calm settled over the household as he returned to work and refrained from drinking. Since he wasn't spending his money in the beer joints, my mother was given more money to manage household expenses, almost twice as much as before. We had more fresh produce, milk, and cereal. My mother didn't have to stretch a small beef roast to feed six people any longer. There was money to buy new clothes and enough for my mother to buy new living room furniture and wall-to-wall carpeting. However, none of what happened after he quit drinking changed my feelings about him. There had been too much pain and suffering in my life to forgive him.

Within two months, my father resumed his fishing trips with a friend who had a cabin on a small lake an hour away. Even though my father wasn't drinking, I still hated being around him. The anxiety and the fear from the past came back every Sunday when he returned home around five o'clock. His friend would park the car at the bottom of our street to drop him off. As soon as I saw the familiar car, I still wanted to hide from him like I had in first grade, but there was no place to go. My friends and I were usually pitching pennies against a neighbor's porch wall at that time. As the car stopped in front of us, I would sit on the ledge of the porch wall as my friends gathered by the trunk of the car to see if he had caught a big fish. By then I was a young teenager, and my father was a stranger to me, just some man who I happened to be living with. Whenever he got out of the car on these Sundays and saw me, he never said hello or anything to me. Sixty years later, those feelings about my father and his returning home from a fishing weekend still haunt me every Sunday as it gets close to 5:00 p.m. My feeling of impending doom hangs around for a few hours and then slowly drifts away, only to return the next Sunday like clockwork.

CHAPTER 9

My Brother Tom

It was time to talk about the elephant in the room that I had ignored since I started counseling. At the beginning of my next session, Dr. Dan asked, "Are you able to talk about your brother Tom?"

Although I loved my older brother so much and wanted to believe that somewhere in his twisted mind he had loved me too, I dreaded this conversation and had put it off. Telling Dr. Dan the full story would take multiple sessions over multiple weeks to cover the entire sad story and my trauma.

As a kid, I idolized my older brothers Tom and Bob. Tom was nine years older than me while Bob and I were six years apart. Unlike my three oldest siblings and my parents, both were nice to me. When I was six or seven years old, each willingly played along when I challenged them to a wrestling match on the carpet of our dining room, fully aware that both Tom and Bob could easily pin me within five seconds. Crying "uncle" each time they did, I would run into the kitchen, grab a handful of Cheerios to boost my energy like Popeye the sailor did with a can of spinach, and return to the wrestling match. Those times were great fun and always ended too soon.

These happy times with Tom ended when he was drafted into the army in 1966 along with at least a dozen of his friends. Focusing their efforts on sports and girls in high school, Tom and his friends did poorly in their classes, so a college defer-ment for the draft wasn't an option. My mother cried for hours when his draft notice arrived by certified mail, although Tom was surprisingly nonchalant over his fate. Men of his age in our culture saw being in the armed forces as service to God and country back in the mid-1960s, portrayed poignantly years later in the movie *The Deer Hunter*. Multiple scenes in the movie were filmed in Mingo Junction, a steel town just south of Steubenville.

For the first time in American warfare, villages being set ablaze (this time with napalm) and sounds of active combat were broadcast into living rooms on the evening news with-out government censorship. In 1966, hundreds of American soldiers were killed or wounded weekly. The scenes captured by the photographers were graphic, showing wounded soldiers sharing space on a rescue helicopter with the body bags of the young men killed in combat in that godforsaken jungle half-way across the world. The infamous photograph of a young Vietnamese girl running down a road naked fleeing a napalm attack depicted the horrors of the war. How could I know that these war scenes would come back to haunt me as an adult?

The morning Tom left for his eight-week basic training at Fort Knox, Kentucky, was one of the saddest days in my life. He left the house carrying a duffel bag slung on his back as he walked alone to the Greyhound bus station. My mother and I waved goodbye, standing on the front porch. Both of us were crying, one of the few times I witnessed my mother shed tears. I was afraid that I would never see my beloved brother again.

Within a month, my mother had a nervous breakdown from the stress, crying all the time, not sleeping, and not taking care of herself. She refused to see a doctor even when she started having increased shortness of breath. In looking back at this period years later through my experienced physician's eyes, my mother had likely had a heart attack, leading to congestive heart failure. She couldn't climb the stairs to her bedroom because of her shortness of breath, so she began sleeping on the sofa in the living room.

During this period, she also started having nosebleeds that lasted for hours, most likely from uncontrolled high blood pressure. Every day was full of fear that my brother was going to be killed in the war and that my mother would die at home from a stroke. While this was going on, my father continued to drink heavily, oblivious to what was happening around him. On school days, my older sister Mary Ellen and I walked home for lunch. When we walked into the kitchen, my mother was often leaning over a sink full of bloodied towels, trying to stop the bleeding. Despite our best efforts in helping, her nosebleeds often continued when we had to go back to school, leaving her to deal with them on her own.

Joanne was aware of these episodes, but I don't recall her or my other siblings being there to help. Since she worked full-time in a clothing store, perhaps making money was more pressing than helping my mom, or she wasn't allowed to leave by her boss. Mary Ellen and I were alone, a fourteen-year-old girl and a ten-year-old boy, taking care of our mother. She refused to go to the emergency room or see our family doctor, despite the urging of my sister-in-law and an aunt who were nurses. Eventually, the severe nosebleeds stopped on their own, and I was able to return to being a child, leaving me with confusion over being my mother's caretaker during that period in my life.

Tom spent his two years of service at Fort Hood in Texas.

Unlike his high school friends who were deployed to Vietnam, he lucked out and spent his time in the army stateside. Pictures from those years show my tanned, blond brother with a big smile on his face, drinking beers with his friends somewhere on the plains in Texas, in stark contrast to the humid jungles of Vietnam where his friends were stationed.

When he was discharged and returned home, he enrolled at the College of Steubenville, now Franciscan University. He took a full load of courses while also working the night shift in the coke plant across the river. He was juggling a handful of balls in the air but doing well in his classes, making good money working in the steel mill, and maintaining his long-distance relationship with Joyce, his girlfriend in Chicago. Along with trendy clothes, he bought a 1966 red Mustang with bucket seats and a leather hardtop, one of my favorite cars.

In the summers during these years, I enjoyed caddying for him when he went golfing. Besides getting a free lunch and extra spending money, I learned the rules of the game and would play two or three holes with him on the course. Riding shotgun in his red Mustang with the windows open as I surfed the breeze with my outstretched hand is one of my fondest memories of those times with Tom. He let me tag along with him to church-league softball and basketball games and the after-game drinking in a local bar. Everything was going well for him. He was friendly, cracking jokes with his friends in the bar, enjoying his Pabst Blue Ribbon, and always ordering a hamburger, one of his favorite foods. Despite my being nine years younger than him, Tom liked me and allowed me to spend time with him, making me feel special, a kinship I've never forgotten.

In hindsight, subtle changes in his behavior began in the spring of 1971. Over a few months, he gradually stopped hanging out with friends for a beer or golfing. Phone calls from his buddies were not returned. Tom began to stay in the bedroom alone for prolonged periods, not joining the rest of us in the living room watching TV.

His smoking habit worsened, to where he became a chain-smoker. The bedroom was always full of smoke as he lit cigarette after cigarette, and he began to reek of the smell of tobacco since he often wore the same clothes day after day. In contrast to the past when sleep for him had never been a problem, he developed insomnia and paced in and out of the bedroom, up and down the stairs, and throughout the first floor almost every night. None of the dozens of different over-the-counter sleep aids he tried ever helped his sleep problems.

The friendly face I had always seen was now replaced with a look of irritation. I heard "Just leave me alone" dozens of times when I tried to engage him in conversation. I was hurt by his withdrawal since we had been close, not understanding what was happening to him.

He started talking to himself, having a conversation with an invisible person in the room. If I asked, "Tom, who are you talking to?" he usually answered "Nobody" and then his mumbling would stop. Eventually he admitted to hearing voices coming from the light fixtures telling him to do certain things and who might harm him. As his paranoia worsened, he would tell us that people were also listening in on his conversations via his radio. When my brother Bob or I asked, "Who's trying to hurt you? What are these voices telling you to do?" he never replied.

Everyone in the immediate family speculated about what was going on. Stas, my oldest brother, was big on conspiracy theories, for example believing that the CIA had been responsible for President Kennedy's death. He questioned whether Tom had been part of an army experiment where he was given a new long-lasting mind-altering drug to enhance his performance. Was he showing signs of brain damage from it? His opinion wasn't too far-fetched since soldiers at the front lines in the Vietnam War (and previous wars) were regularly given steroids, amphetamines, and painkillers to boost performance and reduce the rate of mental breakdowns. A 1971 investigation revealed that the army had dispensed a staggering 225 million amphetamine tablets to soldiers in Vietnam from 1966 to 1969. Had Tom been one of the army's guinea pigs in Fort Hood, Texas?

In 1971, most people knew little about mental illness, hallucinations, or schizophrenia. There was no internet. If you now google "Causes of a person talking to themselves," you get linked within seconds to hundreds of websites pointing to serious mental disorders as a potential cause. Why didn't someone in our family notify our doctor when this all started for Tom? Ignorance, shame, embarrassment, and not being able to convince Tom that he needed help all played a role.

We all witnessed his mental state worsening by the summer of 1971 when I was fifteen years old. The conversations he was having with someone in his head changed to a more nefarious tone. Once when I asked who he was talking to, he slowly turned his head with an expressionless face and calmly replied, "The devil," rattling me to my core and causing a shiver of fear throughout my body. Another memorable incident occurred when my twelve-year-old nephew joined us for dinner one day. When Tom saw him sitting in his preferred chair at the kitchen table, he went berserk and screamed at him to move, making me afraid that he might throw my nephew out of the chair.

A week after this incident, I returned home after football practice and quickly noticed that Tom was not home. When I asked my mother, "Hey, where's Tom?" she replied that he had been taken to the emergency room by the police when he became more agitated and was acting strange. He was just twenty-four years old when he was diagnosed with paranoid schizophrenia, a condition that would alter his life forever.

That fateful day became the beginning of the end of my

brother Tom as I knew him. There was a honeymoon period of about a year when the antipsychotic medicines rescued him from his paranoia and psychosis and he acted and appeared normal. He expected to resume college in the fall, he started golfing with friends, and he planned to drive to visit Joyce, his girlfriend who lived in Chicago. When he asked me to join him on the weeklong trip, I was thrilled. Besides being with my brother, it was the first time I had been to a big city like Chicago, and I was awestruck. Tom and Joyce took me to a popular beach on Lake Michigan, we ate Chicago-style pan pizza, and Tom even bought me a pair of the latest style of bell-bottom jeans.

Unfortunately, the grace period of normalcy didn't last long. His disease progressed like it did with most people who live with schizophrenia. His psychosis, delusions, and hallucinations would come back quickly when he stopped his medications. He frequently stopped them because of the multitude of side effects associated with antipsychotics. He was in and out of the local mental health facility and the state mental hospital in Cambridge, Ohio, too many times to keep track of over the years. Tom's illness took a toll on everyone, especially Bob, Mary Ellen, and me, who were all still living at home.

Tom was no longer my handsome, athletic, successful brother working on a college degree. The dream of marrying his beautiful blonde Chicago girlfriend, having two kids, and living life to the fullest was not to be. No, that picture of his life was now a mirage, replaced by the horrible reality of what happened to a person with mental illness back then. He looked like a drug addict with his gaunt face, now-visible cheekbones from his weight loss, and deep dark circles around his eyes. The medicines caused his flexible athletic body to become stiff, and he began having involuntary muscle movements, facial grimaces and twitching of his hands, similar to Parkinson's disease.

Within our neighborhood and Polish culture, Tom's mental illness was not only incomprehensible, it was an embarrassment to the family. On several occasions, my mother was called to pick Tom up from a local restaurant because he was sitting at the counter drinking coffee in his pajamas and I was sent to bring him home. In 1979, as a precaution, the local police jailed Tom while President Jimmy Carter was in Steubenville campaigning for reelection. I couldn't imagine what Tom, an army veteran, was thinking when he was in jail, having done nothing wrong. I was heartbroken and cried when I heard that he had been jailed because of his mental illness.

My mother could never accept that her son was seriously ill and would never be the same. In those years of the early seventies, mental illness was misunderstood, and patients were not cared for the way they are now. My mother always referred to Tom as "just being nervous."

My loving relationship with Tom changed a year after he was diagnosed with schizophrenia. His thinking clearly had transitioned to envy and resentment. Within only months, it seemed that the more I achieved, the more he resented my success. The affection and support I once felt from him was gone. A photo from my high school graduation day shows him staring down at me from our porch with a menacing look on his face, a permanent reminder of Tom's mental state in those days and how he had transformed into someone I should fear.

Our relationship deteriorated further when I went to Carnegie Mellon University (CMU) in Pittsburgh, and he started competing with me in strange ways. When I bought a 35 mm camera, he bought one. He went out and bought himself a new suit, even though he wasn't working, when I came home once with a new one. I prayed this bizarre one-upmanship between us wouldn't escalate.

In my third year of college, I was thrilled when the dean of student affairs selected me to give an update on student life at a

CMU alum meeting in Palm Beach, Florida. The trip would be the first milestone in my lifelong interest and skill in speaking before a large audience while also being the first time I flew on an airplane and stayed in an oceanside luxury hotel. The weekend trip became a life-changing experience, opening my eyes to a world that I had never seen nor imagined I could be part of.

After I returned to Pittsburgh, my mother phoned, letting me know that Tom had once again stopped his medications and was back in the local hospital. Had my trip triggered more anger in Tom, prompting him to stop his medications? During this admission, he became physically violent for the first time, attacking an orderly, throwing him to the floor, and then breaking two of his ribs when he kicked him in the chest. Tom was subdued quickly and was transferred the next day to the state mental health hospital in Cambridge, Ohio. If he was capable of doing this, what might he do to me in one of his psychotic states?

In the spring of 1978, I approached the end of my undergraduate studies with mixed emotions. I had earned a degree in applied mathematics, had a 3.5 GPA, was ranked in the top ten in the mathematics department, and had been accepted into the master's degree program as a backup to medical school.

All of that was great, but I was crestfallen that I had not been accepted to medical school, primarily because of my low scores on the admissions test (MCAT) in the spring of my third year. Since I couldn't take another exam before I applied in the fall of my senior year, those results had to be used in my school application process. By December of my last year in college, I had been rejected by eleven of the twelve medical schools but had been placed on the waiting list at the University of Cincinnati (UC). After taking the MCAT again in early April 1978, I was confident that I had done well and was hopeful that UC would accept me after the results came back in six weeks.

While preparing for the possibility of my dream of being

a doctor not coming true, I interviewed for a job as another backup plan. Narrowing my choices to three companies, it was easy to rule out the position in Rochester, New York, when the plane landed and there was a foot of snow still on the ground in late April. The second was a computer systems analyst position with a company whose corporate offices were in a high-rise building in downtown Pittsburgh. My third choice was a position in LA, which by far was the most interesting of my options. It was an opportunity to join a startup company developing computer animation for movies, a field that would explode over the upcoming decades. Being on the forefront of a new technology was intriguing, and the potential downstream financial rewards with stock options were an attractive component of their offer. But being a physician was still my real dream, and I wasn't quite ready to give up on it. So, I accepted the job in Pittsburgh, awaiting the results of the medical school admission test.

Graduation day arrived. Monday, May 15, 1978. It was hard to believe that four years had gone by so quickly. No test results over the weekend. Being rejected by medical schools had been discouraging, as if all my hard work and long hours were for naught. It was difficult to be excited about graduating when my dream of being a doctor was on hold pending the results of the MCAT. Bob and Mary Ellen were the only two family members I wanted to be there but, unfortunately, they wouldn't be attending. Bob had been the main support person for me through my high school and college years. He was training for his IRS position in Louisville, Kentucky, while Mary Ellen also would be out of town.

Trying to discourage my mother and others from showing up, I told her that no one needed to attend my graduation since it wasn't a big deal to me, rather than telling them I didn't want them there and getting into another big argument. Bob was the only one who had visited me in college, giving me rides back to school after Thanksgiving or Christmas breaks, taking me out for Chinese food before heading back home, and meeting my friends. Everyone else in my family was like a stranger to me. My mother and I had never spoken on the phone for more than five minutes over the four years of college. As for my father, I never spoke with him at all on the phone when my mother called me, besides having nothing to talk about on my weekend or holiday visits back home. My sister Joanne and her husband regularly visited my nephew who was in his first year of college in Pittsburgh a mile away from where I lived but never stopped to see me or drop off homemade cookies or her famous wedding soup.

I especially didn't want Tom to attend my graduation ceremony. His volatile behavior and progressive downhill spiral made me afraid that my commencement day would trigger another of his psychotic breakdowns, given how our relationship had morphed into this bizarre competition between us. Despite my preference, the entourage of family strangers planned to drive up for the ceremony. On a phone call the day before graduation, my mother said that she and my father, my sister Joanne, and her husband, Angelo, would be attending, and blindsided me with the news that Tom would also be with them. To no avail, I had told her on the phone the previous week that I didn't want him to be there since I was afraid of what might happen between us.

The graduation ceremony was uneventful, outside of the traditional parade of bagpipe players leading the processional in honor of Andrew Carnegie's Scottish birth. I just wanted it to end quickly so that I could minimize my time with my family. Before driving to Steubenville for a family dinner at a local restaurant, I wanted to check my mail at the apartment to see if my admission test scores had arrived. Also, I needed to grab clothes to take with me since I had planned to spend two days at home before I started work the following Monday.

I quickly got out of the car and hurried along the front walk to the mailbox. My recent MCAT scores were there! Tearing the envelope open, I was elated to see that I had scored at the top level for each of the subjects, guaranteeing acceptance to the University of Cincinnati. I couldn't believe it. The sour mood I had been in for months was gone, replaced by a sense of optimism that my life would be changed for the better. I was thrilled and bounded up the steps, taking two at a time to my third-floor apartment.

Following me, Angelo and Tom had stepped out of the car and walked up the narrow stairs to join me. When I shared the good news with them, taking me by surprise, Angelo gave me a hug while congratulating me on my scores. I couldn't help but be cynical in reacting. *So now you're happy for me so you can brag that you have a doctor brother-in-law. Where were you all the times in my life when I needed someone to help or protect me?* I saw the expression on Tom's face darken, looking as threatening as he had on the day of my high school graduation, making me even more worried.

I quickly changed from my suit into jeans and a shirt and packed my overnight bag and then we went back downstairs and got into the car for the drive to Steubenville. Tom's reaction pushed the happiness of that moment aside as I could only think about what might happen to me as we drove the forty miles from Pittsburgh back to Steubenville. Tom was quiet, more so than normal.

My mother had booked a celebration dinner for me and the family at a venue in Steubenville. The meal was awkward and strained. I had little to say to them because I'd never had any support or love from them. What little conversation that broke the silence around the table was forced and trite. Tom sat there chain-smoking and didn't say a word to anyone, just glaring at me throughout the dinner. By the middle of the meal, I realized that I had made a mistake going back home for a family get-together after my graduation. I wished that I had stayed alone in my Shadyside apartment.

It was late afternoon when the gathering ended and we exchanged goodbyes. Angelo dropped me, my parents, and Tom off at the family home. It was dark inside since all the lights were turned off, which I always hated with my ongoing fear of the dark. As he usually did, Tom went upstairs to his room and turned on the radio. Because of his behavior, I was suspicious that he had gone off his medications again. While he was upstairs, I quickly checked the kitchen cabinet where he usually kept his medicine and was horrified to see that the bottles were empty. Agitated, I asked, "Mom, has Tom been taking his medicines?" She admitted that he had run out months ago and she had been unable to persuade him to get refills. "Why didn't you at least call Dr. Manalac?" I was so frustrated with her and Joanne and Angelo, who always stayed out of any interventions with Tom when he was psychotic. My anxiety level skyrocketed, since Bob and Mary Ellen were gone and unable to help me deal with him and his voices.

That night after dinner, I slept poorly, repeatedly awakened by bad dreams and Tom's pacing up and down the stairs into the living room. After waking up the next morning and having a cup of coffee, I tried to talk to him about resuming his medications, which he refused to do. Then, I put a call into Dr. Manalac's office, Tom's psychiatrist over the prior seven years, telling the nurse that once again he had gone off his medicines. Since there was nothing the office could really do at this point to persuade Tom to resume taking his meds, the nurse discussed calling the sheriff's office, as had happened in the past, for transport to the local emergency room.

Throughout the day, Tom's behavior became more erratic. Previously, he would sit in his preferred spot on the sofa, chain-smoking as a TV show was on. He had become agitated, not able to sit still for more than a few minutes before he went back upstairs to the bedroom. His restlessness increased throughout the evening as he was constantly in and out of the bedroom, up and down the stairs, sitting down on the sofa, and then getting up. His pacing woke me up repeatedly in the night as it had in the past when he was off his medicine.

Exhausted from the tension of the past few days, I easily fell asleep around midnight on the second night home. At 2:30 a.m., I was awakened again by Tom's pacing downstairs. As I sat on the edge of my bed, I realized the sounds were different; goose bumps covered my entire body while my heart raced. Tom wasn't just walking back and forth from room to room, he was going in and out of the house through the front entrance in the living room, something he had never done. The repeated sound of the metal against metal from the latch hitting the strike plate and the hiss of the hydraulic tube slowing the door's closure was what had awakened me. Wondering what was going on, I quickly got dressed. This wasn't typical behavior for him.

As I stepped out of the bedroom, I heard my parents quietly snoring, then headed downstairs, nervous about what I might encounter. Approaching the bottom of the stairs to the dining room, the first thing I noticed was the loud sound of crickets chirping filling the room, which confused me at first, then I noticed that the inner kitchen door was wide open. For a moment, the thought that we had been robbed crossed my mind.

Standing on the landing of the stairs in one corner of the dining room, I didn't see anyone and called out, "Tom? Tom?" As he entered the dining room from the living room, he and I were in opposite corners of the small room. Although it was dim, I could see the look on his face and knew he was back into a psychotic state and likely hearing voices again. As he stood there in silence, he occasionally turned his head slightly to the left and right every few seconds, and I could hear him mumbling to himself, presumably replying to the voices that always accompanied his psychotic states. Was he listening to the devil again?

As my eyes adjusted to the dim light, I could see he was hiding something behind his leg. I immediately knew that I was in danger and tremulously asked, "What are you holding?" The answer scared me even further when I saw that he was wielding his army shovel, a tool for digging foxholes but also used as a weapon in hand-to-hand combat.

Based on the threatening look on his face and how he was holding the shovel with the blade open, I was horrified to think what he was considering. In seconds, he made his intentions clear when he said, "Larry, move out of the way." I ignored him and stood my ground, despite having nothing to defend myself with. What had the voices in his head told him to do? My heart was pounding as I questioned my next steps. If I charged at him, he would surely kill me. *Do I scream for help and awaken my parents, or do I quickly call the police if he steps back onto the porch?* Would there be enough time to reach the police before he came back into the room? I stood there quivering inside, mustering the courage to say, "Tom, I'm not going to let you harm them. Please drop the shovel." He didn't say anything and just stood there for a minute, then turned and walked through the living room to the front porch again, and I heard the screen door close. I could hear him mumbling as he responded to the voices in his head, and I imagined what he was thinking in his psychotic state.

Just kill them. Don't let him stop you. Shit, why did Larry have to wake up? God, I don't want to hurt him, but . . . Oh shut up. Just do it . . . I'm sorry, Larry.

By walking out to the porch, he gave me time to think. *Will he attack me as I am calling for help? Do I grab a knife? No, don't do that. That will only threaten him more.* Hurriedly, I went into the kitchen just six feet away and grabbed a fistful of sugar in each hand from the sugar bowl sitting on the kitchen counter and went back to my position on the landing in the dining room. If he came at me, I would at least be able to throw the sugar in his eyes, hopefully blinding him temporarily so that I could get to the phone and call the police.

Within seconds, he came back into the dining room and stood where he had been. I was pleading with him to drop the shovel. My mind was racing. *Why is there no one to help me? Why me? Help me, God. Help me be strong. Protect me, O Lord. If I am killed, please forgive all my sins. Our Father, who art in Heaven, hallowed be thy name. Please, God, let this night be over.* My heart raced, and my hair stood on end.

Tom retreated again to the porch, and I could still hear him quietly muttering. I prayed that whatever emotions were driving him to do this—anger, revenge, delusional thoughts— were easing, and he was having doubts about harming me and my parents.

Oh God, what do I do? Shit, shit, shit. I can't think. Shut up . . . I can't stand this. I can't. I just can't.

When he returned to the dining room, the menacing look on his face was gone, replaced by one of resignation. He looked beaten and exhausted from the chaos and voices in his head. The internal crisis in his head seemed to have passed without him harming me or my parents. I lowered my voice and offered to help him but kept my distance from him across the room. "Tom, I'll drive you to the hospital, but only if you put the shovel down." He refused to give it up. "OK then, how about if I call the police, then they take you to the hospital?" After a moment, he agreed to go to the hospital, but he wanted to walk by himself. I tried to persuade him that it would be easier to drive since the hospital was almost three miles away. He declined my offer and without a word slowly walked out the front door. I waited in the dining room until I was certain that he was not coming back into the house.

I walked quietly to the living room, opened the front door, and walked out into the dark onto the porch, where I saw him walking past the church by the brightness of the lone street-light, still carrying the army shovel. As I threw the sugar onto the street and reentered the house, a profound sense of relief and sadness overcame me as my defenses waned. I was trembling inside and exhausted. The entire standoff had only lasted ten to fifteen minutes, but it felt like hours.

Calling the police quickly, I told them what had happened, then woke up my parents and let them know what was going on; both had slept through everything. My mother got out of bed while my father, as expected, ignored the crisis and rolled over and went back to sleep. I called my sister Joanne, gave her an abbreviated version of the events, and asked if Angelo could help me look for Tom and hung up the phone.

By the time he arrived fifteen minutes later, I had already gotten a call back from the police informing me they had picked Tom up and were transporting him to the hospital. Angelo and I drove to the hospital, quickly parked the car, and entered the emergency room. Standing anxiously at the reception desk, I was told that Tom was already in a lockdown in the mental health unit, so I couldn't see him. I thanked the receptionist for her help as she reached underneath a cabinet and gave me the package of his clothes to take home. We started walking out of the reception room when she said, "Wait, I have something else for you." It was the army shovel. She had a quizzical look on her face when she handed it to me. I froze with fear as I thought about what had just happened to me. The potential murder weapon was in my hands now. After a few seconds of silence, I gave the shovel back to her and said, "You don't want to know," and walked out to the car.

Talking in Dr. Dan's office about Tom and that night forced me to relive the terror and fear. It was difficult. As I sat there in my chair, I was exhausted, with little more to say. I had surprisingly kept my emotions in check. There was still time left in our session when Dr. Dan asked, "So, what happened when Tom was discharged? How did that incident all end?"

I responded, "After sleeping for a few hours at home, I took the bus back to Pittsburgh that afternoon to get away from the house and Tom."

"Did you see him afterward?"

Replying, I said, "Yes, he had been discharged and was back on his medicines when I went home a week later. Within minutes of my arrival, I heard the characteristic sounds of Tom hurrying down the stairs into the kitchen. As he entered, he didn't say hello but acknowledged me by looking over. He poured himself a cup of coffee, lit a cigarette, and sat down at the kitchen table. There we were, the two of us who had faced each other just ten days prior in the darkness of the night, a confrontation that I didn't know at the time would haunt me and forever change the way I'd look at the world. There was little to talk about as we each drank our coffee. Then out of nowhere, in a very matter-of-fact, unemotional tone, Tom abruptly said, 'You know, I would've killed you that night.'

"His words sent chills once again through my body. I felt like I was sitting across the table from a mass murderer instead of my brother. The emptiness in his eyes and the cold-blooded way he threatened me rattled me to my core. I knew that it was not over with Tom."

Dr. Dan and I both stood at the same time. He said, "I can now understand why you didn't want to talk about this. Try to rest this week."

CHAPTER 10

The Dream Comes True

Returning to my apartment that Thursday, I was shaken by what had happened the previous night but was also now struggling over how and what to tell Beth. She knew about my brother's schizophrenia, since I had told her soon after we started dating, but his illness had evolved quickly into a more dangerous state. Keeping it from her wasn't an option, but I was nervous that she might not want to marry a man with a violent mentally ill brother. We had planned to get engaged later that summer, but would this be too much for her to deal with? Unlike in my own family, no one in her father's extended family had an alcohol problem or unstable mental illness. Although I don't remember the details of what I told Beth about that night, she and her parents seemed to take it in stride when we spoke that day, even if they silently harbored doubts about the marriage.

My schedule was free the next morning, so I decided to walk over to the campus midmorning and talk to Mr. Anton, my premed advisor. I was anxious to get an update on my status with the University of Cincinnati medical school since I had done so well on the admissions test. It was an unusually gorgeous summer day in Pittsburgh, with crisp cool air and the sky full of billowing puffy clouds. Although the terror from earlier that week kept spinning in my head, the beauty of the day pushed my fears to the side as I walked past the mansions on Fifth Avenue, where men who made their millions in the steel and coal industry lived almost a century ago. When I'd gone by these mansions on my way to class for the past year, I imagined living in such a house if I became a successful physician. I took a left at Morewood Avenue, then passed the women's dorms and the fraternity quadrangle. Living with forty other guys crammed into a three-story house was a great experience until I grew weary of the endless beer blasts and my drunken frat brothers' reckless behavior, which included punching holes in the wall on several occasions and tossing a vending machine over the third-floor railings. The summer before my last year at CMU, I moved into an apartment in Shadyside, an upscale section of Pittsburgh, to get away from the foolishness.

As I waited at the Forbes Avenue crosswalk for the light to change, there were only half a dozen students standing with me, unlike when school was in session and hundreds of us were hurrying across the road to get to our 8:00 a.m. classes. It was hard to believe how fast the four years had gone by as I strode past the bus stop for the 61-B, which ran the full length of Forbes Avenue, from downtown to Oakland and the University of Pittsburgh and then to CMU, Squirrel Hill, and beyond. When I got off that bus on a beautiful fall evening in October 1973 for an overnight campus visit, I was stepping into a different world as I had my first look at the campus, dotted with dozens of beautiful sycamore trees lining the walking paths, students playing Frisbee on the green space known as

The Cut, and the setting sun casting a lovely light on the old buildings financed by Andrew Carnegie in the early 1900s. Although I had not visited other colleges or universities, I had an overwhelming feeling that CMU was right for me, so I applied for an early decision acceptance process and within a month received the letter that every applicant wants to read: "We are pleased to inform you . . ."

It was a short walk across campus to Chemistry Hall, one of the first structures built in 1900 when Andrew Carnegie endowed the Carnegie Institute of Technology, which merged with the Mellon Institute of Science in 1967 to form Carnegie Mellon University. Mr. Anton's office was on the second floor of this historic structure, next to the three-story marble staircase. The hustle and bustle in his office during the academic year was gone, replaced by the quiet of the summer months. His door was open when I said, "Hello, Mr. Anton. How are you doing? Do you have five minutes? I wanted to talk to you about my MCAT scores. They came in the mail on graduation day." He had always been a big supporter of mine, although he questioned me when I transferred over from being a chemistry major to the math department in the fall of my sophomore year. He and my math advisor, Dr. Richard Moore, both thought it would be too difficult majoring in applied mathematics and taking organic chemistry, biology, and the other premedical courses.

"Hi, Larry. Come on in and have a seat. I had planned to give you a call myself. I saw your scores." Unbeknownst to me, he had received copies of all the premed students' scores.

"Larry, you did great! You placed above ninety percent on all categories. I'm proud of you." I looked up to his wall clock—it was around 11:00 a.m.

He then asked, "Have you heard anything from the admissions office at Cincinnati?" I shook my head no. "Have you called them?" I had been too nervous to make the call, so I said, "No. I'm not sure if I should just wait to hear from them."

"Well, are you OK if I call them now and see if they have made a decision?"

Oh wow! I hadn't thought about this. My anxiety level shot to the ceiling. "Sure, that'd be great!" There I was, facing the moment that I had dreamed about since I was a teenager and had worked so hard and sacrificed so much for during high school and college.

He found the phone number of the admissions office in the file and placed the call. "Hello, this is Mr. Anton. I'm the premed advisor at Carnegie Mellon University in Pittsburgh, calling about one of our students who's on your waiting list. You should have received his recent MCAT scores." A pause. "His name is Lawrence Mieczkowski." Another pause.

With my heart pounding from my nervousness, I tried to read his face as he cradled the phone against his ear. It was probably only ten seconds, but it felt like an hour before I saw a smile come to his face.

"He's sitting here in front of me. Can I tell him?"

Oh my God! I got in. I got in. Tears came to my eyes. *I'm going to be a doctor.*

He looked over at me and said, "You've been accepted. They saw your scores last week and have already sent out the formal letter of acceptance. You should get it in three or four days."

There is no one word that can adequately describe the emotions I felt. I had worked so hard to get to this point. Joy, pride, happiness, acceptance, validation—this was life-changing. I had made it.

Mr. Anton hung up the phone, came around the desk, and approached me with the biggest smile I had ever seen in a mentor. "I'm so happy for you. You deserve this so much," he said as he gave me a heartfelt hug of congratulations.

It was surreal as I left his office and walked back to my

apartment, savoring each part of the visit, replaying the conversation in my mind. Although I had imagined hundreds of times how I would react if I got accepted to med school, the reality far exceeded my dreams. Since it was one of the few times I could celebrate good news in my life, I wanted to freeze those moments in his office in time, to be savored over and over, like listening to a favorite song for hours on a record player. My life was forever changed with that one phone call, in ways that I could never imagine.

I was excited to share the news, especially with Bob, but he wouldn't be available until later in the evening after work. Mary Ellen was still in Florida on her vacation. So, Beth and her parents were the first people I called, all of them offering heartfelt congratulations on my acceptance. I couldn't care less what my father would say, figuring he would start bragging to his drinking buddies that his son was going to be a doctor, trying to take some credit for my success even though he hadn't done a damn thing to support me in my life.

In contrast to the feelings I had for my father, oddly, I still sought approval from my mother. Despite the abuse, the neglect, and her always putting her needs ahead of mine, I still held on to a fragment of misplaced loyalty to her and was still hoping that I might win her love. When I called her with the good news, her reaction took me by surprise. She started crying, asking if I was serious. "Of course, why else would I be calling?" I said. After a short conversation, I put the phone down but had mixed feelings about what to think. Was her response genuine? Was she really happy for me and proud of me? Since I had never seen any demonstrations of love from my mother before, I wasn't certain that her reaction to the news of my acceptance was sincere. Thinking she knew better than me, she had been furious when I applied and got accepted to CMU instead of going to the local College of Steubenville. Now, all was forgiven, I guess. I figured that she would start bragging about my acceptance to her circle of friends, especially to one of the ladies in the group whose son never got accepted into medical school despite applying to dozens of schools.

There was no need to call my oldest siblings, Joanne, Stas, or Patricia. I did reach Bob later that evening. When he greeted me with "Hey, Doc!" I got choked up. I was happy that he was proud of me. Almost in tears, I said, "You know that I couldn't have done this without you. You were always there for me. I can't thank you enough."

CHAPTER 11

The Summer of 1978

The summer after graduation should've been one of the best periods in my life. Medical school was no longer just a dream, and I had a computer systems analyst position for the summer that paid well. Beth and I were planning to get engaged in June, having settled on a June wedding the next summer. I was ready to move on with my life, away from my family and the darkness of living in Steubenville.

Since I had college friends who were staying in Pittsburgh after graduation, I looked forward to having a leisurely summer hanging out with them, exploring local bars and venues, and catching two or three Pirates games, something I had not been able to do in college because of the challenging academic demands. In addition, living in my own apartment and having money gave me the opportunity to do as I pleased.

Being away from my brother Tom gave me relief and happiness more than anything. By living in Pittsburgh, I would no longer have to endure his psychotic breaks and the futile attempts to get him back on his medicines or to resume visits with his psychiatrist. Over the previous seven years, my parents, Joanne, and Stas didn't involve themselves directly with Tom and his behavior, mostly ignoring his outbursts and leaving him to Bob, Mary Ellen, and me as a problem to solve. However, Bob was gone, living in Louisville, Kentucky, working as an IRS agent in the field. His move out of state meant that my mother would turn to me more often in dealing with Tom, but I was done with this chapter of my life. Being one of his caretakers when he was psychotic from being off his medicines wasn't what I had signed on for those years. Like Bob, it was my turn to move on.

I had been traumatized by the events of that horrifying night with Tom, but like most trauma victims I was unaware that what had happened to me would trigger a constellation of symptoms we now call post-traumatic stress disorder, or PTSD, first coined in 1980.

Unbeknownst to me, my world had changed, but it wasn't as if I was suddenly transported into a different reality. The change in my behavior and the ever-present fear began slowly and didn't fully appear until weeks later. The first indication that my brain was acting different occurred one evening in late May after work. After eating dinner, I was putting things away in the refrigerator and noticed that I was out of milk for my usual cereal breakfast. There were two grocery stores near my apartment in a safe area of Pittsburgh; there were always people around, and the parking lots were well lit. That evening, the hypervigilance and fear emerged from the depths of my brain, where the primal instinct of self-preservation resides. I went back and forth in my head. *It's not far to walk. You'll be fine. No, don't go; something will happen to you. You don't need to go out just to buy milk.* This had never happened to me in the past, so was I becoming another Tom? How could I be afraid to go out and buy milk? Fear had taken hold of me and began to rule my life. I had coffee and toast for breakfast the next day.

Within a month, my fear of impending harm increased to the point where I was reluctant to leave my apartment at all after dark. It seemed like the fear from that night with Tom was a permanent part of my brain, even playing itself out in my dreams as well. If Beth and I went out for dinner, I couldn't wait to be finished so that I could return to the safety of my apartment. Washing clothes at the nearby laundromat became a task for Saturday afternoons when it was light outside. Any traveling to unfamiliar places, even to a shopping mall with Beth in the daytime, was unbearable for fear that something bad would happen to me. My illogical anxiety would only go away when I was back in my apartment, safe from the outside world.

I became almost paralyzed that summer, living in a self-imposed prison that would gradually worsen over the next twenty years, even transforming a fun evening of miniature golf while on vacation at the Jersey shore to a test of wills.

CHAPTER 12

Family Life as a Child

My counseling sessions often felt like I had taken a snow globe of my life and shaken it, making the tiny flakes swirl and float in every direction. Talking about Tom had done that for me, causing the intrusive thoughts throughout the daytime to worsen while the war-scene nightmares interrupted my sleep at night. Since this had happened to me before, I knew it would take weeks for things to settle in my head.

As I sat with Dr. Dan in my next session, he could hear the weariness, sadness, and frustration in my voice. I said, "It's taking forever to get through my issues. Honestly, there are times when I feel worse than I did before I started counseling."

He said, "I understand, but you seem to be in a hurry to get everything fixed at once. It's hard to accept that you can't speed the process along. Plus, you don't have to do homework on these issues every night."

"I get it. You're right. But I'm tired of the nightmares, the sadness, and, at home, feeling like I'm just a guy who cuts the grass and pays the bills. Feeling alone in the world is horrible."

The memories from the past were again swirling around me, as my thoughts dragged me back to my youth. Memories of confronting Tom mingled with images of being in the kitchen and trying to get away from my mother. Then the nuns were hitting me. Being chased by my mother as I flew through the glass windowpane. Desperate to be rid of the demons, I was on the edge of crying again. "Why me? Why did this all happen to me? When will this end?" The suicidal thoughts had never gone away and still toyed with me.

He replied, "I'm sorry for all the pain you're feeling. It's understandable."

I had to ask, "Is all of this normal?" I was scared that I was losing my mind.

"Well, as I've said before, it's not normal, but very typical of what happens to people when they've experienced trauma. Your painful experiences were layered one on top of another for years. You were powerless. It's not a surprise that you're afraid when you consider what happened to you as a child, plus having to face a homicidal psychotic brother. And you've tried to bury the pain from the past, and it's coming back to the surface. I'm sure the hurt and fear you're feeling is as real as when it first occurred."

So, I'm not crazy.

I continued, "I'm dragging through the day. I don't know how I can keep going sometimes. The nightmares have worsened. Often, I'm in a house with a tornado approaching. Sometimes I'm trying to avoid drowning in a flood, or I might be on a plane that's crashing. When are these nightmares going to end? It's every night and often a succession of terrifying dreams. Can you give me something to help me sleep?"

He nodded. "I agree. It's time." He wrote a prescription for a medicine to take at bedtime and explained the side effects and how to use it.

Thanking him, I then moved to an issue from the past that I had yet to bring up. "As a child, I was hungry all the time since there wasn't enough to eat. My mother would make a meat loaf or pot roast once a week on Sundays, often the only day we had a full meal. Breakfast was a piece of toast or six saltine crackers covered with a bit of rock-hard butter, washed down by a cup of coffee. We rarely had fresh fruit or orange juice. A box of cereal didn't last long with five children living at home, plus we were always out of milk. There weren't cookies or ice cream for dessert. I would scrounge to see what I could eat in the evening when I was hungry, often warming a can of corn or peas to eat by myself. Sometimes I snuck into the kitchen while my mother was watching TV and quietly opened the refrigerator door and quickly grabbed an uncooked hot dog and gobbled it down or hurriedly ate a cold potato left over from the evening meal. My mother often heard me stirring about in the kitchen and yelled, 'What are you doing in there?' I'd reply, 'Nothing. Just getting a drink of water.'

"We didn't have enough food in the house because my father spent the majority of his paycheck on himself. It was so dire at times that one morning my mother sent Bob and me to redeem pop bottles at a nearby store so that we had money to stop at the local bakery and spend a quarter to buy a loaf of bread.

"Before I started first grade, I was alone with my mother on paydays, since Mary Ellen and my three older brothers were in school. Every other Friday was even more stressful since my mother had to wait to see how much money my father would leave in the kitchen cabinet to manage the household's expenses for the upcoming two weeks.

"After cashing his paycheck at one of the Polish clubs and

paying off his tab, he'd come home at lunchtime, often already drunk. He'd put the money in a specific kitchen cabinet and sit down at the kitchen table to smoke a cigarette and have a cup of coffee. My mother would enter the room and then take the pile out of the cupboard, counting out maybe three or four twenty-dollar bills, two or three ten-dollar bills, and an occasional five-dollar bill, always a fraction of what he was actually paid. The tears and fireworks came quickly.

"'How in the hell are we going to live on ninety dollars? You goddamned son of a bitch! I know where you spend your money.' In these interactions, he never responded, ignoring her tears and frustration while sitting there smoking one of his Salem cigarettes. This scene was repeated every two weeks throughout my childhood.

"Except for the early-morning hours, he was always drunk, and anything could set him off into a rage. One time my mother had prepared one of my favorite meals for dinner, a pot roast with carrots and potatoes. She was waiting for him to arrive before serving us, keeping it warm in the oven until he came home. He was a good thirty minutes late when he came into the kitchen, which triggered a fight between them as we sat at the kitchen table hungry and ready to eat. Instead of sitting down at the table, my dad walked over to the stove, opened the oven door, carried the roaster out to the backyard, and threw the food in the dirt, leaving us hungry with no food to eat while he went back to the beer joint to drink more and have a burger or hot dog for dinner. When I was a young kid, my mother was always yelling about my father spending his money on liquor and whores."

Dr. Dan looked shocked to hear this and responded, "You know that a young child shouldn't know anything about whores."

"I know now, of course, but when I was six or seven, I didn't know what a whore was, but I heard it loud and clear that she, he, or it was at this Polish drinking club taking money from my father—something I would understand much later in my youth.

"Although we were living in poverty like the kids in Appalachia, I never used the word 'poor' in referring to my family. I always envied kids who came from wealthier families and had plenty to eat and wore nice clothes.

"It was embarrassing having to wear hand-me-down clothes all the time. The clothes rarely fit me well and were usually two sizes too large since they had been passed down from Tom to Bob and me. When I was in first grade and had class pictures taken, I still fit in the same sports jacket that I had worn when I was four years old, meaning that I really hadn't grown much in those three years because of inadequate nutrition.

"My trousers were also usually too big for me, so even wearing a tightly drawn belt, my pants drooped from my waist, with the pant legs rolled up several times. Since I didn't have another pair of dress pants that weren't tattered or worn at the knees, I usually wore the same pair of pants a few days in a row to school, then had to wash and iron them on my own, beginning when I was in second grade, because my mother refused to do laundry other than on Mondays.

"Which clothes I wore to school triggered constant bullying by several girls in the neighborhood, who made fun of my pants or shirts. Their taunts were nonstop and humiliating, leaving me with wounds that never healed. By second or third grade, I stayed away from them and other mean kids, and I retreated inward by taking walks by myself in the woods or looking for crawfish to play with in the creek at the bottom of the hill near our house."

Recalling the anger I'd felt when I heard them snickering about my clothes, I stopped talking and took a drink of my coffee to calm myself. Dr. Dan commented, "Childhood experiences often stay with people throughout their lives. Did this bullying as a young boy affect you later in life?"

I replied, "Yes. Once I was in eighth grade, I was able to earn money cutting grass and doing odd jobs for people. So, I started buying some of my own clothes; more so in high school when I worked as a nurse's aide. Even today, I am self-conscious about my clothes and how I look."

I continued, "Besides the beatings and the lack of food, one of the most important parts of a child's development that was absent in my life was the love and affection between parents. It's likely that my very existence came from the drunken desires of my alcoholic father forcing himself on my mother. By the age of five, I had witnessed only contempt and hatred between them, never any sign of civility, let alone love. During one of their fights, my father crossed the line and struck my mother with his fist. Her left eye puffed up and blackened quickly. No one called the sheriff or police when this happened, but I also never understood why my six-foot-five-inch oldest brother, who towered over my father, never protected my mother and me.

"My mother loathed my father so much that I can't recall a time in my childhood when she called him Stan, or Skinny as he was known. He was always the 'goddamn son of a bitch,' 'your old man,' or *'pijak'*—Polish for drunkard. I always questioned, *Why do they hate each other so much? Why do they fight all the time?* It's a horrible reality when the two most important adults in my life had such hate for one another and had become real monsters."

As I finished what I had been saying, Dr. Dan leaned forward in his chair, gesturing that the session was ending. As I stood up, I added, "This is exhausting, trying to make progress fighting against the current. It's impossible to tell if I'm making progress."

He replied, "I understand. It's hard and draining, but you're going through multiple exceedingly difficult experiences. But try to remember, you don't always have to be swimming upstream. It's OK to just float for a while and let yourself rest."

I hung on to his words as I stood up to leave.

CHAPTER 13

Neglect

In the week after the session, I took a break as Dr. Dan had suggested. The self-help books on childhood trauma stayed in my briefcase to be read another time. TV shows and movies that focused on violence or other upsetting content were immediately turned off. And conversations about a divorce with Beth were tabled. I also didn't get into any long discussions over how my counseling was going with my friends at work. By the end of the week, I did feel better and was less exhausted.

As I was sitting down in my chair for the next session with Dr. Dan, I said, "I took your advice about slowing things down. You were right. It was helpful. Thanks."

He replied, "You're welcome. I'm glad you feel better. What's on your mind that you want to talk about?"

I said, "Well, there's much more to talk about from my childhood, centering on my mother. It wasn't unusual for her to leave me alone at home by myself when I was a child."

"How old were you when she did this?"

I thought for a moment before I replied. "The incident that I remember best occurred when I was six, alone at home with my mother. After waking from a nap in the bedroom, I went downstairs, calling out, 'Mom? Mom, where are you?' There was no answer, which made me afraid as I walked into the living room. It was quiet since the television was off, which was unusual since my mother watched her favorite soap operas throughout the day. There was only silence. Where was she? Panic set in as I thought maybe my mom had died and would be gone forever, or had been kidnapped. Where could she have gone? I looked in the basement. She wasn't there. Then I went outside, hoping that she was hanging laundry on the clothesline. She wasn't there either. I ran up the street to a neighbor's home. I didn't know Mrs. Walkowski or her husband well since they didn't have any children to play with. Crying by then, I knocked and waited for someone to come to the door. Mrs. Walkowski appeared and opened the door. 'Hi, Larry. What's wrong?' Between sobs, I was able to ask, 'Have you seen my mom?'

"She looked worried as she replied, 'No, I haven't. I'm sorry. She's not here, but I'm sure she's fine. Have you tried Menia's house next door?'

"I said, 'No. But I will now. Thanks.'

"Running out of her yard, I was terrified, questioning: What if my mother wasn't there? Menia came to the kitchen door quickly after I knocked. Between sobs, I pleaded, 'Is my mom here?'

"Yes, she was there, sitting comfortably in the living room, drinking coffee with Menia and watching a soap opera on the new color TV. I couldn't understand why my mother had neglected me by her actions or why she laughed at me and dismissed my fears by saying, 'Larry, stop crying. Don't be such a baby.' I wasn't a baby, but I was only six years old, and my mother had left me alone for the umpteenth time. If this happened to a child now and it was discovered, child services would be called in to evaluate the family home. But, back then, in the early sixties, there was no one to help me. To this day, a feeling of abandonment hovers over me when I wake up from a long nap, sometimes lasting for hours before I can rid myself of that darkness. I guess those feelings of abandonment don't go away easily."

Dr. Dan replied, "Well, they may not go away completely, but usually over time you may find the frequency or intensity of the emotions diminish as you slowly reprogram your brain's response to a trigger. For example, if you need to close your eyes and rest, set a timer for twenty minutes so that you don't accidentally fall asleep for an hour, which may then cause you to experience that sense of abandonment."

I said, "You're right. I have done that on occasion, and it has worked. Continuing on with my mother, she always made me feel that I was a burden, as if she wanted to rid herself of the responsibility of being a parent. There were dozens of incidents throughout my childhood, but one in particular demonstrated her disregard for my well-being. One summer in early June when I was ten years old, I unknowingly must have walked through a patch of poison ivy, playing hide-and-seek in the dark. Everything was fine going to sleep that night, but something was dreadfully wrong when I woke up the next morning. I couldn't open my eyes and everything was black. I didn't know what was happening and called out to my mother. Panic set in as I waited for her to come upstairs. Why couldn't I see? Once she came into the bedroom and saw that my arms, legs, and face were covered with large, fluid-filled blisters and my eyes were swollen shut, her first response was to yell at me, like the times I had fallen and injured myself. In an angry voice, she yelled, 'What the hell did you get yourself into?' I couldn't open my eyes, for God's sake, and she was shouting that it was my fault. She led me to the bathroom, where I applied cold-water compresses on my own to reduce the swelling enough so that I could open my eyes, while she had gone back to watching TV in the living room."

As I was describing that early morning to Dr. Dan, my anger came roaring back in my head, and I wished she was with us in the room so that I could scream at her: "Why didn't you help me? Why didn't you take me to the doctor or the emergency room?" Instead, I let out my emotions to Dr. Dan, a stranger, just the two of us in his office in Mount Lookout.

Tears rolled down my cheeks again as I continued. "After eating and getting dressed, I walked to the nearby pharmacy by myself and asked the pharmacist for his advice on over-the-counter medicines for poison ivy, when in fact I should've seen a doctor and taken a course of cortisone."

With my voice rising, I said, "Damn it! I was only ten years old and had to take care of myself! My mother didn't help me as I applied topical creams and took baths with oatmeal and soaps to dry up the blisters. The welts scabbed over slowly but got infected on my lower legs, which I had to deal with the entire summer. Because of the obvious infection, I couldn't go swimming. The lesions itched terribly, despite slathering my entire body with calamine lotion. I was miserable. No one took care of me. No one took me to the doctor for antibiotics."

As I let out my anger, I could barely talk, sobbing with tears running down my face, wailing, "Why did my mother treat me this way? Why?" Grabbing two or three tissues, I sat there in silence for minutes until I composed myself. I always hated it when this happened to me in the sessions; it was so embarrassing to lose it emotionally in front of anyone.

My voice was calmer as I continued, "Every time I was injured, my mother would always scream that it was my fault, often hitting me at the same time. It made no sense why I was being punished for an accident. There was another time when a group of us were playing tag on a warm summer evening.

When I jumped off the porch, I misjudged the distance, hitting my head on the corner edge of a brick column. The sharp edge of the brick was like a knife, causing a huge gash in my scalp. Blood was pouring down my head onto my neck and the back of my shirt as I ran home. Stepping into the kitchen, I yelled for help, as the blood was now puddling onto the linoleum floor. Within seconds, Bob, Mary Ellen, and my mother came into the kitchen. It was chaotic. Towel after towel was held tightly over the wound in a futile attempt to stop the bleeding. My mother was yelling at me while Mary Ellen and Bob tried to stop the bleeding. I don't recall how I got to the emergency room, but the doctors in the ER stopped the bleeding by placing a dozen sutures in my scalp."

Dr. Dan was sympathetic. "I'm sure that what I say will never erase those memories and make them get better. It wasn't your fault. It was an accident, and you didn't do anything to justify her yelling at you that way."

"I know that now. But as a kid I thought I deserved the punishment and her yelling at me."

He said, "I'm sure that's not how you are with your own children."

"On occasion, I have found myself initially reacting to an injury like my mother did, then I would catch myself. I mean, that's all I experienced growing up. To answer your question: No, I didn't blame them for an injury or getting into poison ivy, as my daughter did when she was eight or nine years old. It wasn't my son's fault that he had terrible nosebleeds and needed to go to the ER to stop them."

I continued, "Because of how my mother reacted whenever I got hurt, I kept most injuries from her whenever I could, to avoid being yelled out or hit. The most extreme example of how far I went to keep things from her occurred when I was twelve years old. It was springtime, and I had just started Little League baseball practice. On a Saturday afternoon, I walked over to the parish rectory, where there was a large magnolia tree in the yard. It was a great tree to climb, which I did frequently but would get shooed away if one of the priests came out of the rectory and saw me. Like my friends, I was a daredevil. I climbed up the tree trunk and started walking out onto a large branch that held my weight while holding on to another branch just above my head to balance myself. Just like Wallenda's high-wire act! The branch was five or six feet off the ground. I had walked out on this tree limb dozens of times before.

"Then, in an instant, I lost my balance and fell hard onto the ground, knocking the wind out of me. As I landed, there was a loud crunching sound that I didn't recognize. For a split second, I thought I was dead since I felt nothing and everything around me was blurred. There was no pain, most likely because I had gone into shock from the injury. As I stood up, I felt lightheaded and almost passed out when I saw the grotesque deformity of my lower left arm, wrist, and hand. Everything was out of alignment. The crunching sound I had heard came from both bones in my lower left arm breaking.

"My hand drooped inches below my wrist and was twisted twenty or thirty degrees from the arm. I was fortunate that the sharp edges of the two fractured bones had not gone through the muscle and skin, causing a compound fracture. Still in shock and not feeling any pain, I instinctively knew that I needed to straighten my arm, so I pulled my left hand hard and away from me to try to realign the bones, naively thinking that it was only a dislocated wrist. It worked, but within seconds my arm and hand slipped out of place and returned to their deformed appearance. Still no pain, but I became more panicked. Was I going to die from this? *Oh my God! I wish I'd never climbed the tree. What am I going to tell my mother? She'll beat the hell out of me.*

"I attempted again to align the fractured bones. Using my

right hand, I grasped my left hand firmly again and pulled it forward as hard as I could and was successful in straightening my arm and hand. Tugging as hard as I could for several minutes more to keep the bones in alignment, I hoped that would prevent them from slipping back into a mangled, twisted mess. After two minutes, I released my grip and waited. The fractured bones stayed in place. I was not thinking clearly and kept saying to myself that I had only dislocated my wrist and everything would be fine in two days and back to normal, which indicated that I was still in shock from the accident. At that point, reality started to sink in. What would I tell my mother? I couldn't divulge that I had fallen out of the tree since we had been told to stay out of the tree. My mother knew that I had gotten caught playing on the tree before by one of the priests, and I had been punished by her.

"As I stood there, still in shock, pondering the next steps, I heard the rectory's screen door open as Father Gallo walked out. He was different than the other priests who had come through the parish. I liked him and trusted him. He was always good-natured and never yelled at us if we made a mistake in serving mass on Sundays.

"He saw me standing there, and I must have looked ashen, since he said hello and walked up the yard to where I was standing holding my left wrist. He said, 'Hi, Larry. Are you OK? What happened?'

"'Hi, Father. I'm all right. I fell out of the tree, and I must've sprained my wrist.' He came closer and looked at my arm and wrist. Fortunately, he didn't try to check the wrist for range of motion or anything else, because by then the pain had started. 'I'm glad you're OK, but make sure you tell your mother what happened.' And with that he walked over to his parked car and drove off.

"Since it was midafternoon on a Saturday when this happened, I didn't have baseball practice or any other activities that day, but I was scheduled to be an altar boy for the 9:30 a.m. mass on Sunday. After thinking about what to say to my mother, I finally decided not to tell her about the fall, despite Father Gallo's insistence that I do so. He didn't know our family, and he sure didn't know about the abuse I suffered at my parents' hands."

I paused and looked over at the clock. Dr. Dan looked shocked when he said, "You must have been in agony."

Continuing, I said, "Yes, it wasn't long before the pain became excruciating. I walked home and entered through the back kitchen door and went upstairs to my room, knowing that my mother was in the living room watching TV. Hiding the injury from my mom and others was the plan, as I naively thought the discomfort would get better by the next day. My wrist and hand throbbed even more if I bent my wrist at all, so I stealthily tried to immobilize it by wrapping an Ace bandage numerous times around my wrist. I put on a long-sleeve shirt to cover my homemade splint, finding it almost impossible to button the shirt with one hand. At dinner that evening, no one noticed that I was favoring my left wrist and was wearing a long-sleeve shirt. After watching television until ten o'clock, I went upstairs to go to sleep. By then, the wrist was swollen and throbbing, while the pain level was ten out of ten. The two aspirins I took didn't help at all. That night, I slept fitfully, waking up every time I turned over and moved my arm.

"Sunday morning came. After breakfast, I got dressed for serving mass and wore a long-sleeve shirt again to cover the bandage. Somehow, I made it through the religious ceremony by only using my right hand. By then, if I tried to use my left arm and wrist for anything, I would almost double over from the intense pain. Afterward I went home and kept myself out of view, hoping that the sensations would ease.

"That afternoon, my mother attended an event in the church hall where Father Gallo and the other priests were as well. He saw my mother and asked, 'Hello, Eleanore. How's Larry doing?' As I heard about the interaction later, she said, 'Hello, Father. What do you mean, "How's Larry?"' He replied, 'Didn't he tell you that he hurt his wrist yesterday when he fell out of the magnolia tree? I said he needed to tell you.'

"After the church event, my mother came home and immediately called for me in a stern voice. 'Larry, come downstairs now.' With that tone, I knew she must've heard what had happened, and I went into the living room and sat across from her. She said, 'Father Gallo told me that you had fallen out of the tree yesterday and hurt your wrist. Is that true?' I had to fess up since the pain was unbearable, but I was guarded, waiting for the yelling and punishment that typically would have been coming. 'Yes, I did. I was afraid to tell you.'

"My mother didn't yell, scream, or hit me as she had before when I hurt myself. To my surprise, she genuinely seemed concerned and perhaps felt guilty that I had lived with the pain for twenty-four hours for fear of being punished by her. There was almost tenderness in her voice when she asked, 'Which arm did you hurt?'

"I said, 'My left one' as I held my arm up and rolled my long sleeve back. She looked at the improvised splint I had placed around my wrist and said that I needed to go to the emergency room to get it X-rayed. I don't remember who drove me to the hospital or if my mother went with me. As it turned out, the doctor covering the ER that day was our family physician. He recognized me as one of his private patients and, to my surprise, asked if I wanted to see the X-rays. Since I had already started thinking about being a doctor, I jumped at the chance. He showed me the two out-of-position broken bones on the X-ray hanging on the brightly lit box on the wall in the dim viewing room and said, 'You have a significant injury. I'll have to keep you in the hospital overnight and put you to sleep to fix it in the morning. I have to ask, how did you put up with the pain?' I was hesitant to tell him the truth, but I admitted that I had been afraid of what my mother would do to me if I told her.

"Word spread quickly throughout our neighborhood that I had broken my arm and had gone twenty-four hours without telling anyone. Since there were no widespread child protective services in the 1960s, no one at the hospital questioned why a child with a fractured arm showed up in the ER over twenty-four hours after a fracture. Now, a social worker would see the child and assess the family situation. Well, that wasn't the case for me. I just went home to the same environment. No hugs or words of support and understanding. It's when I realized that I was on my own and had to take care of myself. Even though she had not beat me, which was a huge surprise and actually demonstrated concern, I knew she was partly to blame, as I would never have gone that long with such horrible pain if I hadn't been afraid of being punished."

I finished the last of the coffee and then tossed the cup in the trash can between Dr. Dan and me.

He said, "I can't imagine how you must've felt. That's one of the most horrifying stories I've heard. I can understand why you didn't trust your mother to help you. This must've been very traumatic for you, like when you flew through the windowpane."

I replied, "It was, and it's the reason I never considered going into orthopedic surgery. Just thinking of how my arm looked after the fall still makes me squeamish. I can't forget the bloodcurdling screams of pain from a patient with a fractured thigh bone in the ER at Mercy when I was a resident, admitting a patient with a heart attack down the hall. That's the level of pain I had for over twenty-four hours."

It was time to go. I was relieved to have finally told him the story of when I broke my arm, one of the darkest secrets about my mother that I kept hidden from others. He was still in the doorway of his office, looking at me as I started down the stairs, and I looked back.

I said, "Thanks for your help, Dan. I appreciate it."

"You're welcome."

A man of few words.

CHAPTER 14

The Gun

Sitting in Dr. Dan's office for another session, I wasn't sure how to bring up the gun incident from when I was young. Having already spent hours in the sessions talking about my childhood, I didn't know whether to continue with memories from that time or move on to other issues.

I was guarded as I started to tell him the story. "I need to tell you about another thing that happened when I was a child, probably five or six."

He asked, "Is this connected to the other things we have covered previously?"

Shaking my head, I said, "No, it's different. Sometimes I can't believe this had really happened since it's so mind-boggling." I took a moment before continuing. "One evening, I overheard a conversation between my parents in which my father said that several older teenagers were harassing him as he walked to work early in the morning. He then said angrily something like 'I'm going to teach those kids a lesson.' A couple of days went by, and it became clearer what he meant by those threatening words when he told my mom that he had purchased a gun and was carrying it with him in his pants pocket on the way to work. An argument ensued, with words being exchanged. My mother yelled, 'Why the hell are you carrying the gun? What are you going to do with it?'

"He shrugged her question off. 'It's none of your damn business.'

"She warned him that he would go to prison if he shot one of the boys, which was scary to me. Even at a young age, 'prison' was not a foreign word in my vocabulary, since I had firsthand knowledge of this type of situation when a neighbor, a man known to be an alcoholic, showed up intoxicated in the middle of mass at Saint Stan's Church brandishing a pistol. Police were called to resolve the standoff, arrested him, and kept him in jail. Fortunately, no one was shot. I was old enough to realize what it would mean if my father was sent away to prison. Sure, he wouldn't be abusing me anymore, but there would be no source of income, no food, and I didn't know how we could survive. As much as I already hated my father by then and wished he were dead, I was terrified by the thought that he would go to prison. Steubenville police may have had the reputation of looking the other way for gambling, prostitution, and drugs, but shooting and killing someone on an open street with multiple witnesses meant jail time.

"So, to deal with the situation, my mother came up with the insane idea that I crawl under the bed after my father had passed out, to his boots where he was hiding the gun, and retrieve it. Why me? Because I was a small child and would regularly hide under my parents' bed when playing hide-and-seek in the house with my siblings.

"All of the boys in our neighborhood had plastic guns and rifles to play army or cowboys and Indians. I knew TV shows were make-believe. But this was different. I was terrified, plus

I had never seen a real gun and didn't know what it felt like or whether it could go off if I grabbed it the wrong way. My heart was racing while my head was pounding from the anxiety, terrified that I might wake my father before I got the gun out of his boots. Once again, my mother had put me in the middle of them. At this point, I can't remember where my mother was, although I know she wasn't upstairs, and she was not in the bedroom with me as I crawled under the bed.

"I slowly crawled on my stomach on the dusty floor from my mother's side to the middle of the bed. Directly underneath where my father was sleeping, the bedsprings were pushed down two or three inches from his weight. *I'm not going to fit.* As I made my way in, I could hear the bedsprings squeak as they moved closer to me as he shifted from one side to another. Holding my breath and not moving an inch, I waited a moment for him to settle and listened to make sure he was still asleep. Once he was quiet again, I resumed scooting across the floor and made it to the boots. Slowly reaching in carefully and quietly, I felt for the gun. It wasn't there. Maybe my mother had been wrong about my dad carrying a pistol. I removed my hand and placed it in the other boot, then felt the cold hard piece of metal against my hand—it was the gun. As lightly as I could, I grabbed it by the handle and lifted it out. Thinking it might explode like a grenade, I held it in my open palm, making sure my fingers stayed away from the trigger. Then, I crawled backward until I was no longer under the bed. My father was still snoring loudly and hadn't moved a bit.

"I stood in the bedroom for a moment as I looked at the revolver. It was heavier than I had imagined. It was a small pewter-colored handgun, likely a type of cheap revolver called a Saturday night special, about the size of an adult's palm, which could easily be concealed in a pants pocket. It didn't have any distinctive markings.

"Mary Ellen was in her bedroom down the hall, waiting

for me. I quietly carried the gun down the hallway. She and I figured out how to get the cylinder out of position to remove the bullets. The image has been with me forever, five bullets in my little hand. They were about an inch long and had smooth, rounded, copper-colored tips. After that, my memory abruptly stops. Where the gun was hidden, where the bullets went, or what happened when my father discovered that it was missing the next morning are mysteries. Although I don't remember the last details, I'm sure my father was furious—but fortunately he didn't buy another one."

As I sat there in Dr. Dan's office, I could picture every detail about the small pewter-colored revolver, the copper-tipped bullets, the fear, and the recklessness of my mother ordering me to retrieve a gun when I was a child. Who does this to their kid?

It was obvious that Dr. Dan had not expected to hear about this experience, since I had never mentioned it or alluded to this incident in any previous session. If I had spoken about it earlier, would he have believed me, or would he think that I had made the story up since it was so fantastical? Surely, no child would have been put in the situation of retrieving a loaded gun from his father's boot by crawling under his bed while he was sleeping. As I left the session, I knew there was little Dr. Dan or anyone could say that would lessen the impact this had on me.

CHAPTER 15

Hidden Skeletons

As a young grade schooler, I did not talk to friends who lived outside of Polish Hill about how my parents treated me or what my daily life was like. They existed in a different world than mine. They had nice parents, clean and more comfortable houses, and enough food to eat. I didn't invite them over for dinner, to work on homework together, or for sleepovers because I was too ashamed to bring them into our dirty and disheveled house. My mother had stacks of old clothing, torn sheets, newspapers years old, and other clutter spread out on every flat surface, which she refused to discard and make the house more presentable.

There wasn't enough food for our own family members at dinner, let alone anyone else. And why would I risk having a friend see my drunken father or listen to my parents fight? My miserable childhood was hidden from my friends by choice since I didn't trust that others liked me for who I was and thought they would reject me if they saw how I lived.

In high school, I became best friends with two guys in our first year; both lived in the nicer areas of town. We became inseparable. Neither of them was aware of the beatings I had endured, the negligence, my father's alcoholism, the lack of food, and the humiliation over wearing worn-out hand-me-downs as a kid. How I lived as a child was never to be shared.

By my first year in high school, I had become focused on being a doctor, while dreaming that I might be good enough in football to get a college scholarship. My guidance counselor suggested volunteering or working in the local hospital to gain experience. Taking his advice, I started working full-time as a nurse's aide on a cardiac care unit the summer after my sophomore year and one eight-hour shift a week during the academic year. Surely, I needed the money, but the experience would help me understand a little of what it would be like working in the medical field as a doctor.

In 1971, all nurses I knew were women with just a few teenagers or young men working as orderlies. It didn't take long to realize that it was emotionally safer for me to divulge aspects of my past with the women I worked with instead of my guy friends. They listened, and I became close friends with a few of them, occasionally visiting them and their families.

In the first summer, I became especially good friends with one of the nurses on the unit named Carolyn. Her husband, Ed, a Polish American guy with a name almost as long as mine, had been one of my football coaches in grade school. She was outgoing, had a great sense of humor, and constantly teased me about almost everything that could embarrass a fifteen-year-old boy.

There's often a fair amount of downtime on a nursing unit after patients were bathed, given their medicines, and beds were made every day with freshly pressed sheets and pillowcases. I found myself frequently paired up with Carolyn, so when it was time for a break or lunch, we sat together in the nurses' conference room or in the snack bar or cafeteria.

She was in her mid-thirties, old enough to be my mother. Perhaps her warmth, knowledge of the Polish culture, and her own father being an alcoholic made her approachable. I had never opened up to anyone before about the depths of the abuse from my childhood, but I trusted her and shared part of my past and my family's issues, especially how I had been physically beaten. When I told her about the incidents of running through a windowpane as a young child or falling out of the tree and hiding a broken arm from my mother for twenty-four hours, she teared up and hugged me like a mother, trying to find the words to console me and assuring me that my life would be better. Her confidence that I would make a great doctor and find someone who loved me dearly were welcome words that I had not heard from my parents or oldest siblings. I was somewhat overwhelmed by her concern but grateful that I had opened up to her. What had happened to me in my childhood was no longer just my secret; someone outside of the family was now aware of what had happened all those years in our home.

Once I started college, I had a clean slate to start a new life. No one from Steubenville would be at CMU to judge me or dredge up the past. I discovered quickly that having a brother with schizophrenia piqued people's interest. On the first day of freshmen orientation, I met an older woman who was majoring in psychology. Given her field of studies, I casually mentioned Tom's illness. She was interested in hearing more, and she asked if I was comfortable in sharing. Since she had not done any clinical work yet in her studies, schizophrenia was just a mandatory read for one of her classes. In broad strokes, I shared the personal side of what happens to a person with severe mental illness. A comparable situation occurred in my psychology class when we were discussing manic-depressive disorders and schizophrenia. Since I had spoken to my professor about my brother's illness, looking for advice, he asked if

I was willing to share a few of my experiences with my class-mates, several of whom approached me afterward with kind words of support.

The earliest effort to write about my life came in my first-year English literature class at CMU. We had to read William Faulkner's *The Sound and the Fury* and then write a piece of fiction in the author's style. As I devoured his words, I could not help but compare my own family life, parents, and siblings to the characters in the novel. Had Faulkner grown up in such a dysfunctional family?

My story was a not-so-veiled invocation of my own life and family. For the first time, I wrote about my alcoholic fa-ther; my brother suffering from schizophrenia; the beatings; the conflicts, resentment, and jealousy among my siblings; and my efforts to survive and rise above the evil and wretched side of my family. The assignment was meant to be at least three pages; I had written three times as much. I was proud of the work, confident that I had captured the spirit of William Faulkner's writing while allowing me to put my feelings onto the page. My English professor gave me an A+ for the paper. If he had any reactions to the story, he never shared them with me. Disclosing my experiences through a writing assignment or buffered through a discussion in a psychology class allowed me to open the closet full of skeletons in a safe way without fear of judgment.

Trust issues with friends, however, continued, and de-spite making connections with others, both men and women, at the various stages of my life, I always drifted away from them. As an adult, I envied guys I knew who had main-tained friendships from grade school, high school, or college. Throughout my life, I was never part of a foursome playing golf twice a month. It was easy to blame my fractured rela-tionships on the stress and demands of being a physician. Yet, I knew physicians who had regular golfing friends or went out for dinners in a group. I knew it was my issue, but I didn't fully know why I was like that.

As I approached my upcoming session with Dr. Dan, I had to admit that I had not seen any major improvement in my depression, irritability, frequency of nightmares, or the intrusive thoughts of ending my life. I knew that I was one of a million others who had been physically abused by their parents. Reading about child abuse and its long-term effects on survivors helped me see that what I was feeling was not normal, but typical. Hearing Dr. Dan use those words was helpful, but it was more powerful coming from the mouths of others who had lived through similar experiences.

It was another session in the summer of 2001. Most sessions started with Dr. Dan asking, "How did the week go? Did you find the books I gave you to read helpful?"

I replied, "I guess I'm not the only person who has horrible nightmares and doesn't have a healthy marriage. It was weird to see myself and my life depicted so accurately on the pages I read, almost like the author was writing about me."

He said, "Like others you've read about in the books, you've lived through a lot of trauma in your life, and it's a long process to heal." Sometimes I just wanted to hear him say that my parents were horrible people and deserved a place in hell, just to validate how I felt about them. But I never heard that, since he was never judgmental.

Nodding in agreement, I said, "As a doctor I can see that, but as a patient I still feel like my life has been a failure and no one really cares about me. Certainly, my parents and siblings didn't care. I believe that Beth checked out of our marriage a long time ago, leaving me to deal with my depression on my own."

He asked, "So why do you feel this way?"

I tried to hide my annoyance with the question. "That's just how I feel. It's easy to understand that it was my parents' fault in the past when I was hungry and there was no food in the house. It was also my parents' fault then that I didn't have new clothes. It's however much more difficult to understand why I have so few friends now or why I didn't stay in touch with people from my past or why I have had problems with sexual relationships since high school. These are difficult and painful subjects. It feels like everything in my life is screwed up."

Relationships and trust were major problems in my life, but Dr. Dan and I had only talked briefly about them in previous sessions. Our discussions had centered on my childhood and the physical abuse I had suffered from my parents and the experience with my brother Tom. The physical abuse and confrontation with Tom had been out in the open since I was fifteen years old and thus easier—and emotionally safer—for me to talk about. It was much harder to figure out why I didn't have any close male friends.

I reached for my coffee, to take a break from the conversation. My frustration with my progress was showing, since I just wanted him to fix me. He said, "Look, over the span of your childhood, you were subjected to multiple kinds of abuse. I'm sure you saw that your experiences were similar to those depicted in the books."

I replied, "OK, yes, I get it objectively, but how am I going to move forward with all this in my head? It never stops. And there's a hundred things that I don't want to think about. Can we talk about adding an antidepressant? I can't stand living like this."

CHAPTER 16

Columbine

April 20, 1999. The day of the Columbine High School massacre. Like most people, I reacted with horror and sadness for the victims and family members. We didn't know that this tragedy was a seminal event that would usher in an onslaught of mass shootings across the country over the next quarter of a century. Nor did I know that it would further unleash the demons from my past and trigger my spiral into a deep and dark hole.

Before the Columbine mass shooting, I would go for stretches of time in a good mood and optimistic about the future. I had my nightmares and fears to contend with, but I thought I was coping well with my life. Then, without any obvious triggering event, the balance in my emotional state would shift toward depression, anxiety, and fear, causing me to withdraw from my wife and others.

When I fell into these periods of hopelessness, bills weren't paid on time, the grass didn't get cut, and I was more irritable and judgmental. I wanted to scream at noncompliant patients,

You're wasting my time being here! My disagreeable emotional state also affected my immediate family, forcing them to walk on eggshells when I was in the doldrums. When asked, I always lied and said that nothing was wrong. It was not possible for me to link the bad-tempered mood I was in on a beautiful spring day watching my daughter play soccer to events that had happened to me thirty years prior.

After Columbine, nothing slowed my free fall into the deep, large black hole. There were fewer periods of good humor and contentment, and although I had considered seeing a therapist as my life worsened, I wasn't willing or able to cross that threshold for another two years. During this time, I kept going deeper into the darkness.

Fear came roaring back into my life, as it had after the incident with Tom and the shovel. In my mind, I became certain that strange men might be hiding in the parking lot of the TGIF restaurant, waiting to kidnap my daughter. A man walking behind me in the dark airport parking garage might be stalking me, and every department store or movie theater could be the site of another massacre by another lunatic with an assault rifle. The intensity of my fears was overwhelming. My internal fears transferred over to my daily life. I was afraid of allowing my daughter to stay out past 11:00 p.m., not able to give her a rational explanation. I observed a stranger's movement more thoroughly than usual, noting what they were wearing, where they could be hiding a gun, and how or if they could hurt me. Anytime I did go out with my family, I never verbalized my fears to them. Scanning for the best escape route when at a restaurant because second nature.

I continued to isolate myself, just wanting to be left alone. Being a key opinion leader in the medical community, I was frequently invited by pharmaceutical sales representatives for an after-work glass of wine at a local restaurant and then dinner afterward. These obligatory outings were part of

the give-and-take of being a speaker for the company's medications and were part of the contractual obligations I had.
Ostensibly they were social get-togethers, but in reality it was
always about business. I slowly stopped accepting the invitations for drinks after work, declining for a number of reasons.
"Let me check my calendar and get back to you. Is that OK?" I
just didn't want to be around them.

I avoided dinners out with my wife or another couple for
fear that something bad was going to happen to me. It didn't
take long or require effort to isolate myself from people around
me. The paradox, though, was that I saw others' behavior of
not checking in on me as a sign that no one cared, even though
in truth I had pushed them away.

When two employees in the office observed that I was falling deeper into depression, they encouraged me to seek help.
I couldn't see how counseling could help me, given that I felt
that I was better off dead. Like others with suicidal thoughts,
I let out little clues about my mental state while trying to keep
up the facade with my immediate family and my office staff.
I'd say, "Good morning, everyone. How are you doing?"

By the spring of 2001, I finally accepted that I needed
help when one of my employees left a bottle of St. John's wort
on my chair before work, an over-the-counter supplement
for depression. I walked down the hall to her office, holding
the bottle, and spoke to her. I admitted that all I could think
about was ending my life. She strongly encouraged me to
start taking it if I wasn't willing to see a psychiatrist. It was
time to make the call.

Now, as I had feared, the months of counseling had taken
a toll on me. My depression worsened, my fears of being killed
increased, and my nightmares continued throughout my sleep
with scenes of tornadoes, floods, and violence, including one
horrific dream of being in the army in Iraq watching as our 35
mm gun mowed down civilians, cutting them in half. In one

particularly gruesome nightmare, I was lying in a field next to decomposing, decapitated corpses as blood trickled down the street.

Dr. Dan was right about the frequency of counseling sessions. I know that I had pushed him on this, but two weekly sessions were too much. He had advised me that things might get worse. He was correct about that as well. Since I had started counseling, the images and noises of my past kept getting louder and more vivid, constantly distracting me during my workday. On top of the fifty-mile drive every morning, I was now even more exhausted by waking up every hour or two from the horrible nightmares of war scenes. Patients who had been with me for years noticed the fatigue that showed in my eyes and face. I used to greet every patient in an upbeat mood and with a warm handshake—a hallmark of my bedside manner—but that changed as well. My smile was replaced by a flat affect—a term used to describe a depressed person's unemotional facial expression.

"Good morning, Dr. Mitch." They could see that I didn't have my typical smile on my face. "Is everything OK?"

God, if you only knew.

"Yes. I'm fine. I gave a lecture last night in Columbus and got home late. I'm just tired."

I became short-tempered with my patients, pharmaceutical reps, and other physicians. I didn't suffer fools gladly, as the expression goes, especially in dealing with arrogant physicians or with out-of-control diabetic patients referred to me. For example, within minutes of talking to one patient, it was clear that his daily consumption of two liters of regular Coke was the reason his blood sugar was out of control. With frustration in my voice, I said, "Look, what don't you understand? Your blood sugar is out of control because of your Coke consumption. You need to make the change to diet soda."

"Well, Doc, I don't like the taste of Diet Coke."

"Too bad; it's either starting insulin or you get rid of the regular Coke."

"Not going to happen, Doc."

"Well then, you're wasting my time. We're finished here. I'm sending you back to your family doc, and I'll send a letter letting him know what's going on." I closed the chart, made it clear that the visit was over, and walked him up to the check-out receptionist, saying, "No follow-up. I need the chart back for sending a letter."

In the past I had been tolerant of patients not taking their medications regularly and would try to work with them to improve their compliance. I no longer had patience with this behavior, saying, "Your family doc can easily prescribe the medicines you're not going to take as well as I can." It would take most people two or three seconds to process what I had just said as I ended the visit and walked them down the hall to be discharged back to their primary care doctor.

My staff were not immune from my irritability and moodiness. In looking at my schedule for the day, I would angrily question out loud to no one in particular, "Why was I double booked at eleven o'clock? Now I'm going to have to work through lunch to be on time." As my outbursts at work became more frequent, I knew my staff were also wary around me. At that point I really didn't care and rarely apologized for my behavior, unlike what I would've done in the past. What they didn't know was that I had to get consultation letters typed at lunch rather than after hours to leave the office earlier to get to my appointment with Dr. Dan. Outside of three close staff members who knew I was in counseling for depression, the others were kept in the dark. I couldn't trust them to keep it to themselves. *Will someone report me to the state medical board as an impaired physician? Will they gossip with other doctors' offices? Will my referrals drop off if other doctors find out?*

Once, I lost it when one of my nurses was standing in my

office doorway trying to engage me in a non-work-related issue. After ten minutes of sending signals that I was busy and occupied with the piles of charts and labs to review, I erupted. "Karen, is there something you need? I don't have time to listen to your rambling on and on. Can't you see that I'm swamped and that you're interrupting me?"

I noticed the hurt look on her face as she stepped away and headed back to the nurses' room. At the end of the day, another one of my nurses asked if I had a minute to talk about the incident. Since she had been with me for over ten years, she was usually the most likely of my staff to mention a sensitive issue with me. I invited her into my office and asked her to close the door. She was aware of my depression and that I was seeing a psychiatrist.

"Hi. What's up?" *Great, now I must rehash the incident.*

She hesitated for a moment, then asked, "Larry, are you OK? Karen told me what happened. She said that you got so angry with her earlier. She was upset and was crying when she told me what happened. Is there anything I can do to help?"

What could I say? I didn't really understand why I got so angry either. My short temper was also becoming more frequent at home with my wife and my children.

"Sue, I'm sorry. There are a thousand things on my mind. The counseling has been difficult. I'm not sleeping well, and things aren't going well at home. I will talk to Karen tomorrow."

"You know that you can always talk to me."

I let out a long sigh. "I know. Dozens of childhood issues have been dredged up from my sessions. This is difficult for me. It's as if all the horrible things from my past are actually happening to me again, all at once."

As she opened the door and left, all I could think was *What the hell is happening to me?*

CHAPTER 17

Cambridge, Ohio

During my first year of medical school, my mother would call every few weeks at 7:00 p.m. on a Sunday evening. During these short phone calls, we had little to talk about. After five minutes, she always shifted the conversation to my sister Joanne and how her children were doing. My mother never asked about me or my life, something you would expect from a caring parent in a healthy relationship. Questions like: How were my classes? Were they interesting? She never asked if I was eating enough, which I wasn't, or needed any extra money, which I did. It was pointless to tell her that one of my good friends was also from Steubenville. She wouldn't care.

One Sunday, I heard the dreaded words "Tom is in the hospital again." Since Bob and I were not available, my mother was on her own to deal with him. My father wasn't going to help, since he hated Tom, and the feeling was mutual. They had been close to physical confrontations on dozens of occasions.

Even though Mary Ellen was also still living at home, she was able to emotionally remove herself from the family drama and Tom's erratic behavior.

When his delusions and hallucinations returned within a week of stopping his medications, my mother would eventually call the sheriff's department, which knew the routine with Tom and his long-standing mental illness. Two deputies would be dispatched to transport him to the local mental health unit, where he would be placed on a forty-eight-hour psychiatric hold. He was caught in the revolving door of hospitalizations and short periods of living at home. Group homes for individuals with serious mental health illnesses were not available back then.

After Tom had gotten into a fight with an attendant and broke two of the man's ribs, at the first sign of trouble the local mental health unit would quickly transfer him to the state mental hospital in Cambridge, Ohio, located seventy miles west of Steubenville. Unlike other state hospitals for the mentally ill, Cambridge State Hospital had a storied past. In 1942, to meet the medical needs of the men and women injured in World War II, the US Army appropriated a sprawling farm a few miles north of the city and began building a hospital and other facilities. Fletcher General Hospital, named in honor of the deceased Lieutenant Colonel John Fletcher, treated over seventeen thousand patients while also serving as a World War II POW camp.

In 1946, after the war, the hospital and other facilities were given to the State of Ohio and renamed the Cambridge State Hospital and transitioned to caring for mentally ill patients, the criminally insane, and patients with alcoholism. It was not unusual for patients to stay confined to the hospital grounds for years. Like other insane asylums, as they were often called, its horrific reputation was not far off from reality, with patients undergoing frontal lobotomies or electroshock convulsive therapy to modify behavior while also being shackled to their beds with leather restraints.

I visited Tom once when he was in the Cambridge mental hospital—that was enough. In the spring of 1979, I was driving home from Cincinnati for a weekend to join Beth and her family on Easter. Tom had been in Cambridge for two weeks when I decided to pay a visit.

Despite everything that happened between us, I still cared about him, loved him, and wanted to see him. Even though this would be the first time I would be alone with him since the confrontation the previous May, I wasn't too nervous since he would be back on medications. Plus, guards and attendants would be nearby.

When I arrived, the building looked more like a prison than any hospital I had seen. It was an imposing structure with bars on many of the windows and stone walls, gray and black from years of wear and exposure to the weather. I didn't know what to expect since I had never seen pictures of it nor any state mental health hospital.

Once I passed through two security doors and registered as a visitor, I was cleared to enter the facility. Inside, I felt like I had been transported back in time. What struck me immediately was the horrible smell, a combination of urine, sweat, and feces, which permeated the entire complex. Barred doors. Guards everywhere. Dimly lit rooms. Peeling paint. The loud voices—even screams—of patients echoing throughout the cavernous waiting room like the sounds of crows circling overhead. As I sat at a table waiting for Tom, I became afraid that he might try to harm me again. My heart was pounding just like it did on that night almost a year ago. *What if he pulls out a shiv or a knife from his shoes and lunges at me? What was I thinking when I decided to stop for a visit? What is he going to do when he sees me?*

It was only a few minutes before I spotted him across the

large room scattered with benches and tables where other guests were visiting with patients. He was smoking, as always. After being first diagnosed with schizophrenia in 1971, he looked like his old self for two or three years, whether he was on or off his medication. In recent years, he had easily lost twenty pounds and didn't look healthy. There was little expression on his face when he saw me. He walked over and sat across from me on a metal picnic-style bench bolted to the concrete floor. I could tell he was heavily sedated by his cocktail of psychotropic medications. His face contorted with a grimace every few seconds from involuntary muscle spasms.

"Hi. How was the drive?" he asked.

Like most patients taking antipsychotics at the time, he had developed tardive dyskinesia, a common side effect of long-term antipsychotic use. Besides affecting his face, his neck would twist involuntarily, and his hands and arms would twitch and shake like he had Parkinson's disease. He had no control over them and said that the involuntary muscle movements were painful, like a muscle cramp might feel.

I don't recall if he was wearing street clothes, pajamas, or a prisonlike jumpsuit. He immediately lit another cigarette, asking me if I wanted one. I accepted the offer since I had started smoking again. I gave him the carton of cigarettes I had purchased for him.

"Thought you could use the cigarettes. I'm fine. School's going well. How are you doing?" I asked, knowing full well that life there had to be horrible. I couldn't imagine what went through his mind when he was back on his meds and saw the reality of where he was. With bitterness in his voice, he replied, "What do you think? Look at this place. I'm locked up with a bunch of crazy people." He went on. His description of what he had to deal with was too graphic for me to bear. I had no idea it was that horrible there. After about thirty minutes, I told him that I needed to get back on the road. He thanked me for the cigarettes and for taking the time to visit. No one else in the family ever visited him when he was in Cambridge.

I was shaken by the visit. The mental health unit in Steubenville looked like a standard hospital floor. I had not expected to see him in a prisonlike facility. As I walked to my car, I was choked up by sadness over how his life had turned out and for the first time felt guilty over my success and good health. Survivor's guilt would stick with me for the rest of my life.

The experience was emotionally difficult for me in so many ways. I became convinced that Tom was past the point of ever being normal again. Since he had already crossed the threshold into being violent toward me and my parents, I couldn't stop thinking of when he would act out again, perhaps the next time with a gun. Although I felt horrible about it, I didn't want him at my wedding with Beth, which was scheduled for June, only two months away. I was determined to hold my ground no matter how much my mother or Joanne pressured me to give in and let him attend the wedding. After my visit with him in Cambridge, I couldn't stop thinking about whether he would use the event as an opportunity for harming me or others.

As I drove back to Cincinnati after my visit back home, I started obsessing over the possibility of Tom figuring out a way to show up at my wedding in June. However, the farther I got away from Steubenville and past Cambridge, the less I worried about what might happen in the future. Cincinnati was over two hundred miles away from my hometown, providing enough of a distance that I started living my life without irrational fear. Plus, I didn't have to talk with my mother or Joanne on a regular basis. The first year of medical school was going well, and I had made dozens of friends to hang out with. Given the way the summer of 1978 had gone, I was surprised that I felt relatively safe living alone in my one-bedroom apartment. I was appropriately cautious, but I didn't fear going out for a beer in the evening or meeting one of my best friends, also from Steubenville, for a late-evening snack at Skyline Chili in the Clifton neighborhood, just six or seven blocks from where we both lived.

Beth and I had discussed whether to invite Tom to the wedding. Whatever doubts I had about the decision went away after the visit to Cambridge. I couldn't have him attend. As I went through the first year of medical school, I learned more about schizophrenia and other mental illnesses, the theories of how it develops, and the limited treatment options. Although I had a better understanding of the disease, everything I read pointed to an increased risk of suicide or homicide by patients with schizophrenia. Tom fit the profile of being at elevated risk: white male, single, younger, never married, with a long history of the disease and noncompliance. My concerns were justified.

As the wedding day approached, I didn't worry about Tom attending since he was back in Cambridge again. In a phone call a week before the wedding, my mother pressured me on allowing him to be there. "How's it going to look if he's not there?" Once again, how my mother was seen by others was more important than what I wanted. I said sarcastically, "And you're sure he's not going to ruin my wedding or try to harm me like he attempted last year? Besides, why are we even talking about this since he's still in the hospital?" I held my ground and believed I had made my point clear.

I drove back home on the Wednesday before the wedding and had planned to stay two nights at home in Steubenville and then overnight in a hotel Friday night in Washington, Pennsylvania, where Beth and her parents lived and where the wedding was to be held on Saturday morning. When I drove into our neighborhood and parked the car, I was in a good place, excited about the wedding, grabbed my duffel bag, and walked up to the kitchen door. Before opening the door, I smelled cigarette smoke through the screen, thinking it was my father smoking. As I opened the door, I was dumbfounded: Tom was there, sitting in his favorite chair, drinking a cup of coffee and smoking a cigarette. I thought, *What the hell is going on?*

"I can't believe this." I asked scornfully, "What are you doing here? How did you get out of Cambridge?"

My mother had walked into the kitchen once she heard me arrive and answered for him. "He was able to get a weekend pass so he could attend the wedding."

I was beside myself, full of anger and disbelief. This couldn't be happening to me. In a tone I rarely used with my mother, I glared at her, asking, "Did you arrange this behind my back? There's no way they would've done this without your approval." I was furious with her, Tom, and everyone in my family who was in on the scheme. I paced back and forth in the small kitchen as my mind was racing.

Tom said, "Well, since I'm out on a weekend pass, that means that I can go to the wedding, right? Look, I'm not going to do anything, I promise."

My mother pleaded, "Why don't you just let him attend?"

She had tried to box me into a corner, but I was not going to let that happen. I needed time to think and stepped away from the conversation, went out the back door, slamming it shut in anger, and took a long walk in the neighborhood to calm down. How could I prevent him from attending the wedding with my family unless someone supported me on this? Bob was scheduled to arrive the next day, and I was hopeful he would back me on this as he had on multiple other occasions. Tom clearly enjoyed the chaos he and my mother had created for me.

The next morning, I got into another heated conversation with my mother about the rehearsal dinner, traditionally paid for by the groom's family. Even though we had discussed the plans half a dozen times and came to an agreement, she was in a huff again about the location of the venue and the cost. It was frustrating and disappointing that she was reluctant to help cover the cost of my wedding. For years, she had paid all of Tom's expenses and had given money to Joanne and Stas when they had needs while never helping me out with any financial support when I was in college.

After the argument, I left earlier than planned and drove over to Beth's parents' home in Washington. When I arrived, I discussed the situation and went over the possibility of Tom showing up at the wedding. I didn't care whether anyone from my family would show up for the rehearsal dinner or even the wedding. Bob was my best man, so I knew he would be there, as would Mary Ellen. I had run out of patience in dealing with my family.

My parents and others showed up for the rehearsal dinner, and Tom stayed home. It was a stressful evening. Beth left the room for over ten minutes at one point in the middle of the dinner. When she came back to the room, I could tell that she had been crying, likely from the stress. When she wouldn't tell me what was going on in her head, it made me think she was questioning moving forward with the marriage. The silence between us was not the best way for us to begin a marriage, foretelling hundreds of conflicts we would have over the years regarding communication and sharing feelings.

The wedding ceremony and reception the next day went well despite the chaos of the previous days. My parents and siblings arrived at the church, acting like nothing had happened. Tom was not with them, to my relief. Surprisingly, all my father's siblings and their spouses showed up. It was awkward making small talk with my paternal aunts and uncles, whom I didn't recognize or even know by name. They were very friendly and grateful to have been invited to the wedding while also offering congratulations on my acceptance to medical school.

On the other hand, my mother was unhappy with the wedding protocol at the country club, compared to the more casual approach at the hundreds of wedding receptions she had attended in our local church hall. My father had stopped drinking years prior, so I didn't have to deal with him staggering around the room drunk like he had done at other wedding receptions. During the gaiety of the evening, I was unable to get Tom out of my head. I kept looking for him over my shoulder, as if he could suddenly somehow appear at the reception with a gun in hand to take his revenge on me.

I naively thought that being married would shield me from having to deal with Tom. I was wrong.

CHAPTER 18

A Phone Call in the Night

Transitioning to just one counseling session weekly meant I needed to prioritize which issues to discuss among the multitude of problems swirling in my head. At times, I gave Dr. Dan the CliffsNotes version of events at one session and then elaborated on what had happened in a session the following week. The relationship and history with Tom were complex, and it took multiple sessions to explain what had happened, what had led up to "the night," what had happened in the months afterward, and the drama surrounding my wedding a year later. Unlike the memories from my childhood, the events in my adult life were more vivid and easier to recall.

Dr. Dan asked, "So how'd life go after you married?"

I sighed, since it wasn't an easy question to answer. I replied, "Living together had a learning curve, as you would expect, since we really hadn't seen much of each other in the previous year while she was working on a master's degree in Virginia, and I was busy in medical school. A weekend visit every six or seven weeks wasn't comparable to living together as a married couple, a lesson I learned early on when she insisted on renting an apartment without air-conditioning in an old house on the fringe of a high-crime area of Cincinnati. That became a source of frustration as we sweltered in the hot and humid summer.

"It was a big adjustment in all areas as we disagreed over basic issues like who does the shopping and which foods to buy. Other areas of contention arose when she went to work as a paralegal for a law firm downtown and we were trying to adjust to living on a tight budget. At the beginning of my second year of medical school in September 1979, the routine in our daily lives was shattered suddenly, though, with a phone call late one evening."

I paused to toss my empty coffee cup in the trash, then continued. "It was Tuesday, September 25. I was awakened by the loud ringing of the phone on my bedside stand. Seeing that it was 10:15 p.m., I immediately thought that something had happened with Tom. Preparing myself for the expected bad news, I was taken aback when I heard my father's voice. A sense of confusion came over me, as he had never called me on the phone. 'Larry, your mother died this evening. She was found dead on the sofa. You'll need to come home tomorrow.' There was no emotion in his voice, no crying, just a matter-of-fact statement. Stunned by the news, I asked, 'What happened? Who found her?' So many thoughts were going through my head. Beth sat up and listened.

"He said, 'We don't know what happened. Mary Ellen came home and saw that the living room was dark and turned on the light and saw your mother on the sofa, not moving. She must've died watching TV.'

"It was a shock because I had just talked to her a week before. She must've had a stroke or a sudden heart attack, given that her mother had died suddenly in her sixties in a comparable manner. I told my father that we would head out the following morning, hung up the phone, and then filled Beth in on the details that she had not been able to hear. Choked up by the news, I started crying over her death, and my head was swirling with the sad memories of the past. Although as a child I had wished so many times that my father would die, I'd never thought of the consequences afterward. Now, my mother's sudden death would change everything in my life. Thinking of Bob: How would he manage her passing away, since he had been close to my mother? What was going to happen to Tom? My father most likely would kick him out of the house, since my mother wouldn't be there to prevent that from happening."

Dr. Dan said, "You must've had mixed emotions about the news."

I replied, "I did. The years of abuse and neglect and lack of affection from her had taken a toll on me. I didn't hold any deep feelings for her in my heart. In my childhood or teen years there were only a few times when I received a hug from her to comfort me when I was injured or after she or my father had punished me. Physical touch, outside of being beaten, was foreign to me as a child. Even when I was a young man leaving for college, she pulled back from my attempt to give her a hug. Her arms stayed at her side, and she quickly turned her head away from me and squirmed out of my embrace."

Dr. Dan asked, "How old was she when she died?"

I continued, "She was young, only sixty-six years old. Besides my grandmother, my oldest brother Stas was diagnosed with coronary artery blockages when he was only forty-two years old. My family history of premature heart disease prompted me to specialize in the prevention field."

Dr. Dan said, "Tell me about the funeral and how things went with your family."

"When we headed out the next morning, Beth drove since I hadn't slept well. I dreaded the family drama that I knew was to come. My siblings were likely squabbling over which casket to choose or which floral arrangement to lay on top of the coffin. Not important decisions, if you think about it, but for Joanne it was all about the show and how it would look to the visitors. She would try to assume the matriarch role in the family, even though my father was still alive. As a physician, I had seen firsthand how families react to the death of a family member. Sadly, deaths and funerals often brought out the worst in people. I wondered how I would react to seeing my mother in the coffin.

"On the drive to Steubenville, I had waves of sadness and tears with periods of silent introspection. Whatever sorrow I had in my heart paled in comparison to the abuse and neglect I had suffered at her hands. By the time Beth and I got off the interstate and were driving along the Ohio River to my hometown, my tears had dried up, replaced by anxiety as we got closer to Steubenville. As we drove through town to Polish Hill, I let Beth know that my family's grieving process would be much different from the experience she'd had when her grandma Rose, the matriarch of her father's family with nine children, had died four years prior.

"The parking lot off Highland Avenue in front of our house was nearly full of my family's cars. All my siblings and their spouses were there. Bob had decided to drive home late at night from Lexington immediately after getting the phone call from my father.

"As Beth and I entered, everyone was in the kitchen or the dining room. The table and counters were covered with food trays and casseroles that friends and family had dropped off. The smell of coffee was in the air, bringing some sense of normalcy to the occasion. I knew that everyone grieves in their own way, influenced by their previous experiences with death, whether the death was sudden or expected, and their individual relationship with the deceased. Knowing this, I wanted to

be understanding of how my siblings would be and braced myself specifically for Joanne's behavior. My siblings didn't feel
the same about my mother as I did. My father would not be
shedding any tears over her death. He likely was more upset
over the money he'd have to shell out for the whole funeral
process while finally being rid of the wife who hated him and
called him every name in the book.

"Joanne was talking with someone when she saw me.
Suddenly she screamed, 'Larry, our mother is dead!' Then the
wailing and the cries of anguish began. Taken aback by this,
I questioned whether she was looking to me for comfort and
support. Thrown off by her reaction, I wasn't sure what to do,
say, or how to respond. Although Joanne had a special relationship with my mother, her reaction on seeing me had not
been expected.

"My mother's death should not have come as a complete
shock to the family. She had not been to a doctor since she
gave birth to me in 1956. Then, when I was twenty years old
and in college, her shortness of breath worsened; she was finally coerced by Mary Ellen to go to the emergency room,
where her blood pressure was 240/120. In addition, her heart
was enlarged from years of uncontrolled hypertension, causing heart failure. Considering there were few treatment options for patients with the condition in the seventies and early
eighties, it was remarkable that she had lived over ten years
with severe heart disease. Studying to be a doctor, I was aware
of how she had beaten the odds, but I'm certain that Joanne,
Patricia, and Bob thought she'd live forever. Since I never held
the same feelings about my mother as Joanne and my other
siblings did, I didn't echo her words with my own expressions
of grief or crying.

"With so many people there, the house was chaotic as
Both and I made the rounds greeting my siblings, nephews,
nieces, and aunts. Patricia let me know that the family had just

returned from the funeral home. Everything for the service had already been arranged, the coffin, the burial day, the time of the funeral mass, the flowers for the coffin, hours and days of visitation, and even which funeral car Beth and I would ride in on the way to cemetery; there was nothing left for me to provide any input on. Beth knew how I felt about being excluded from family decisions in the past and looked over at me for how I would respond. At that point in my life, I accepted my position in the hierarchy: I was the youngest, the baby of the family in Polish culture. Years prior, I might have still tried to get my voice heard, but I had given up on my siblings listening to anything I had to say.

"Not wanting to make a scene, I quietly asked Patricia in a nonconfrontational tone, 'Why didn't you wait for me? You know that I left early this morning to be here by the afternoon.'

"She replied with a judgmental tone in her voice, 'Well, we didn't know for sure what time you'd arrive, and since everyone else was here, we went down earlier than planned.' I thought sarcastically, *You're right. Since I didn't drive through the night, I must not care as much.*"

I paused to take a sip of coffee, and Dr. Dan asked, "Why didn't you press the point of how you felt being excluded from a ritual that helps family members come to grips with the reality of a death?"

"I thought, what was the point? Neither of my oldest sisters would change, and the decisions had already been made. I had dealt with these types of situations in the past so many times that I was used to it. Even though I was no longer the five-year-old child Patricia put in place by smacking me or yelling at me, she, along with Joanne and Stas, would never see me differently."

Dr. Dan asked, "How did the rest of the weekend go for you? I'm sure it was difficult and brought up a lot of unpleasant memories."

I replied, "Yes, it was grueling, but although I had a hint of sadness, I couldn't deny that I was relieved to be free of the person who had abused me my entire childhood. It was hard reconciling these opposing emotions."

Dr. Dan said, "It's common for survivors of abuse to feel relief when their abuser is dead, yet struggle with some guilt for thinking that. How did Tom deal with her death?"

I replied, "Not well. He looked terrible, and his mental state was delusional again since he was off his medications. Barely speaking to anyone, he mostly stayed in his room, chain-smoking. When Tom would come downstairs to get something to eat, he would go right back upstairs to his room. His restlessness reminded me of the night with the shovel. It seemed that I was the only one who noticed or cared that he was in bad shape and likely hallucinating again. I had hoped that Patricia and her husband, George, might help with Tom, but they had never been around in the past when he was psychotic, so they were inexperienced in dealing with an out-of-control brother and didn't step up to help. I was worried that Tom might do something to harm others, given where his mental state was."

Dr. Dan checked the time on the clock. There were twenty minutes left in my session.

I added, "It was incredibly stressful being around my family so much. We'd all gather at the family home in the morning, then drive down to the funeral home for an afternoon two-hour visitation period, talk to dozens of family friends and relatives, then go back home to eat, and then another visitation period in the evening. Joanne continued with her loud lamentations of grief in the funeral home, almost throwing herself on the coffin. My family, like others, judged a person's sadness by how much they cried at a funeral. Both Joanne and Patricia questioned why I wasn't crying over my mother's death. I replied with something like 'this isn't a contest for who cries the most' and walked away from them.

"Tom made only one appearance at the funeral home, dashing in and standing by the coffin for just seconds and then hurrying out just as quickly, not saying a word to anyone. He was unshaven and looked like he had not changed clothes or showered in days. I didn't approach him in that setting to avoid triggering a scene.

"Before the mass and the trip to the cemetery, the family gathered in the funeral home around my mother's coffin for prayers before it was sealed. It was emotional for me, probably the first time I had cried since my drive back home. The coffin was not closed until everyone left the room, dabbing at their tears with tissues, and went outside. The funeral staff had their list of who was going in which vehicle and directed us to our seats.

"Having served as an altar boy for dozens of funerals when I was young, I had witnessed the raw emotions and tears triggered by the traditional Polish recessional song as the draped coffin is slowly wheeled out of the church and then lifted into the hearse by the six pallbearers, with the music from the grand pipe organ resounding through the church. The funeral procession of limousines and cars with headlights on and a purple flag stuck to the roof slowly made its way to Mount Calvary Cemetery, located five miles west of the church. As was customary, a police officer on a motorcycle blocked traffic to let the steady stream of vehicles pass by uninterrupted. It was September and the weather was beautiful, so a graveside internment service was planned in the Saint Stanislaus section of the cemetery. After a prayer service blessing the coffin and the soul of my mother, we returned to the church hall for a traditional reception. Polish funeral receptions are no different than wedding receptions—hundreds of people, dozens of meat platters and roasters filled with cabbage rolls, traditional Polish cookies, and an open bar.

"Tom had not shown up for the ceremony at the funeral

home that morning, nor did he attend the funeral mass, instead staying at home mired in the darkness of his schizophrenia that none of us could ever understand. I overheard my aunt, the matriarch of the extended family, make cruel, disparaging remarks about Tom being absent and what a shame it was that he didn't join the family for the funeral service. This was the same aunt who had slapped me repeatedly as a child to fess up about throwing a stone when I hadn't and who had once dragged Tom to school when my mother didn't know how to deal with his refusal to go to his third-grade class.

"But then in the middle of the reception, Tom entered the church hall and headed directly to the food tables without saying a word to anyone. He quickly filled his plate and left. Stepping outside, I watched him walk the few hundred feet back home as quickly as he had come, still wearing the clothes from when he appeared at the funeral home. His appearance was similar to when I visited him in the Cambridge mental hospital: exhausted from insomnia, eyes sunk into the sockets, and constantly grimacing from the permanent side effects of his medications.

"There wasn't time to discuss Tom's situation with my siblings since Beth and I needed to get back to Cincinnati and not miss another day of classes. With my mother's death, I knew that my father wouldn't deal with Tom's current state, suspecting that he would eventually kick him out of the house. Bob was returning to Lexington the next day. After Beth and I said our goodbyes at the reception, I approached Joanne and pleaded with her to help Tom by calling his psychiatrist for guidance as soon as possible, considering how poorly he was doing. She was noncommittal in her response, brushing off my concerns about him and what he might do in this frame of mind. 'Will you give Dr. Manalac a call tomorrow?' I asked, but I didn't have much faith that she would at least call his psychiatrist.

"Driving back to Cincinnati, I found myself replaying the events of the past three days in my head. Those days had drained me both emotionally and physically. The thoughts of the funeral and my mother's death receded in my mind the farther we were from Steubenville, replaced by concerns over Tom and what would happen to him."

CHAPTER 19

A Lecture in Portsmouth, Ohio

Talking about my mother's death, Tom, siblings, Steubenville, and the drama surrounding the funeral stayed with me the week after my session. It had brought back a flood of emotions from that time, even though it had been nearly twenty years since she died.

On the next Wednesday, I left my office in Kettering early since I had to drive to Portsmouth, Ohio, a little over two hours away. Decades ago, it was a town of forty thousand people with thriving businesses frequented by the families of men working in the local steel and brickmaking plants. Now, like Steubenville, Portsmouth had joined the ranks of once-prosperous mill and factory towns left on the river to wither away. There was no capital investment fund ready to tear down these old factories and develop the land to attract high-tech companies in the way that Pittsburgh had done successfully in the 1980s.

I had agreed to give an hour-long presentation on diabetes

for a pharmaceutical company, to be followed by thirty minutes of questions and discussion. Over the previous ten years I had received hundreds of invitations from pharmaceutical companies to lecture in small cities across the country such as Macon, Georgia; Tupelo, Mississippi; or Hazard, Kentucky, since I was one of the few national speakers willing to travel to these towns for a single evening lecture. These day trips worked well for me since I could easily drive or catch a direct flight to just about anywhere on a Comair regional jet from Cincinnati, often making it back home the same evening or early the next morning. Unlike the academic physicians who pocketed the honorarium for themselves, the checks I received for my services went directly into the business's account as a secondary source of income, adding to the revenue from Medicare and other insurance companies.

Since the lecture in Portsmouth was my first out-of-town venture since I had started counseling, I was nervous about the trip. I had driven to this rust belt steel town ninety miles upriver from Cincinnati dozens of times since my first lecture in the late eighties and had always looked forward to the two-hour trip. Driving from my office in Kettering, I went past the strip malls and car dealerships and then entered some of Ohio's lushest farmland. Beyond Xenia, a town that had been almost totaled by a massive tornado in the seventies, the highway carved out a path through thousands of acres of corn and soybeans on both sides of the road, stretching to the horizon. Before the fall harvest, when the six-foot cornstalks were topped off by brown tassels, grain silos towered over the fields like lighthouses on the edge of an ocean.

Since the stress and demands of being a physician were overwhelming, I often daydreamed of what my life might have looked like if I had not pursued medicine as a career. Minimal traffic on the road and wide-open spaces made it easy for my mind to wander as I drove alone with a Rascal Flatts song in the background easing my worries. Despite dealing with the vagaries of Ohio weather and corn prices, the farmers who came to my practice loved what they were doing and usually spoke of their vocation as a calling to continue the family tradition.

As I approached Portsmouth, the flat fields gradually changed to the gently rolling foothills of the Appalachian Mountains, a beautiful scene any time of the year but especially so in the autumn months with the trees painted crimson, yellow, and orange, harmonizing with the lavender, pink, and blue of the sky while the sun set in the west. With the acres of cornfields running all the way up to the edge of these hills, the spectacular view could compete with the best that Napa Valley had to offer.

When I saw a sign after crossing the Appalachian Highway that Lucasville and the Southern Ohio Correctional Facility were ten miles away, I started having some mild tightness in my chest as my anxiety returned. The closer I got to the prison, the more fearful I became. Ever since I was a small child, I had carried an irrational fear of ending up in jail for a crime that I did not commit, which made no sense since I had only had a few speeding tickets in my life, never stole anything, nor had I assaulted anyone.

The Southern Ohio Correctional Facility is one of Ohio's largest maximum-security penitentiaries. On Easter Sunday, April 11, 1993, one of the country's largest and most violent prison riots broke out there, involving four hundred inmates who took control of three cellblocks. Before order was restored, one prison guard was killed and nine inmates died, either at the hands of other inmates or prison guards. Since the riot, I had been even more anxious driving near a prison for fear of something happening to me. As the road leading to the prison faded in my back window, I felt relieved and loosened the grip I had on my steering wheel. I was out of immediate danger, but Portsmouth was approaching. *Get a grip. You're not going to jail.*

As I entered the city limits, the bridge spanning the Ohio River to Kentucky was in front of me. I quickly turned left onto Main Street, passing the Bob Evans restaurant I occasionally patronized for an early dinner or a cup of coffee. Driving slowly down the main street, I scanned left and right at the empty business fronts, looking for the venue. After a minute, I finally saw it on the right.

Oh no, it's a bar. I hate giving a talk in the back room of a bar.

Memories of living in Steubenville with its dozens of beer joints in bad neighborhoods popped up in my mind. Even having a beer with college friends in Pittsburgh at a local bar or joining others from medical school at Fries Café after exams made me anxious, and none of those places were in shady areas of town. As I wrestled with my irrational fear of something bad happening to me, I went farther down the street and then pulled into a large parking lot that was nearly empty. I put the car in park and kept the motor running as I struggled with my anxiety and fears.

I can't do this. What's wrong with me? Why do I feel so afraid? If I drive back, the rep is going to be upset, and I won't get paid at the end of the lecture. I need this check to make the payroll in two days.

As I had done numerous times before, I tried to tamp down my fear some by listening to another Alison Krauss CD, and I took half of the Xanax I had brought with me. The need to make payroll took precedence over my inclination to leave. I took a deep breath, turned off the car, got my laptop and briefcase out of the back seat, put on my suit coat, and walked up to the front entrance of the restaurant on the town's Main Street. When I entered the bar through the front door, there were two men sitting at the bar. Suddenly, I was back in Steubenville, dealing with two older guys in a bar who threatened me when I was seventeen. Panic set in as I did a quick scan of the room, looking for exits to flee. *Shit! These guys are scary-looking and could beat me up. Calm down. How will I defend myself?*

These two men sitting at the bar got off their stools and walked toward me. Each of them was dressed in jeans and T-shirts with the name of the restaurant on the front. The taller of the two looked at me in my suit and tie and said, "Hi, you must be the speaker for tonight. Right? I'm Greg, one of the owners. Let me show you the room and help you get set up. You have your laptop?"

"Hi. Yes, I'm Dr. Mieczkowski. My laptop's right here. Good to meet you," I told him, sighing with relief. As I shook his hand, my anxiety and fear went away as quickly as it had come on when I first spotted them. My hypervigilance, my internal Doppler radar danger system—"DANGER, WILL ROBINSON! DANGER!"—had been wrong. Once again, there really had been no real danger.

Through my career of giving lectures to physicians in Ohio or the neighboring states, well before Columbine worsened my mental state, I had to overcome my anxiety at being out late and driving home in the dark because my business needed the money to help with the financial constraints of being self-employed. The evening programs were generally enjoyable until it came time to leave. If it was dark outside by the time I finished lecturing, I limited my time answering questions from the audience in order to get on the road.

After Columbine, though, my anxiety about driving home after dark and my hypervigilance became disabling. Unlike years before, when I traveled almost everywhere, I began declining offers to lecture in places that were new to me or more than a two-hour drive away. Certain cities like Columbus or Indianapolis were always safe, whereas Toledo, because of its run-down sections of town, was off-limits for me. For evening lectures, I began to tell the waiter upfront what time to box up my dinner selection and have it ready to go when I had finished fielding audience members' questions. Invariably, one of the pharmaceutical reps would overhear my request and ask, "Dr. Mitch, you aren't going to stay and have dinner afterward with us?" Despite the anxiety of driving at night, in the past I had always enjoyed the camaraderie around the table with the reps, three or four of whom I had worked with for over ten years. I could loosen my tie and take off my suit coat, enjoy a relaxing dinner and a glass or two of wine, and catch up on family and kids. But those days were gone after Columbine.

I can't stay. It's a long drive home. It was going to be dark when I left, and I was afraid.

Instead of revealing the truth that it would be dark and scary driving home, I usually said, "Thanks, but no. It's been a long day and I'm tired."

Sometimes on my trips to these smaller towns, I would just grab an early dinner before the lecture at a place where I felt safe, like the Bob Evans restaurant on the edge of Portsmouth. This made it even easier to leave right after the program.

After Columbine, I no longer felt safe anywhere, even at home. I felt completely exposed, like people were staring through binoculars, watching me in the yard, on the porch, or inside as I walked from my bedroom out onto the landing. On elevators, everyone seemed to be looking at me, passing judgment on how I looked. Even with Dr. Dan's help, I wasn't sure that I would ever stop looking over my shoulder.

CHAPTER 20

Being Hunted

I was enjoying my coffee at Lookout Joe's before another therapy session, thinking through how to finish Tom's story. Because of my worsening anxiety, Dr. Dan had written a prescription for Xanax that I could take as needed in stressful circumstances. Although I had an initial fight-or-flight panic response on arriving to the venue in downtown Portsmouth, the low dose of the medicine I took in the parking lot had helped. At this point in my counseling, I was still not sleeping well even with the trazodone, so he had also given me an Ambien prescription for insomnia. The night I returned from Portsmouth, I couldn't fall asleep, so without guilt I took one of the Ambien tablets, as I began to accept that I needed anti-anxiety medicines and a sleep aid as much as counseling.

Dr. Dan was always prompt with our appointments, the benefit of his diligence in ending all his sessions on time. After we sat down, he asked, "So how did your program go the other night? Wasn't it in Portsmouth?"

Even though he had most likely refreshed his memory from his notes of our previous visit, he made me feel that I was a real person to him and not just his five o'clock appointment when he connected my past sessions to the present.

I replied, "It went all right. I did take half a Xanax in the parking lot when I saw that the venue was a bar and started panicking. Then I walked in and saw two rough-looking guys sitting inside at the bar, giving me the same feeling from when I was back in high school and a guy in his twenties threatened to beat the crap out of me for a snide remark I had made to him. But it turned out these guys in Portsmouth were the owners of the place and not a threat to me. The trip had rattled me, so I took an Ambien to sleep, which you don't really approve of."

Dr. Dan said, "I'm not saying that you shouldn't take it. I'd prefer you to wait fifteen minutes to see if you can fall asleep with just the trazodone and then take the Ambien if needed."

I replied, "I understand, but my mind was still running through the trip, driving past the prison, getting panicked when I walked in. I hear you." *I hear you* was my signal that I wanted to change the subject.

Dr. Dan asked, "Where do you want to start?"

"I need to fill in what happened after my mother died. As relieved as I was about getting out of the war zone, I also felt guilty being able to walk away from Tom. My brain knew that I was justified for not wanting to deal with him, but my heart wouldn't easily let it go since I felt an obligation to help him; he was still my brother."

I continued, "I did call Joanne a week after the funeral to check on Tom's condition. Not surprisingly, she had not reached out to his psychiatrist, claiming she was too busy. From her description of him, it seemed that he was about the same as when I had left. I implored her to do something, get Stas involved, whatever needed to be done to get him back in the hospital. When I brought up the possibility of Tom hurting someone in his state, she dismissed my main concern. I hung up, frustrated over inaction, and told Beth that Joanne hadn't done anything—she was too busy to call his doctor. My sister always drove me crazy. She was the oldest and acting like she was the matriarch of the Mieczkowski family, but she wouldn't step up to help Tom."

Dr. Dan asked, "What made you so concerned that he might hurt someone?"

I replied, "The state he was in, and the menacing look on his face the day of my mother's funeral was the same expression I had seen before on two separate occasions, the first being on my high school graduation day and the second when he was brandishing the shovel that night after my college graduation. It's difficult to describe, but it was terrifying."

Dr. Dan asked, "Did you feel safe being back in your apartment here in Cincinnati?"

I nodded. "Yes, with regard to Tom. But my concerns about living in that location came true. It reminded me so much of living in Polish Hill where our nearby grocery store was just two blocks from our home and I ran the risk of being mugged after shopping. Things got even scarier in my mind when one summer evening, Beth and I heard shouting in the distance and went over to the bedroom window to see what was going on. A couple of blocks over, a man was chasing a woman down the street with a gun and fired three shots at her. Fortunately, he missed while she kept running away. Stepping away from the window, I quickly called the police. Although this shooting incident made me more anxious, there wasn't anything we could do. I wished we could have moved out immediately, but we were stuck there, without enough money to break the one-year rental agreement."

Dr. Dan knew that I was afraid of guns ever since my terrifying ordeal as a child crawling under the bed. He followed with "How did you deal with this incident? I'm sure this must've upset you."

"It did. I became even more hypervigilant and on edge. It wasn't hard to convince Beth that we should find an apartment in Hyde Park when the one-year occupancy ended."

Wanting to move on, I said, "Can we go back to talking about Tom? I can't recall whether it was in the fall after my mother died or in the spring months when I got a phone call from Bob midmorning on a Saturday. His call surprised me since I had just talked to him recently while he was in Steubenville on a weekend visit.

"I answered, 'Hey, Bob. What's up? I wasn't expecting to hear from you. Is everything OK?' I started getting nervous, feeling that something must've happened. Why else was he calling?

"He asked, 'Have you had any phone calls from Tom recently?' My panic alert was screaming louder in my head.

"Feeling more anxious, I asked, 'No. What's going on? You're making me nervous.'

"He continued, and I could tell he was trying not to scare me too much. 'I'm calling to give you a heads-up. Tom is on his way to Cincinnati. If he shows up at your door, don't let him in. You'll need to call the police.'

"At that point, I was in full panic mode. Lightheaded, trembling inside, skin crawling—everything I felt that night from hell after college graduation. My voice was tremulous as I asked, 'What do you mean, he's on his way to Cincinnati? Is he driving here to kill me? What the hell did he say?'

"He responded, 'I don't want to tell you. Just keep your doors locked, and don't open the door if he shows up.'

"The three-story building where we lived had a side door with glass panes that provided access to our apartment on the second floor. It would be easy to get into the building by breaking the glass and undoing the lock on the first floor.

Fortunately, our apartment door was solid wood with a good deadbolt lock.

"With fear in my voice, I replied, 'Bob, c'mon. You have to tell me. I want to know what he said. Does he have a gun?'

"I sensed he wasn't telling me the truth when he said, 'I don't know. All I can say is that you need to be prepared and keep an eye out for him. Don't open the door if he shows up.' I could detect the seriousness of the warning in Bob's voice, as he had never spoken to me that way. I kept throwing question after question at him, wanting more information as I tried to cope with the shock of his warning. I asked, 'Is he on his way?'

"'Yes. He left a short while ago.'

"Paralyzed with fear, I checked the time. Damn, he would be in Cincinnati within two or three hours. I didn't know what else to say or do.

"I said, 'OK, I'm going to go now. Thanks for the heads-up. I hope you're wrong.'"

I told Dr. Dan, "I was sick to my stomach and felt faint as I hung up the phone, walked out of the bedroom, and sat on the living room sofa, saying to myself, 'Oh my God, not again.' I must've lost all the color in my face, since Beth commented on how badly I looked and asked what was going on. When I gave her the details of the conversation that she had not heard, the color in her face drained as well."

As I sat there safely in the counseling session, the terror of that morning was with me again. One of the demons had resurfaced in my brain. I had thought that I was safe in Cincinnati. What was I supposed to do, since I didn't have anything to defend myself with if he showed up? Calling the police would be futile since nothing had happened.

Dr. Dan asked, "What did you do?"

Looking at him as I remembered my reaction, I said, "I didn't know what to do. There was no place to hide. Leaving the apartment and having to come back at night wasn't a good option. Since we didn't have any family nearby and we weren't close enough with any friends to say that my psychotic brother was on his way to harm or kill me, we stayed put, making sure the downstairs door was bolted. The third-floor tenant was away for the weekend, so I didn't have to worry about her leaving the door bolt unlocked. We stayed in our apartment reading or watching TV while I silently prayed that Tom would turn back. Beth was shaken from the phone call. I felt terrible that she had to be involved. She hadn't agreed to love, honor, and put up with Tom when we exchanged wedding vows the previous June. It would've been understandable if she had said to herself, 'What the hell have I gotten myself into?'

"As the day progressed, I couldn't concentrate. I'd read three or four pages in a textbook, go off into my mind's dark and scary shadows for a minute, and then snap back and have to reread what I just covered. I kept checking the time and got more anxious hour by hour, wondering whether he had passed Cambridge and was near Columbus, only two hours from Cincinnati. I prayed that the police would come quickly when I called them on his arrival. It helped to know that he would be visible at the outside door below from our dining room window. Beth and I ate lunch and waited as the hours went by, expecting him to be in town midafternoon. The anticipation of his arriving was torturous, as I thought this might be my last day alive. The clock ticked and the hours went by slowly until around five o'clock when the phone rang. It was Bob.

"I prayed he had good news. 'Hey, Bob. Any news?'

"'You can relax. Tom's back home. His car broke down outside of Wheeling before he got on I-70. Since he couldn't get it restarted, he had to hitchhike back home. He just got back a short while ago.'

"'Thank God, I'm relieved. Thank goodness that old car wasn't dependable. We've been on edge all day waiting for him to show up. Did he say whether he was going to try again?'

"'He didn't say much at all when he got back since he was exhausted. I don't know what he's going to do with the car since he doesn't have any money and Dad sure isn't going to help him out like Mom always did. I don't think he's going to come after you again.'

"'Thanks for letting me know. It's been a rough day. Give me a call if things change. Otherwise I'll catch up with you next weekend.'"

My time was up for the session. I said, "The terror from that day never faded to a distant memory. Tom was the stalker, and I was the prey. Even though I kept questioning when it would all end with him, I knew in my heart that it would only be over when he was dead and couldn't try to harm me anymore."

CHAPTER 21

Silver Dollars

Throughout my life, it was difficult to accept that my own brother wanted to harm or kill me. Sure, I understood it was coming from his altered mental state, but what had I done to trigger his deranged desire to do me harm?

Post-traumatic stress disorder (PTSD) wasn't a topic that was covered in my psychiatry classes, since it didn't become a formal mental health diagnosis until 1980. In looking back, I had all the symptoms of PTSD, which worsened after this second threat from Tom.

A week later in a session, Dr. Dan said, "How'd you do last week after our session? Did it trigger nightmares you've had before?"

I replied, "It did. The war scenes of bloodied streets and dead soldiers came back several nights, plus several of Tom chasing me while I'm running away in slow motion and can't yell out for help. I used the Ambien more this past week, which helps but really knocks me out."

Dr. Dan asked, "Do you want to continue talking about what happened after the day you got the phone call from Bob?" I replied, "No, I'm OK with moving on. As I had thought would happen, the situation at home deteriorated. My father and Tom didn't get along at all with my mother gone. A tipping point occurred when Tom found my father's collection of old silver dollar coins, at least a dozen of them in a cigar box, dated back to 1890. Each was probably worth at least ten to twenty dollars apiece, with the oldest ones in good condition worth as much as a hundred dollars. Since my father wasn't giving him any money to buy cigarettes like my mother had, when Tom found the box of silver dollars, he used the coins at their face value of a dollar to purchase cigarettes and treat himself to a restaurant meal. It wasn't clear how my father discovered that the coins he had collected were missing, but when he did, he went into a rage over what Tom had done and started a fist-fight with him. Considering that my father was all of five foot six and one hundred forty pounds and was in his early sixties and Tom was thirty years younger, six foot two and one hundred eighty pounds, my brother got the best of him. Then, my brother threw the iron resting nearby and hit my father with it. The details of what happened after that are murky, but my father boxed up all of Tom's belongings, placed them outside, and insisted he leave, else the police would be called to arrest him."

By this point in my counseling, Dr. Dan was no longer surprised by what I revealed and asked, "Had he ever gotten into a fight with Tom before?"

I said, "They always exchanged words about everything but had never gotten into a fighting match. Regarding my brother's schizophrenia, my father believed that Tom was faking every-thing and just lazy after being babied by my mother. When I heard about the fight between them from my brother Bob a week or so later, I wasn't surprised that my dad had thrown him out. Sandy, my brother Stas's wife, helped Tom find a run-down, low-rent apartment on the hilltop owned by a Polish lady who had known my mother. The landlord was particularly good to him and regularly provided Tom with meals and leftovers to eat. Sandy paid the monthly rent since Tom didn't have any money, wasn't working, and wasn't going to get any help from my siblings as he waited to get on disability for his mental illness."

Dr. Dan asked, "Did you ever visit him in the apartment?"

"Yes, two or three times a year when I was in medical school and more frequently after moving back to Pittsburgh for my residency training. Despite my fear and everything that had happened between us, I wanted to help him as much as he would allow. After completing my inpatient psychiatry rotation, I'd seen dozens of patients with schizophrenia. To me, Tom was a typical patient, and our family dynamics were like that of other families. When I discussed his condition with my professor, he offered advice on how to deal with him when he was off his medications, which helped me to overcome my fears.

"Before each visit, I would reach Tom on the phone and ask if I could stop over. When we spoke, sometimes he sounded more coherent than other times. On the way to his apartment in Steubenville, I would always stop at the local Kroger and buy two bags of groceries for him. However, no matter how many times I had visited him, I was always nervous and on guard when I walked up the stairs to his apartment and knocked on the door, holding on to the fear that he might ambush me. Hearing him yell that it was open, I would walk in and was usually welcomed with a smile and a handshake.

"There was a routine to my visits. After entering the apartment, I helped him unpack the bags of groceries. Usually there were only a few items in the refrigerator and freezer, with two or three cans of soup and Dinty Moore stew in his kitchen cabinet. He said that I didn't need to buy groceries, but he always thanked me. Overall, once he was living on his own, Tom seemed to be in the best shape I had seen him for years. When I asked, he said that he was taking his medications, which I was able to verify when I used his bathroom, since the bottles had pills in them and were consistently laid out on his counter. His living room had a sofa and a matching side chair that were in decent shape and a TV. Like the bedroom at home, his apartment always smelled of tobacco, with his chain-smoking habit. I usually sat in the chair closer to the front door while he sat on the sofa next to a small table holding his smoking gear, the ashtray overflowing with cigarette butts. When we chatted, Tom asked with genuine interest how medical school was going. I always wondered what he remembered about the threats against my life, but I never risked asking him. Seeing him happily living alone and calmer than ever was a joy, something that I had lost hope in believing could happen for him.

"To get him out of the apartment for a while, we would have lunch at McDonald's, his favorite burger place, usually eating inside, sitting across from one another, no more than twelve inches apart as if nothing had ever happened between us.

"When we were together eating out, I often thought about the trip to Chicago when he was twenty-four and I was fifteen, and how much fun I had. Eating at a McDonald's in Steubenville wasn't the same as sharing a deep-dish pizza in Chicago's Old Town ten years prior, but it was the best I could've ever hoped for."

Dr. Dan said, "Well, I never would have expected this, based on what you had dealt with in the past. What do you think helped Tom get to a better place?"

"I believe my father throwing him out was the best thing that could have happened to him. I hated my father for the things he had done to me, and I knew that Tom shared the same hate. So, maybe being away from the house where Tom may have experienced horrible things as well removed him from a major source of his problems, our father. Honestly, I don't recall Tom being hospitalized again once he was living on his own."

Dr. Dan replied, "That makes sense if there had been traumatic events in Tom's past that came from your father. The conflict with your dad didn't cause his schizophrenia but certainly could have worsened things."

I continued, "After my graduation from med school, Beth and I moved back to Pittsburgh in June 1982 for my internal medicine training, so I was able to visit more frequently. However, on occasion during my residency, I had to cancel a planned visit at the last minute because of work responsibilities from spending over one hundred hours weekly in the hospital.

"I had underestimated how much effect the residency training and fatigue might have on my moods and stress levels. I had not expected to care for so many patients dying from cancer, heart failure, lung disease, women almost paralyzed with end-stage multiple sclerosis, and other serious conditions. One night was particularly traumatic when I had to pronounce three patients dead and talk to their families within hours of each other, while also being responsible for over thirty or forty patients on multiple floors of the hospital. One of the patients was an eighteen-year-old young lady with leukemia who was no longer responding to therapy. Her death was the most difficult during my training. I can picture her and her family now like it was that night when she drifted off and passed away."

Dr. Dan had trained a few years earlier than me, so he was aware of the demands placed on residents. He asked, "Were your program directors aware of these issues or the emotional impact the training had on you and your fellow residents?"

I scoffed, shaking my head. "Really? No, back in the early eighties none of the directors listened. No one was interested in changing the system since it had been that way for a hundred years. Back then, there wasn't a therapist available to help us deal with the trauma. I found it harder and harder to cope with these losses and the responsibility I had as a first-year resident, leaving me depressed, irritable, and angry over an abusive educational system that required us to work over one hundred hours weekly. I directed my anger and frustration at the hospital's program directors, especially when I joined the graduate medical education committee after being elected house staff president. Given the opportunity to voice my concerns, I expressed our frustration that the one hundred twenty residents training in the hospital were being taken advantage of with long hours, poor pay, no disability insurance if we contracted AIDS or hepatitis from an accidental needle stick. Midway through my one-year term, I was crestfallen when our internal medicine director moved for my dismissal from the committee, with all other members in agreement. Talking to the hospital's president and CEO did nothing to reinstate my position, leaving the residents without a voice in our demanding training programs."

He responded, "I'm sorry to hear this. It must've been a surprise to you."

"It was, and hurtful. I think the experience with these dowdy men sitting around the table making decisions for me only added to my mistrust of men in authority."

As I stood to leave, I said, "Thanks for listening."

"Of course. See you next week."

CHAPTER 22

A Voice from the Past

Doctors in training after medical school are traditionally referred to as interns in their first year. The internship year of transition from a student to a licensed physician was the most exhausting and emotionally trying twelve months of my career. Amid all the issues I had dealt with on the hospital wards, I never could have foreseen what else would come my way.

I had another session with Dr. Dan. As he and I sat down in our chairs, he asked, "How was your week?"

As I settled and placed my cup of coffee on the table, I replied, "It went well. No major conflicts at work. Can we go back to what happened during my internship year?"

He replied, "Sure. What's on your mind?"

I let out an audible sigh as I started. "It was April and I had made it past the winter months, leaving the house before dawn and coming home after dark. On the rotation, I had a third-year medical student from the University of Pittsburgh trailing me, doing his mandatory internal medicine third-year clerk-ship. He and I were together on the floors, halfway through an exam on a new patient admitted through the emergency room, when I received a page from the operator that she had an outside call on hold for me. I picked up the phone on the patient's bedside stand and dialed the operator. 'Hello, this is Dr. Mieczkowski. I was paged for an outside call?'

"She said, 'Hello. You do. It's a woman.'

"It wasn't Beth, or the operator would've said so. 'Did she give you her name?'

"The operator continued, 'No, she didn't want to tell me. I'll patch her through. You're on the line with Dr. Mieczkowski. Go ahead, Doctor,' and then got off the call.

"I said, 'Hello, this is Dr. Mieczkowski. How can I help you?' I was expecting it to be one of my outpatient clinic pa-tients whose diabetes was out of control, a common cause of an outside call.

"I vaguely recognized the slurred voice on the other end. 'Hello, Larry. This is Jill Prebills. I need to talk to you.' It took me a second to place her; it was my high school girlfriend. She was crying and sounded desperate. Instantly, I thought, *Oh my God! Why is she calling me? How did she find me?* Other ques-tions erupted in my head. It had been over six years since I last saw her.

"Regaining my composure, I said, 'Hi. I can't talk now since I'm in a patient's room. Give me your number and I'll call you back.'

"I wrote it down on my clipboard, hung up the phone, and told the patient that I had to step out and take the call. I walked down the hall to the nurses' station to call her back, while wrestling with bewilderment. Why had she reached out to me in the middle of her crisis? She had married a guy in law school and was living in Pittsburgh. She must've known that I was married, since her parents came to my wedding ceremony.

Why was she involving me in her life now? I had enough of my own problems to deal with.

"Jill was a year older than me. She and I dated in high school and for half of her first year in nursing school. Our relationship in high school was intense, as we spent the majority of our free time together. She knew about my background, the physical and mental abuse from my parents, my father's alcoholism, the struggles with my brother Tom's mental illness, as well as my dreams and aspirations to become a doctor. Like most teenage romances, we believed our feelings for each other would continue to grow, perhaps even lead to marriage in the future.

"However, when she was in her first year of college and I was a high school senior, our social life and emotional connection drifted away, replaced by spending hours in the privacy of her dorm room. Sex, whether I wanted to engage or not, was always part of the time we shared alone. I didn't understand why this contributed to my pulling away from the relationship, but within months we made a mutual decision to stop dating. I was too timid to share my true feelings with her, believing there must be something wrong with me as a guy when I didn't jump at the chance to have sex. I had seen her a few times after our breakup, but we had not crossed paths for years.

"When I dialed her number, she answered quickly and said, 'Thanks for calling back.'

"I had a mix of emotions—apprehension, confusion, anxiety—as I responded. 'Hi. What's going on? I'm kind of shocked that you called me. How did you know that I was here at Mercy?' I could hear her crying softly.

"'I'm in a terrible place. I called you since you're the only one who understands what I'm going through.' Understand what? It wasn't what I had expected to hear. Thinking the worst, I thought maybe one of her parents had died. But I was still disoriented by her phone call, not being able to place what was happening in the context of my life. I couldn't process what she had just said. I kept thinking, *Who is this? Why are you calling me? Where's your husband? Have you been stalking me?* It brought back terrifying memories of my brother Bob warning me about Tom driving down to Cincinnati.

"Needing to know the answer before I could continue, I asked her again, 'How did you know that I was a resident here at Mercy?'

"'I've been a nurse in the ICU since I graduated from nursing school. I saw your name on the list of the incoming residents last summer.' Since I hadn't had a rotation in the ICU, I would not have run into her.

"Our separate lives had intersected, but I didn't want to be involved in her life since I had enough drama in my own.

"I asked, 'So, how can I help you? It sounds like you're crying.'

"She replied, 'I am. I don't know what to do or who to call. But I knew you were at Mercy, and you'd understand.'

"Hearing the desperation in her voice, I lowered my guard. 'What would I understand? Tell me what's going on.' I wasn't prepared when she said, 'I just couldn't take it anymore. I've slit my wrists and I'm bleeding.'

"In an instant, I froze as the air was sucked out of the room where I was sitting and everything went silent. I didn't hear the next few sentences she said, as everything in my world just stopped. After what seemed to be an eternity, I could feel the air come rushing back into my lungs as I was able to breathe again; someone had turned the volume back up, and I could process what I had just heard.

"I asked typical triage questions quickly. 'How bad are you bleeding? Are you at home? Are you alone? Do you feel faint?'

"'I'm home alone. I've been able to stop the bleeding, and I don't feel faint.'

"I said, 'Jill, please listen to me. You need to call 911. OK?'

"Crying harder now, she said, 'I can't call the paramedics. I just can't.'

"I wasn't going to argue with her. 'OK. Tell me where you live so that I can call them for you.'

"'No, I'll just drive myself to the ER. I don't live that far from the hospital. Will you meet me in the emergency room?'

"What was I supposed to do? Sighing, I quickly agreed. 'OK, I'll come down to the ER when you arrive. I'll call ahead and let them know you're on your way.'

"Hanging up the phone, I sat there processing another surreal experience. My personal and family life had been relatively free of drama for a while. Calling the ER, I spoke to the attending physician and gave her the details of the situation, without making any mention of our previous connection. Hanging up the phone, I put her issues aside and went back to finishing the exam on the patient with my third-year medical school student.

"About thirty minutes later, the ER nurse paged me that Jill had arrived. By that point in my training, there were few patient situations that I hadn't seen. That wasn't the case this time as I walked down to the ER, wondering if I could handle seeing her in this condition. I wasn't her doctor, only just an old friend. What would I say? What did she want from me? Why did she call me and not her husband or anyone else? When I arrived, her nurse pointed to the room where she was. I could see through the glass panes of the closed door that the curtain was pulled around the bed to give her privacy. I knocked, then cracked the door open a bit and asked if I could come in. She recognized my voice. 'Larry, you can come in.'

"As I opened the door and walked behind the curtain, I immediately recognized the smell of stale beer and vomit. She looked the same as she had when I had last seen her, but thinner. I hadn't remembered her to be so petite. But I was bigger than when I had seen her last, having grown four inches in college, and was no longer the skinny guy I was in high school. A portion of her last meal was on the flannel shirt she was wearing. Both wrists were bandaged with fresh gauze.

"Sitting down, I asked, 'How are you? What's been going on?'

"She said that she had been depressed and just couldn't cope any longer, and she started to cry. As I sat there without saying much, she admitted to struggling for years and said she didn't have anyone to fully confide in. She focused her attention on me and asked, 'How did you do it? How did you manage all the issues you grew up with and make it through medical school?'

"The question didn't take me by surprise, but I didn't have a good explanation for how I had not let my past deter me from my goal of being a doctor and having a relatively happy life. I was just able to move forward.

"I replied, 'I don't really know. Maybe the abuse in my childhood enabled me to build up the walls around me to protect myself.'

"She asked, 'Have you ever seen a counselor?'

"'No, although I have considered it multiple times. I saw and read dozens of informative articles about depression and schizophrenia on my psych rotation in medical school. What about you? Have you seen anyone?'

"Jill said, 'No.' Since she did not have her own psychiatrist, I would need to talk to one of our staff physicians for admission to the behavioral health unit. I checked the time on the wall clock, reminding me that I had a dozen patients upstairs to see with my medical student.

"I told her that I had to go. As I stood up to leave the room, she quickly asked about my family and how my wife and I were doing. It was an awkward moment as I was hesitant to say much to her about my personal life. Beth was four months pregnant with our first child at the time, my mother had died since I had last seen Jill, Tom's mental health had continued to deteriorate, and residency was draining the humanity out of me. I didn't have time to chat. 'Everyone is doing well. Thanks for asking. Good luck, Jill.'

"The experience was so surreal. I was sad for what she had been going through. God knows, I did understand. Everything about the situation was traumatizing. I couldn't get the image of her wrists laid bare out of my head. She wasn't a stranger coming into the ER for care. She was someone I had once loved and cared for as a teenager. When I had left for work early that morning, I never could have imagined being faced with this near tragedy.

"The nurse then told me that Jill's husband had arrived. As I walked into the waiting room and saw him pacing, I assumed he would be shocked by what happened but also questioning why she had called me for help. 'Hi, Mark. I'm Larry Mieczkowski. Wasn't sure you'd remember me.'

"He shook my hand and said, 'I do. How's she doing?'

"I replied, 'She's in decent shape considering what she's gone through, and lucky there wasn't more damage.'

"He asked about her mental state and why she had called me, rather than the unsaid question of whether we were having an affair. I assured him that I was unaware she worked there and that she had called me out of the blue, knowing that I was a resident, adding that she had likely reached out to me knowing my own history in dealing with mental illness in the family and would understand her depression. After giving him the names of the physicians who would be taking care of her, I told him that I had to leave, while reassuring him that she was in good hands.

"Those few hours had been the most emotionally draining experience in my young career, leaving me exhausted and wishing that I could go home. Asking another resident to cover for me, however, wasn't an option since all my colleagues were just as busy as I was and were reluctant to take on more work. I resumed my rounds, taking care of a dozen patients, knowing that once again I would be late getting home."

Dr. Dan asked as I took a drink of coffee, "Do you know what happened to her afterward?"

I replied, "A few days later, I ran into the psychiatrist caring for her, who said she was doing well and would be discharged soon. Since then, though, I've not spoken to her or heard anything about her."

Time was up. Leaning forward in his chair, Dr. Dan asked, "Are you all right? This interaction must have been difficult."

I told him that I was fine. At times, in our past sessions, he had seen my emotions erupt to the surface, sometimes sadness with uncontrollable crying, while other times anger, and frequently both. The session had brought back a portion of the sadness I'd felt for Jill, her husband, and their kids, but in this case the sorrow wasn't about me.

CHAPTER 23

Another Phone Call

Sitting in Dr. Dan's waiting room for my next session, I was preparing myself to tell him about the rest of that traumatic week in 1983. My heart was already heavy as I climbed the stairs to his office.

He said, "You look like you have something heavy on your mind. What's going on?"

I began, "I need to finish telling you about the next few days after helping Jill. It was early afternoon two days later when I got another page from the operator for an outside call. I wondered who might be calling me, since I had just left my outpatient clinic. Maybe my nurse needed to speak to me about something that needed to be signed. Calling the operator back, I said, 'Hello, this is Dr. Mieczkowski.'

"She said, 'Doctor, I have Karen Parker on the line. She said she's your niece.' Karen, my oldest sister's daughter, and I were close; she was just four years younger than me. Since she was calling me at work, I knew she must be the bearer of bad news, causing me to be on guard.

"'Uncle Larry, hi, this is Karen.' I could tell she had been crying as she struggled to say what had happened. 'There's some bad news, and you need to come home.'

"Already prepared for bad news, I wasn't going to drive to Steubenville just to hear what happened. Based on her emotional state, I figured someone had died. 'Just tell me what's going on!'

"She replied, 'I can't tell you over the phone.'

"Getting annoyed as I easily did when I was in training, I said, 'Karen, I'm a doctor, for God's sake.' With growing frustration, I said, 'I can manage it. Just tell me.' She was triggering a reaction from my past, treating me like a child, just as her mother had done for nearly thirty years.

"Finally, she said, 'It's Uncle Tom. He was found dead in his apartment this morning. The landlord went up to the landing of the house to give him breakfast and saw that he was not moving in his bed through the window of the apartment and called my mom. My dad went over and found him lifeless. Uncle Tom was already stiff, cold, and blue and must've passed overnight.' Tom was only thirty-six years old when he died.

"Since Tom was diagnosed with schizophrenia when he was twenty-four years old, I had questioned how I would react if Tom committed suicide. So, I shouldn't have been shocked by his death since I'd thought about it so many times. I fought back the tears and retained my composure outwardly as I asked my niece other questions. Although suicide seemed the most probable cause of death, I had doubts that he would've done it since he had been doing well and I had just spoken to him on the phone the previous Sunday. She said that the coroner was going to do an autopsy, which would include analyzing the blood for toxic substances. Tom had smoked heavily for over twenty years, plus there was our family history of heart disease. Was it suicide, a fatal heart attack, or underlying lung cancer with his smoking history and years of exposure to cancer-causing chemicals when he worked in the steel mill?

"Still composed, I told her that I would be in Steubenville by five o'clock and hung up. Then, the floodgates opened, and I started crying and sobbing from grief. The nurses' station was always busy, and there were RNs, unit clerks, and other medical residents around. My raw emotional reaction was obvious to everyone, but I didn't care. I was alone in my world, leaning forward with my head resting in my hands, unable to move or stop crying as I sobbed uncontrollably over the sudden death of my brother.

"Chris, the head nurse on the floor, heard me, walked over, and calmly asked what had happened. I told her that I had just gotten the news that my older brother had died. She said that I could sit in her office, which was just around the corner from the nurses' station. I didn't say a word as she sat down at her desk after closing the door for privacy. Every time I tried to control my crying to say something to her, the grief swelled, making it impossible to talk amid the tears. I cried for the loss of a normal life for him, getting married, having children, an excellent job, golfing with his friends. I cried for the times he was placed in Cambridge, the restraints and handcuffs holding him down when he was psychotic, like he was an animal. I cried for the loss of his friends as his mental illness forced him further away from the real world. Letting out my grief went on for almost fifteen minutes before I was able to compose myself. Chris left the room for a minute to get me a cup of coffee. When she returned, I was calm enough to explain Tom's story and our relationship through the years. Grateful for her kindness and support, I thanked her profusely, while also apologizing for losing it. It was always embarrassing to me when I cried in public. She quickly dismissed my apology. I was ready to move on and stood up. 'Thanks for your support and kind words. I appreciate it.'

"My next step was to inform my program directors of Tom's sudden death and request a few days off. Although I don't remember calling Beth, she was home when I arrived at our apartment. I started crying again as she hugged me and said how sorry she was, knowing that I loved him despite all the problems in the past. The relief I thought I might feel on his death was replaced by the love I had for him and the pain he had suffered over the past fifteen years.

"We left for Steubenville after I changed from my dress shirt and tie and white pants into more casual attire. My mind was filled with mostly the good memories of Tom from the past. Although sad over his death, I was relieved that years of suffering were over and he was at peace in the afterlife.

"As we arrived at the family home, the church parking lot next to our house wasn't filled with my family's cars like when my mother died four years earlier. Since the neighborhood had deteriorated a great deal in recent years and was home to break-ins and theft, I was uncomfortable leaving our car out in the open, but there were no other places to park. As we entered the house, Joanne and Angelo were in the kitchen along with Mary Ellen. Mary Ellen's sadness over his death was evident as she dabbed at tears. My niece Karen was crying and gave me a big hug when I walked in. However, for my father and Joanne, it seemed to be just another day at 815 Pekruhn Court. My father showed no emotion that day other than grumbling over what the funeral was going to cost him. He and my sisters Joanne and Mary Ellen had already gone to the funeral home and planned the schedule of visits and chosen the casket. If my father had his way, I'm certain he would've put Tom in a wooden box and buried him in the woods above our neighborhood to save himself the expense of having an actual funeral. Since Tom didn't have any life insurance, my father was left paying the cost of the funeral. He, of course, chose the lowest-cost burial option.

"Suicide was discussed as the cause of death among my family members at the house. Although a complete autopsy can take days to complete, the coroner is often able to give a preliminary cause of death in hours, based on results of drug and chemical levels in the blood and urine. His office had already called earlier with a preliminary cause of death: salicylate poisoning from an overdose of aspirin. I questioned whether it was accidental instead of intentional since Tom had been a chronic user of aspirin for over twenty years, taking them for his constant headaches. He could go through a bottle of two hundred tablets a week back when I was in high school. When a person takes excessive amounts of aspirin on a daily basis, ingesting a small amount of additional aspirin can rapidly raise the concentration in the blood to toxic levels and cause death from the lungs filling up with fluid. Knowing that my family wouldn't listen to what I had to say as a physician, I kept this possibility to myself.

"Beth and I didn't stay long, since there wasn't much to decide or talk about. On the short drive back to our apartment, I explained the possibility that Tom's death could have been an accidental overdose. We reached our apartment around eight o'clock and I poured my favorite drink, a double whiskey on ice, and wanted to relax by watching TV. Exhausted by the stress from the past days, I just wanted to be left alone before going to bed. There was nothing Beth could say that would ease my pain.

"The visitation hours at the funeral home were respectful and subdued. No one threw themselves on the coffin or engaged in any other drama. A sizable number of our cousins showed and offered condolences. I had the chance to talk with four or five of his old high school friends; all had been close to Tom before the onset of his schizophrenia. They expressed their sadness and confusion over what had happened to him. None of his friends or even our cousins really knew the extent of his mental illness or the threats of violence he had demonstrated. I skirted questions from anyone who asked whether he had killed himself, although I overheard a handful of visitors refer to Tom as being crazy.

"After the traditional funeral mass with its Polish songs, the religious cloth covering Tom's coffin was removed and replaced by a large American flag. It was then wheeled slowly out of the church, lifted off the catafalque by the six pallbearers; four of them were close cousins and two were his closest friends from high school who he had cut off from his life. They carried the casket down the set of concrete steps and placed it in the waiting black hearse. It was a tradition that funeral attendees stood in their place outside of the church or on the steps until the door to the hearse was closed. Once that happened, everyone dispersed to their cars to be part of the long funeral procession to Mount Calvary Cemetery, led by a police officer on a motorcycle to direct traffic along the way.

"While this was going on outside, the church's choir, consisting of aging gray-haired women, continued singing the mournful recessional song. The brass bells high up in the church's towers tolled the end of another funeral service. Regardless of my age or who had died, I was always brought to tears by the sound of this particular song as a casket was lifted into the hearse. That day was no different.

"Tom was buried in a plot next to my parents'. My father's name and date of birth had already been carved into the large pink granite headstone, awaiting his death. At the grave site, I was angry when Mary Ellen told me that my father had refused to pay for a headstone for Tom. The VA would mark his grave with a large bronze plaque with his name, birth date, date of death, rank, and dates of his army service engraved on a brass plate. This last spiteful act for his own son furthered my disdain for my father.

"I have no recollection of being at the church hall reception, eating lunch, leaving for our apartment, or saying goodbye to family. It's all just a blur. I suppose the trauma of Jill's attempted suicide and then Tom's death two days later was too much for my brain to process, and I put those memories somewhere deep in my mind."

Dr. Dan had taken in the details of events that I had only barely touched on earlier in my counseling sessions. Those three days in April had been very painful for me. He said, "I appreciate your sharing what happened. You had never mentioned Jill and the suicide attempt that happened two days before Tom's death plus all the other trauma we've discussed in the sessions."

Nodding in agreement, I said, "I have lived a life of nonstop painful ordeals." Dr. Dan had always used the metaphor of how the sound of one train may drown out the sound of another train running on another track. That's how I felt, one train after another barreling into me.

Our session was just about over. He asked, "How did the days and weeks go after Tom's death?"

"It went as expected. Before leaving for Pittsburgh, Stas, Angelo, and I met at Tom's apartment to go through his belongings. As we entered, I first walked over to the bedroom and stood looking at the unmade bed where he had died. On his dresser were various bottles of aftershave and cologne, a watch, a college fraternity ring, and photos of him and his army friends.

"As I looked in his bathroom, I spotted two or three bottles of aspirin. Seeing firsthand the medicine that had caused his death, I immediately teared up. If it was intentional, I figured that he'd finally had enough of the pain and suffering he had dealt with for over a decade. From the hallway, out of the corner of my eye, I was startled to see his army shovel in the bedroom closet. Unbeknownst to me, he had it in his apartment all of the times I had visited. The hospital must have given it back to him when he was discharged days after the early morning standoff between us in the dining room of the family home after my graduation in 1978. Although the fear from that night came flooding back, for some illogical reason, I decided to take the shovel with me.

"Looking back at Tom's dresser, I thought Bob would like to have the fraternity ring from the College of Steubenville, where they had been studying together. Walking back into the living room, I stood there for a few minutes silently watching Stas and Ang go through Tom's few belongings like vultures picking at the carcass of a dead animal. Neither of them had ever really helped Tom through the years.

"Disgusted by their conduct, I needed to leave to avoid a verbal confrontation. I walked out of the run-down apartment, headed down the stairs, and sat in the car until they had satiated themselves with a set of golf clubs, a winter jacket I had purchased for Tom, the quilt from his bed, and a collection of well-worn pots and pans, the few tangible possessions of Tom's thirty-six years on earth.

"I knew what I wanted as a keepsake of Tom's life. After the graveside ceremony, the military guard had presented my father with the triangular-folded American flag as a lasting symbol of Tom's service to our country. Since he couldn't care less about his own son or the flag that had draped the casket during the ride to the cemetery and the graveside service, I took it from my father's house later that day and have kept it since Tom's death in 1983."

"What happened to the army shovel?" Dr. Dan asked as our time was ending.

"I still have it. I never told my children the complete backstory of the small army shovel I used to dig in the sand and make castles on our summer vacations in Cape May, New Jersey."

Dr. Dan said, "I'm surprised to hear that. Why have you kept it all these years?"

"I'm not sure. I think a part of me saw it as a medal for my years of service helping Tom. It wasn't a Silver Star like soldiers receive for bravery in combat, but for me it came close. I also figured that if I held on to it, no one else could ever try to use it against me again."

CHAPTER 24

What About Bob?

"Where did your older brother Bob fit in all of this?" Dr. Dan asked in another session. "You've shared bits and pieces, but you haven't really talked much about him."

"You're right. I haven't discussed my relationship with Bob because it's another painful chapter of my life. I haven't seen him, spoken to him, or had any communication from him since 1991, nearly three years after my father died."

Dr. Dan had never been lighthearted in any of our sessions, but he seemed to take on a more serious face as I started to discuss Bob and our relationship. It was apparent to me that he had not expected to hear that there was another troubled brother in my life who had been a source of further trauma.

I continued, "It's been years since any of my relatives have seen him about town. If he's still in Steubenville, he's not living in the family house. He had mentioned moving to Florida to a close cousin at one time, but for all I know he's homeless somewhere, or he may be dead."

Focusing on the abuse from my parents, dealing with Tom and his schizophrenia and the night he could have killed me, had allowed me to delay talking about Bob and what had happened to him and to our relationship. My emotions over our estrangement were still very raw, despite the separation happening over a decade ago. I already had tears in my eyes as I continued, "I lost my best friend when he walked away from me."

Dr. Dan asked in a soft voice, "What happened?"

I sighed as I said, "It's a long story. Despite being six years apart, Bob and I had always been close from childhood. We had a special relationship, often fishing together on the riverfront, sled riding with me on top of him holding on for dear life in the middle of a snowstorm down the steep hills above our home, shopping for groceries at the local supermarket when we were both just kids, or simply washing and drying the dishes together after dinner. He was also the big brother I could count on to protect me from older boys in the neighborhood. As I got older, he came to all of my grade school and high school football games, always encouraging me, unlike my oldest brother, Stas, who always criticized my performance, even when I scored a touchdown or had an interception.

"How I viewed Bob through the eyes of a twelve-year-old, though, was vastly different from what I saw when I was in college and he was still living at home, or when I was a thirty-three-year-old physician and he was thirty-nine, living in Pittsburgh. As a child and young teenager, I idolized him. Clearly our family wasn't like the Cleavers, but as a kid if I had to choose the best characterization of our relationship growing up, he was like the older brother, Wally, and I was his younger brother, Beaver, in the TV series from the sixties, *Leave It to Beaver*. Just like in the show, my brother Bob seemed to do no wrong and never got into trouble as a kid. I don't recall my mother or father ever punishing him, nor do I recall hearing about Bob getting summoned to the principal's office in grade school like I was. I don't remember anyone disliking him or ever calling him a pest, deserving of punishment. He helped my father with household projects, whereas when I tagged along, I was told to get out of the way. My grandfather across the street trusted him to take care of his yard and garden, paying him with a half-dollar coin each week." I chuckled to myself, saying, "He really was a lot like Wally in his younger years." My description brought a rare smile to Dr. Dan's face as I made the comparison.

"But he changed as he went through high school. He had a different group of friends, and I knew that he was partying with them on the weekends. I usually stayed up late watching TV on Friday and Saturday nights, and Bob would come home after my parents were asleep. He'd look at me with a drunken gaze and with slurred words he'd say, 'Don't tell Mom.' I never did. He was still a great brother, but I started to see a different part of him. For a couple of years, I thought he was drinking only beer or wine but occasionally heard bits and pieces of conversations between him and his friends in our home or when I was in the car with them—pot, pills, and even the mention of LSD. After all, it was the sixties. Bob always changed the conversation if I was within earshot of them talking about getting high.

"There were a couple of things Bob did in high school that really bothered me. Like other guys who lived downtown or whose fathers worked in the steel mills, Bob belittled the smarter guys in his class. He also always boasted that he and his friends were better football players than the guys on the team, despite Bob and his friends never trying out. He became rebellious in the face of authority. One time when he was a senior in high school and had been drinking, he got into an altercation with a priest chaperoning a school dance who refused to let Bob in since he smelled alcohol on him. The police

were called, and Bob was taken into custody. Because my father refused to bail him out, he spent the night in jail. This
was the first time I recall that Bob was ever defiant and angry,
showing a side of himself that made me question what was
going on in his head. There was a juvenile court hearing with
a type of punishment handed out, but fortunately he didn't get
sent to a detention center. Of course, my mother was morti-
fied that he had gotten into trouble, since Bob was clearly my
mother's favorite son who could do no wrong. As the youngest
of seven, I witnessed dozens of examples of behavior from my
older siblings, especially my brothers, I did not want to emu-
late. The mental notes I took helped me make better decisions
for the most part about studying hard and hanging out with
the right crowd.

"Bob had stopped dating after high school, which was
unlike his friends or Tom. If he did have a girlfriend, he kept
it to himself. I didn't think he was gay since he had *Playboy*,
Penthouse, and other adult magazines lying around in his
apartment, and he would talk about women he and his friends
had met. He never did marry."

I paused to take a drink from my coffee cup as I looked over
to the clock to see how much time remained in my session.

Dr. Dan questioned, "What do you think was going on
with Bob through the years? I assume he wasn't showing any
signs of depression or mental illness like Tom."

"He always seemed upbeat in college despite his life changing when Tom was diagnosed with schizophrenia the summer
before the two of them were starting the fourth year at the
College of Steubenville. Tom didn't complete his studies because of his illness, but although Bob did graduate, he never
looked for a job in the accounting field."

Dr. Dan asked, "Why not? Did he do poorly in college?"

"No, actually, he did very well in college, which made his
decision not to pursue an accounting job even more difficult to

understand. One of his professors, well respected in the region, wrote a glowing letter of recommendation for him. Everyone in the family expected him to have a professional white-collar job after graduation, but he took on various manual jobs and after a year went to work for my aunt's garage-door company. I'm not sure why he went in that direction. Maybe he hoped she'd eventually sell him the business, which unfortunately didn't happen. During those years after college, besides working for our aunt, he was still generous with his time, helping others on house projects. At times, Stas and Joanne took advantage of his willingness to help out by not paying him much for his efforts or only buying him a case of beer as compensation for his hard work.

"He was twenty-two years old at that point and living at home. I never understood why he didn't break away from my parents and at least move into an apartment on his own. It seemed like they had a psychological hold over him; certainly my mother played with his head, saying how she couldn't imagine dealing with things if Bob moved out, as if he had to sacrifice his life for hers. What do you think?"

Dr. Dan replied, "Well, it's certainly not typical, but in and of itself it doesn't mean his behavior was abnormal. Maybe he just didn't have the confidence to pursue a professional position and needed the security of staying at home. You were adventuresome in high school and college, which obviously was to your benefit." I hadn't really thought of it that way. Dr. Dan was right. Throughout my life, I hadn't been afraid to fail or make a mistake and then move on. Bob was always less outspoken and tentative in his interactions with family and friends.

"Through my college years, Bob and I didn't see each other as often since I was overburdened with my academic work. Whatever free time I had, I spent it at the fraternity or playing intramural sports. But he remained helpful, picking me up after exams at the end of the semester or before holiday breaks and then driving me back to campus. He also shared in confidence the negative remarks Joanne and Stas were saying about me behind my back. Their behavior didn't really surprise me, as I had lived with their resentment toward my success and their belief that they had been shortchanged by our parents, whereas I was the youngest and got everything I wanted out of my parents. It was really absurd. Stas was an all-state high school basketball player and received a full scholarship to a Division I college but flunked out after his first semester and lost his scholarship. Joanne had the opportunity to enroll in business school after high school but instead blamed my parents for her not pursuing further education.

"Bob's life changed for the better in the spring of 1978, two months before my college graduation. Although it came as a major surprise to me, I was thrilled when he told me about his interview with the IRS in Louisville, Kentucky. When he was offered the position and accepted, I was so happy for him. Finally, he was getting away from Steubenville and would be free of our dysfunctional family. Somehow, he found the strength not to succumb to my mother's effort to guilt him to stay in the area. He was starting a completely new and different chapter of his life."

I continued, "Bob stayed with the IRS for five or six years before he accepted a position with the Department of Defense based in Pittsburgh, although he eventually ended up spending the majority of his time working at the Pentagon. Since he was in a high-security-clearance position, he couldn't talk about his work. He had a nice apartment in a high-rise building with a magnificent view of downtown Pittsburgh. It was next to Duquesne University, where a niece and nephew of ours were studying pharmacy. It seemed that everything was falling into place for him.

"In 1984, my father became ill, requiring hospitalization. Testing showed that his exhaustion was coming from an enlarged heart and atrial fibrillation, a common but seri-ous heart arrhythmia often seen in patients with alcoholism. A head CT scan showed brain damage from a series of small strokes he'd had throughout the years, which explained his ob-vious memory loss. Because he had liver disease from exces-sive drinking, he could not take prescription blood thinners to help prevent further strokes and damage, because the risk of bleeding with their use was too high. Despite the ongoing mini-strokes and his heart problems, he did relatively well with a daily aspirin and medications to treat his blood pressure and control his heart rate. His strength and stamina improved, but his memory loss continued to worsen. Somewhere around this time Bob moved back home, but I'm not certain of the actual year as my memory of the details is a bit fuzzy."

Anticipating the question Dr. Dan might ask, I said sar-castically, "Why did he move back home in his late thirties? Who knows! I certainly didn't. He said that he wanted to get answers to some questions that had been bothering him for years. I never knew what those questions were nor whether he got them answered. From my perspective, I thought it was a mistake to leave his high-rise apartment in Pittsburgh to live with my father back in Polish Hill and presumptuous of him to think he would get explanations from our father for anything. I don't know. Maybe he had issues with my father that I didn't know about. If so, he never shared any of them with me or Mary Ellen.

"Once he was back in Steubenville, I was confused and hurt when Bob began to spend more time with our abusive father than me. I didn't understand his devotion to him. He would boast about home improvements my father had done, such as installing tile in the shower. His conversations extolling my father's virtues grated on me, as if he expected me to suddenly see how great a guy our dad was. Bob had soft-pedaled my feel-ings toward our father by often saying, 'I know you and Dad don't get along.' It wasn't a matter of not getting along—I hated him and had no interest in seeing him or involving him in my life. I wanted Bob—and my other siblings as well—to hate him as much as I did, and I didn't understand why they didn't. My father was like a cult leader who had brainwashed Bob and my sisters to drink the Kool-Aid and become his loyal followers.

"While employed with the DOD, Bob had started investing in the stock market. He was exceptionally good at it, raking in profits for himself and others to whom he had given advice. I was in training, paid poorly, and had no extra money for buying stocks and selling them for quick profits. He let me know one day that he was leaving his DOD job and was buying a stock brokerage franchise with a partner. I was excited for him and proud of him for making such a big step. He got through all the certifications that were required in the mid-eighties. Everything was going well, and then it all crashed down on him and his partner on Monday, October 19, 1987, when the stock market dropped nearly twenty-three percent, the largest drop in a single session since the Great Depression.

"At the time, I was working in Dayton as a faculty member at the medical school. When I heard about the market crash on the news that evening, I called him immediately. The stress he was under was obvious in his voice. Since I had generous credit lines from multiple banks, I offered to give him a loan. He was grateful for the offer but declined, saying that he and his partner needed much more to stay in business than the amount I could lend. The bottom line for Bob and his partner was that within forty-eight hours they were bankrupt and had to close their business.

"After the loss of his business, Bob went off the grid. He rarely ventured out, would only take handyman jobs where he was paid in cash, and did little that would make him visible. In the years after, he didn't file tax returns in order to remain invisible to anyone trying to find him. It seemed to me that he was hiding from someone, perhaps from a person he owed money. It was all speculation about his behavior since he wouldn't talk about it. The bankruptcy was a pivotal event in his life, which he didn't recover from financially or emotionally. It didn't cross my mind at the time that losing his business was traumatic enough to trigger a full-blown depression."

Dr. Dan replied, "It's common for that type of loss to cause depression, especially if it runs in the family and he didn't have someone in his life to offer emotional support. It sounds like from what you've said that although he was withdrawing from others, he declined any help. Would you agree?"

I said, "You're right. Mary Ellen and I were worried about him and talked frequently about what to do. He kept pushing us away. I knew he was tormented by his business failing. For years, he had talked about wanting to be a millionaire before he was thirty years old. In his view of the world, financial success translates to respect, which he was desperately seeking. Although I knew he was happy for me and my success, I suspect he grew tired of people asking about his brother the doctor.

"Whatever stability there was in the family dynamics was shattered when my father had a major stroke on a Friday in April 1988. Our house phone rang in the early evening around dinnertime. Beth answered the phone and said that it was Mary Ellen. As she handed me the phone, she added, 'It's about your dad.' Since I figured she was calling with unwelcome news, I wasn't surprised to hear that my father had just had a major stroke. I was expecting this day to come years ago when he was first diagnosed with his heart problems and evidence of brain damage from small strokes. Mary Ellen painted a dismal picture of how he was doing: he couldn't talk, was paralyzed on his right side, and was having trouble breathing. When she asked when I would be able to drive home, I explained that it would be midafternoon the next day, since

I had been scheduled for six months to give a lecture at the state's American Heart Association annual scientific meeting the next morning in Columbus. At the end of our short conversation, I specifically asked her to tell Joanne about my obligation the next morning and that I would drive directly to the hospital after my talk. Overhearing the conversation, my wife asked what had happened. 'My dad had a major stroke earlier today. He's in the hospital. Sounds bad, since he can't talk and is paralyzed on the right side.' We discussed the logistics of driving to Steubenville. I had the lecture in Columbus early the next day, plus our daughter was only four and a half years old and our son was a toddler. It wasn't feasible to have them join me on the drive.

"I left immediately after my lecture the next morning instead of staying to chat with other doctors in attendance, as I would have normally done. While I drove, memories of the past came flooding back: my dad hitting me and Mary Ellen, his physical abuse of my mother, hiding from him in the schoolyard, and the alcohol addiction that had affected my life is so many ways. Based on what I was told about his condition, I didn't think he'd survive, but if he did, he would likely have to be placed in a nursing home. I couldn't help but think that my father was finally getting his comeuppance for the abuse and neglect he had caused. He would at least be out of my life.

"Pulling into the hospital's parking lot, I was anxious about seeing my siblings and how our interaction would go. Joanne, Patricia, and Stas had never sought my opinion as a physician. On the rare occasions they did ask, my recommendations were usually ignored. Since Patricia ignored advice from everyone including her own doctors about her health and the health of her children, I didn't think her feelings came from resentment. She had always been stubborn and hardheaded in that regard.

"I ruminated on how to tell my siblings that most patients don't survive a massive stroke even when previously healthy, but my father also had severe heart disease, liver cirrhosis, and chronic lung disease from his decades of smoking. If a patient survives the first forty-eight to seventy-two hours, over the ensuing weeks pneumonia often will set in and become the ultimate cause of death.

"It felt strange entering the lobby of my hometown hospital as a physician where I had worked for years as a nurse's aide. When the elevator dinged its arrival at the eighth floor and the door opened, I stepped onto the floor where I had worked as a teenager. It didn't look much different. As I walked over to the waiting room where I knew my sisters Joanne and Patricia would be sitting, I became more apprehensive when I heard them crying. Bob had been in earlier but had gone home to take a shower and get something to eat. After routine greetings, they provided a brief update about my father's status. However, it didn't take long before the conversation shifted from my father to criticism of my behavior, which I had expected. Even though she knew the answer, Joanne, with her typical judgmental tone, questioned why I had not driven to the hospital yesterday after Mary Ellen had called me. She wasn't going to let me off easily, so while staying calm, I let her vent for a few minutes. Getting into a quarrel with her would not serve a positive purpose, so unlike in the past, I didn't take the bait.

"'Look, Joanne, I asked Mary Ellen to let you know what was going on with my schedule. I had agreed to give the lecture this morning in Columbus six months ago, and I couldn't break my commitment at the last minute.' I knew what she was likely thinking: *So, Dad isn't important enough for you to be here for him.* Whether I was there or not, his outcome was clear to me as an experienced physician; either he would pass away in the hospital or spend the rest of his life in a nursing home.

"After she spewed out her vitriol, Joanne must've felt she

had given me enough of a tongue-lashing, and the conversation shifted to when my other siblings would be there. Since I hadn't planned to stay overnight, I was hoping that I could talk to Mary Ellen and Bob face to face before I returned to Cincinnati. Back then, hospitals kept stricter visiting times than currently, so the three of us waited, watching the hands of the clock on the wall tick slowly to the top of the hour. I sat in the small room with them for about an hour, and as we talked—in truth I listened to them, mostly—it became clear that they weren't going to pay attention to my medical opinions. Hopefully, Mary Ellen and Bob would heed what I had to say.

"It was two p.m., the start time for visiting hours. I walked down the hallway, seemingly in slow motion, to my father's room. I was anxious, not knowing what I was going to say to him. He was in the bed near the door. The five-year-old boy who was scared of him was gone. Instead, I towered over the monster who had beaten me repeatedly and made my childhood a living hell. He had shrunk to a shell of his former self: old, frail, unable to talk or lift his right arm. He seemed surprised to see me as he tried to say something, but I couldn't make out the words. In my head I thought, *You son of a bitch. You deserve this, and I hope you burn in hell when you die,* but instead the words 'Hi, Dad. I'm sorry this has happened to you' came out of my mouth.

"Based on my experiences overseeing the care of patients with major strokes like my father had, managing expectations and being honest about the prognosis was challenging. I had seen family members of my patients bring in cards, flowers, and voice their unrealistic hopes that everything would be fine, as my sisters did. 'Dad, you're going to be fine. You'll be back fishing before you know it.' As I sat there listening to the two of them, I kept silent, shifting my gaze from my father to Joanne and then to Patricia. He was unable to communicate since his speech was so garbled, plus he couldn't write legibly with his left hand on a pad of paper in response to a question or a comment. My sisters were struggling to hold back their tears, seeing him in that state. I didn't doubt that they loved and cared for him; I just couldn't understand why. They both had fawned over him despite his long-standing mistreatment of my mother, Mary Ellen, and me. He had often spent his six-week summer vacations with Patricia, his clear favorite of the seven of us.

"My mind wandered away from the room and the chatter from my sisters. As I kept checking the clock on the wall, I was hoping that Bob and Mary Ellen would arrive soon so that I could talk to them about the stroke and help them understand my father's condition and prognosis. When the clock ticked off the minutes and then the hours, and they hadn't arrived, I was disappointed, since it was time for me to leave and start on the five-hour drive back to Cincinnati. It was more difficult to make that drive at night since there were long stretches of nothing but cornfields on both sides of I-71. Knowing that I was damned no matter what I said, I stood up and told my sisters and my father that I had to leave. My sisters reacted as I had expected. 'What? You're leaving? You haven't been here that long.' Wanting to be polite despite Joanne's attitude, I said, 'I'll try to reach Bob and Mary Ellen by phone before I get on the road. I'll check in tomorrow. Let me know if his condition changes.' Deciding whether my father should be given CPR wasn't a question to discuss with them without Mary Ellen or Bob present. Over my career, I had seen dozens of patients like my father get intubated and then placed on a ventilator and linger for weeks before getting transferred to a nursing home. Even though I could convey my thoughts to Bob and Mary Ellen, it wasn't clear who would make the decisions about my father's medical affairs. This was the late eighties, well before living wills and medical power-of-attorney documents became routine. Most likely, Joanne would step in and appoint herself as the main contact person, as she had done when my mother died in 1979.

"As I gathered my jacket, I knew this would most likely be the last time I would see my father alive, since I had already decided not to return to Steubenville until he died and there was a funeral to attend. The hatred I'd felt for him when I first entered the room had burned out. Only embers of deep sadness remained, and I actually pitied him at that moment. He was a stranger who helped give birth to me and had never really been a father to me. I don't recall whether I first gave my sisters a hug goodbye, but I did something that I never had done before—I kissed my father on his right cheek and squeezed his hand as I said goodbye. I don't know where that gesture came from, but it was spontaneous and the right thing to do for me to move on in my life. I've always wondered what he was thinking about me at that moment as I left his room.

"On the way out, the nurse allowed me to use the phone, and I was able to reach both Mary Ellen and Bob. Since Mary Ellen had worked in the same hospital for nearly twenty years in various roles, she was familiar with patient care issues and what protocol to follow if a patient worsens. When I spoke to Bob, however, I picked up quickly from the tone in his voice that he was not himself. He was distant, anxious, and in denial about our father's poor condition. Talking face to face is always the preferred method when delivering important news to family members of hospitalized patients, but it's not always possible. It's always difficult to accept unwelcome news about a loved one, but more so when it's conveyed over the phone. In hindsight, talking to him on the phone wasn't the right way to have approached it. I should have taken the extra time to drive down to our family home in Polish Hill and speak to him over a cup of coffee. Talking to him as a brother rather than as a physician would've been a better approach. However, that type of wisdom and understanding were skills I had not yet mastered. I truly had little to give to others, including Bob, at that time, because coping with all the demons that had come back and were chasing me again took every ounce of energy in my body.

"As the weeks went by, my father dwindled away, and a feeding tube was placed into his stomach to provide some nutrition. Mary Ellen reported in our phone calls that he was getting weaker each day. Although familiar with these types of situations, she struggled from the stress and the emotions of my father's failing health while balancing working full-time in the same hospital, being married, cooking and cleaning at home, and caring for a two-year-old son. She sounded exhausted each time we talked.

"Beth asked me repeatedly through that six-week period whether I wanted to make the drive for a visit. Each time, I declined. There was no guilt about my decision not to visit my dying father. I was sorry that Mary Ellen and Bob had so much stress since they lived in town. Besides the issues from my past, my current family life was strained, and my career at the medical school was in jeopardy because a new dean had been hired, replacing the person who had recruited me.

"The few times that Bob picked up the phone when I called over those six weeks, I could tell he was struggling emotionally, although he always said that he was fine. His frustration with me about not being around surfaced with jabs thrown my way about how my nephew and niece had been more helpful explaining Dad's medical issues than I had been. Plus, he always mentioned that I had been wrong about Dad and how strong and brave he was and was still alive and fighting week after week. I listened to him and understood his feelings toward my father, but I never would have expected that those six weeks were the beginning of the end of my friendship with my brother Bob.

"My father eventually died from pneumonia as a complication of his stroke, lingering on for six weeks before he passed with my siblings present. They had agreed to a "do not resuscitate" status for him, as I had suggested at the onset. When Beth called with the news, I was in Houston preparing for a conference. In that period from his stroke to death, I never drove back to see him. Mary Ellen understood my reasons for staying away and never judged me, unlike my other siblings, nephews, and nieces.

"Beth and I adjusted our hectic schedules to attend the funeral. Whenever she and I traveled across Ohio for family visits, we stayed with my in-laws in Washington, Pennsylvania. It was only a thirty-minute drive from Washington to Steubenville through the West Virginia panhandle, an easy drive in the daytime but a treacherous road I avoided at nighttime or in the winter. We dropped the kids off and drove over to my family home, where everyone was gathered. I could feel the tension as Beth and I walked through the kitchen door and greeted the others. There were plates of cookies and other platters on the kitchen table, dropped off by a constant stream of neighbors. The coffee was freshly brewed, so I grabbed a cup and joined the others in the dining room.

"Bob wasn't there in the kitchen with the others. When I questioned where he was, no one knew, and I surmised from the conversation that he wasn't doing well emotionally. Besides reeling from my father's death, he was hurt and angry over an incident with Joanne and Stas, centering on donations from friends.

"Besides bringing over food to the family home, a Polish tradition when someone dies is the generosity of friends and relatives giving five or ten dollars to help cover funeral expenses. The funeral home provided a gift card that people could fill out—designating the money either for a mass in the deceased's name or for food—and enclose in a small envelope.

Usually, the envelopes were placed in a box in the viewing room and emptied out by the family at the end of the visitation period.

"These donations were mostly used to buy food and beer for guests staying at the home of the deceased in the afternoon and early evening between visitation hours at the funeral home. As Mary Ellen told the story, Bob took two or three of the envelopes to buy a couple of cases of beer from the store down the street since the supply at home was low. Joanne and Stas were upset by his actions and heatedly challenged him about taking the money, implying that he had dipped into the envelopes for himself. Their accusations were unwarranted and only made the situation worse among the three of them. Bob was hurt and angry over their words and pulled back from interacting with my siblings, as well as friends of the family. He spent much of the time in his room when others were around or left the house for hours, only to return once the house was empty. This resemblance to Tom's behavior concerned me greatly. Had Bob fallen into the darkness of mental illness also?

"When Bob showed up at the funeral home the first evening, it was well after visitation hours had started. The room with the casket was crowded and filled with flowers, and almost all the chairs in the outer room where guests signed the funeral guest book and gathered to talk were full. When he arrived, I was immediately taken aback by his appearance and manner, since I hadn't seen him for at least six months. His hair was shoulder-length, like he had worn it during his college years in the early seventies, and he was unshaven, with a scraggly beard. He had a wild and angry look in his eyes that reminded me of our brother Tom and generated a tinge of fear that he might harm me. *Oh my God! Is he psychotic?* I tried to calm down, telling myself, *Bob will never be like Tom. He's just struggling with his grief and anger toward Joanne and Stas.*

"The room was so crowded that he didn't see me at first.

Beth and I made our way over to him. It was obvious by the brief conversation we had that Bob was distant and didn't want to talk to me. He was struggling to keep his emotions controlled as he moved on to greet others. I talked to Mary Ellen after he stepped away, and she agreed that Bob had not been doing well. She advised me to just let him be and not push him."

Dr. Dan offered, "I'm deeply sorry to hear that your brother had to go through that on top of everything else. What happened next?"

"The events and drama of the following days and months unfolded like a nineteenth-century novel: the funeral, the absent mad son, exchange of words that could not be retracted, the lost will with accusations that it had been burned, with the youngest daughter battling to settle my father's affairs amid conflict, anger, greed, sibling rivalry, and estrangement. Tolstoy opened his novel *Anna Karenina* with one of literature's most famous expressions: 'All happy families are alike; each unhappy family is unhappy in its own way.' It couldn't have been more descriptive of my family.

"Before my father was even placed into the ground, squabbling among my siblings erupted, just as it had when our mother died. Because of the issues after she died, I had persuaded my father to get a will, to minimize the arguments that might arise when he passed. Beth's father was an attorney and agreed to draw up a will, so Bob, my father, and I met with him in Washington, Pennsylvania, where his office was located. After a week or so, he mailed my father two copies to keep in his records. My other siblings were told about it.

"After my father's death, Bob said that he couldn't find the copies of the will, and my father-in-law, who had drawn up the will, hadn't kept one either, which meant the estate, as small as it was, would have to go through probate court. There was no doubt in my mind that Bob had destroyed the copies to spite

Stas and Joanne over his long-standing grievances, worsened by the recent exchange over a few dollars. Plus, in the will, my father had designated Stas, the oldest son, to be the executor, which Bob didn't want. At this point, though, none of us wanted Stas in that role. Except for Patricia, none of us trusted Joanne either, so Mary Ellen became the de facto executor, reluctantly agreeing to take on the thankless position. Patricia and I lived out of town, so neither of us was a suitable choice.

"The arguments weren't about an estate worth millions of dollars. Likely, my father's house, possessions, and cash in the bank totaled twenty thousand dollars at most and was to be divided among six children.

"Stas was furious over Mary Ellen taking charge, since he swore that my dad designated him to be the executor, which in fact had been codified in the will, and he was incensed that the will was missing. 'I'm the oldest son. I should be executor. I don't give a shit that Bob destroyed the will.' His claim may have been true in the 1800s, but it was 1988, and his jockeying around was ignored since none of us trusted him. I pled ignorance of the matter, saying that I couldn't remember what was in the will. He wanted an early-1900s double-barrel flint-style shotgun my father owned, insisting that he had been promised this by Dad as well. Without a will, though, promises meant nothing. Word got back to Bob that Stas intended to retrieve the gun from the house on his own in a week. Well, Bob boarded up the windows while claiming that the two doors were booby-trapped with explosives to thwart any entry. His threats were taken seriously since he had been a demolition expert when he served in the Army Reserves. He truly had become the mad son in this outrageous family drama, increasing my concerns that Bob had crossed the line into mental illness.

"Although the major family drama centered on what to do with the house, there was conflict over everything. Bob had recently purchased a new TV for the family home, and everyone should have agreed that it belonged to him, but my two greedy siblings wanted it to be considered part of the estate.

"Of my siblings, Joanne and Stas wanted to sell the house, which would effectively kick Bob out unless he was willing to buy it himself, whereas Mary Ellen and I wanted to deed it fully over to Bob since he had been living there with my father for at least four years. I don't remember where my sister Patricia stood on these matters, but she had usually sided with Joanne in the past on family conflicts. The house wasn't worth much, since the neighborhood had deteriorated so much that homes were selling for a fraction of their value. Since my father had been unwilling to buy Tom a headstone after his death, I recommended the estate purchase one for his grave site that would be similar to the large one in place for my parents. Even this recommendation was balked at by my three oldest siblings.

"This back-and-forth among my family members went on for over a year. Mary Ellen was able, with great skill and near exhaustion, to get everyone to agree on dividing up the estate to put before the probate court. Bob got the house, with its barricaded windows and booby-trapped doors, and its possessions at no cost. A headstone for Tom's grave was purchased from the cash in the estate, and Stas got his shotgun. I recall that Mary Ellen had gathered a dozen tchotchkes that my father hadn't thrown away after my mother's death. But Bob was unwilling to let Joanne or Patricia in the house and wouldn't budge on this. The prized possession in the house that Joanne craved, our mother's mink stole, remained in the cedar chest where it had been stored for over thirty years. As for me, I didn't want anything from that wretched prison, since the horrible memories of my father and the house that stood so vividly in my mind were enough.

"The six of us would never get together again, sitting around a table at Christmas enjoying homemade Polish sausage and Joanne's Italian wedding soup. Connections had been permanently broken. To paraphrase a well-known quote regarding wars, which seemed to apply in my family's squabbles, 'There are no winners, but all are losers.'

"Although he cut off ties with others in the family, Bob maintained a relationship with Mary Ellen and her husband. He and I were no longer close as we had been. I don't think he ever forgave me for my decision not to drive back after my first visit to our father, and the heated words we exchanged on the morning of the funeral. I regret saying he needed to stop behaving like an immature teenager when he didn't show up at the funeral home for the closing of the casket and was not yet dressed as the funeral mass was to begin.

"Bob occasionally would show up at Mary Ellen's house when Beth and I and the children were in town to visit, but within a year after my father's death, we never saw him as he retreated further into the isolation of the boarded-up family home. Eventually, he was nowhere to be seen, either walking downtown or buying his cigars from the tobacco shop he frequented. Since he claimed the house was booby-trapped, no one felt safe breaking in to find more information about where he might have gone.

"I had lost another brother, the best friend I had and the godfather to my son. After we were estranged, I never forgot any of the good times I had with Bob. I prayed every day that I would be surprised by a message from him on our answering machine. 'Hey, Larry. How are you doing? I know it's been a long time, but can we talk? Give me a call back.' Even a decade later, I prayed to hear from him, even just a card. In the first few years of our estrangement, I sent him a card or a letter and enclosed a check or cash on his birthday or around the holidays. Two or three came back unopened, stamped in bright red letters, 'Return to Sender.' Once when a card was addressed to me with his name written in the upper left corner of the envelope, I got my hopes up, only for them to be dashed when I opened it. He had returned the check I sent, cut in half, writing 'I don't want any of your money,' signed Robert M. Mieczkowski. In some of the letters I sent to him, I had encouraged him to seek help from a counselor, which to my knowledge, he never did. At some of my most conflicted times, I questioned whether it would have been easier for me to move on if he had died rather than being stuck in limbo. Our estrangement was hard enough for me, but the bitterness and anger he had conveyed to me were difficult to bear, worsening my depression and contributing to my thoughts about suicide. I couldn't manage the pain of having lost him.

"I was always on edge whenever I asked Mary Ellen about him on a phone call. 'Have you heard anything from Bob?' Hearing the same answer month after month for a year and expecting it to be different was the very definition of insanity, so I eventually stopped asking her about him, expecting one day that someone would call and let us know that he had been found dead under some highway overpass.

"I've not had closure. Sometimes I felt like the parent whose child was kidnapped and never found, dead or alive. Ten years after he walked away, I am still heartbroken over his absence in my life."

This session was bringing back so much sadness from the past. Choking up once again, I looked away from Dr. Dan and did everything I could to stop the tears. I was suffocating and couldn't breathe, like I had felt in the past when I saw another unopened letter from him in the stack of mail marked "Return to Sender" or when he didn't pick up the phone when I called, letting the message go to the recording machine. "Leave a message." Beep. "Bob, please pick up. I need to talk to you. I can't do this. Please call me back. I love you, and I miss you."

When Bob pulled away, there was no one in my life who understood what I had experienced as a child. Mary Ellen had walled off the trauma from her childhood and had no interest in dredging up the past. My wife, like others I knew, grew up in a lovely home in a safe neighborhood with loving and caring parents, had enough food, and had never been physically or emotionally abused. She couldn't comprehend the depth of my pain like Bob did, even though I never knew for certain if he had gone through the same abuse Mary Ellen and I had endured. He never talked about his early years, even later in life.

Everything about my brother was swirling in my head, the good and the bad. The warm memories from the past mingled with the hurt and rejection I felt as an adult when he cancelled at the last minute meeting me for a drink after a workday or joining Beth and me for dinner when we were living in Pittsburgh. Pain and sadness came back and tumbled over me like a tidal wave of grief, causing another panic attack. My chest tightened and I couldn't breathe as the intensity of my emotions overwhelmed me.

No longer able to hold back the tears, I said, "I need to stop. This is too much."

We both looked at the clock. Sixty minutes had passed since I first sat down. I rose from my seat, grabbed a few tissues, and said, "I'll see you next week."

CHAPTER 25

A Strange New World

Cincinnati's summer days were always hazy, hot, and humid, more akin to weather in New Orleans than what I was used to growing up in eastern Ohio. On my drives to Dr. Dan's office, despite having air-conditioning, my shirt would always be drenched, making me miserable and upsetting the routine I had developed over the past months. Fortunately, I arrived early enough to sit in the cool waiting room and was able to get comfortable before starting the session. I had a lot on my mind that day to discuss.

Dr. Dan was on time as usual for my appointment, and as we sat in the room with the window air-conditioning unit blasting, we made small talk about the summer heat for a few minutes before he started the session. "How have you been?"

I replied, "Not so well. It's been a stressful week."

"What happened?"

I sighed, still struggling to find the right words to explain my feelings. "It's about my marriage."

My sessions with Dr. Dan had focused on unraveling the pieces of my past life. As painful as the process was, dealing with my emotions and how I reacted to the trauma, my parents, Tom, and other issues and events had oddly been easier than deciding what to do with my marriage.

Continuing, I said, "I've been unhappy for years and want a divorce, but I am scared to death of what might be on the other side of that decision."

There was this paradox I was living with. How could I get divorced without going through the painful process that would follow? Sitting there, I questioned whether I would be able to live alone for the first time in decades or deal with the sadness of not seeing my son every day. Could I cope with my daughter's reaction?

He asked, "Did something happen this week?"

"Yes. Beth and I got into a big argument the other day about how we were going to pay for my daughter's college expenses. I said that we would need to borrow more money to cover the costs, adding to our debt. We have always fought over money and how to make ends meet."

He asked, "Did pursuing a divorce come up?"

I replied, "Yes, I said that I've been considering a divorce for months and that our marriage was one of the core issues I was trying to work through in my counseling with you. I did say that I wasn't happy and had built up a lot of resentment and anger from the twenty years of being together."

Dr. Dan asked me, "How did she respond?"

I replied, "Well, since she usually kept her emotions and what she was thinking to herself, I couldn't tell you what she felt. There were no tears of sadness, if that's what you're asking, but she at least acknowledged the rift between us by asking if we could start over, which I didn't believe was possible given the differences between us."

Beth and I had a dozen arguments in the past where

separating and getting a divorce seemed the only way we could settle our differences. When these fights occurred, after two or three days of silence between us, she and I would make amends and continue on, but each time this happened the wounds went deeper as we pulled apart from each other even further. I hadn't envisioned such a contentious marriage when we exchanged vows in 1979.

Before we got married, I had an expectation that both of us would have financially secure careers, which allowed me to dream of easily affording a lovely family home and a small cabin on a lake in Michigan with a dock and a sailboat. However, my hopes were dashed by the reality of our lives, income, and jobs.

Dr. Dan asked, "How old were you when you got married?"

"I was young, only twenty-three years old when we married, and didn't understand at that age how important compatibility and communication were to a successful marriage. None of this was covered in the pre-marriage classes we were required to take before a Catholic wedding. I accepted that there would be issues between us since we were very different people. You know, the whole thing about opposites attract, but I was so wrong, and the differences did matter once we were married. We liked doing different things. She preferred antique shopping on a Saturday afternoon whereas I preferred watching college football on the TV. Having a nice wardrobe of clothes was much more important to her, in contrast to my more casual approach, owning one pair of jeans and being comfortable wearing the same shirt for a few days. We fought about money, her uncertain career paths, how to raise the children, and dozens of other issues.

"Financial problems that had begun soon after our marriage continued over the decades. I was frustrated that she wasn't carrying her full share of the financial responsibility, which made me resentful over time and became the source of almost monthly arguments about money. The pressure I felt was immense as I struggled to keep the bills paid."

Dr. Dan interrupted. "It sounds like you and Beth didn't communicate well about expectations and working together to solve your problems. Is that fair?"

I replied, "Yes, conflict was rarely resolved through talking and compromising. Besides not being able to work out our financial needs, there were several other issues that put distance between us. After we were married and Beth started working in a downtown law firm as a paralegal, it seemed that all she and her coworkers ever talked about was their boss, which just drove me crazy."

Because I was insecure and jealous, her grade-school focus on this attorney made me feel I wasn't good enough, leading me to believe she regretted marrying me. We also argued about her going to after-work gatherings on Friday evenings at a local bar that went on till nearly midnight. These parties with the attorneys, paralegals, and secretaries present without spouses were bewildering to me. The image of other men dancing with my wife, their arms around her waist, rattled me after she acknowledged dancing with a few of the attorneys.

I continued, "We muddled our way through medical school, my residency in Pittsburgh, and then returned to Cincinnati in 1985. Our relationship worsened from the stress after we had a second child and went through several other major changes. That's when Beth chose to enroll in law school, coinciding with my accepting a teaching position at the medical school in Dayton, Ohio, a sixty-mile drive from our home. Then, she decided on her own to have major elective surgery. Initially, I didn't know what to say or how to react. Why did she not involve me, her husband and a physician, in this? She kept it from me because she said that I wouldn't agree with her having the operation. By then, near our tenth wedding anniversary, we were on the path of becoming two people going through the motions of being partners."

Dr. Dan asked, "Were you angry?"

I replied, "No, I was more frustrated and hurt than angry, questioning in my mind who this person was in front of me. I still loved her and wanted her to be happy, so I supported her decision and took on as many extra duties around the house as I could handle."

He said, "You know that you don't have to confront your marriage problems now. You have a dozen other issues on your plate. As I've said before, it's OK to just float for a while instead of swimming upstream all the time." I remembered his words from previous sessions about being in a hurry to fix everything, but I didn't want to wait anymore on dealing with the unhappiness in my marriage.

I replied, "No, I don't want to put off the decision any longer. I need to deal with this now, acknowledging that my life will dramatically change."

Dr. Dan looked at me. "Ultimately, you're the only person who must decide whether the marriage can be salvaged. From what you've shared, it sounds like you don't think it can be."

I replied, "You're right. I don't."

During the following week, I was in agony yet was also sad over the decision, but I just couldn't muster the courage to sit down with Beth to tell her. Each morning, I said this would be the day. Our dinners eaten in silence came and went. I'd watch some TV and then would sleep in the same bed with her as I promised myself every night I'd talk to her the next day. Nervous and shaking inside one evening after dinner, I went upstairs to our bedroom and asked her to come down to the office as I wanted to talk to her. As we sat on opposite sides of the sofa, the words finally came out: "I want a divorce." There was no argument, no negotiating, just a few tears in her eyes as I trembled inside knowing that everything would change for all of us. As she stood up and went back upstairs, I still questioned whether I had made the right decision.

Over the next few months, whatever hesitation I had was replaced by a confidence that I had made the right decision. Beth and I separated in October 2001, when I moved out. As expected, it was painful for the entire family. My daughter was understandably hurt and angry, whereas my son, if he was troubled, did not share those feelings with me. My kids, however, weren't surprised by the decision to divorce, having seen their mother and me frequently argue over the years and grow distant from each other.

In addition to the emotional trauma from the separation, I found moving into an apartment as distressing as I had feared. No longer was I living in our lovely home on an acre of land, sleeping in a four-poster bed, eating family meals on a country white-pine dinner table, and having all the comforts of home. That part of my life was gone and replaced by a five-hundred-square-foot apartment with a foldable card table for eating meals, one recliner wing chair to sit on for watching TV, and an old twin bed that was my daughter's when she was young. Although Beth had offered, it was my decision not to divide up the family furniture; I didn't want to further disrupt life for my children, since I was the one who wanted the divorce.

The two-bedroom apartment was in a complex only a few miles from Wyoming, enabling me to easily see my son throughout the week on school nights and have him with me on weekends without having a major impact on his academic work, high school tennis and golf matches, or hanging out with his friends.

Beside the personal turmoil I was experiencing, just two months before my separation, there was the agony of the terrorist attacks in New York and Washington, DC. The world changed suddenly and dramatically. As I watched the collapse of the towers and people jumping to their deaths, my anxiety and fear of everything and everyone rose to an even higher level as my world had become more dangerous. It was a sobering realization that things I had taken for granted when flying to various sites across the country for lectures were now chaotic and unsettling. I no longer felt safe waiting to board a flight. Every passenger sitting near me in the gate waiting area or in a restaurant was a potential terrorist. Had the man with the beard snuck a bomb past the security check-in? The new security process in airports was clumsy and time-consuming, not surprising since it had been stitched together almost literally overnight. Since lines in the airport were long, it took hours to get through.

The security agents adopted the position that every passenger was a potential terrorist, requiring intense scrutiny of all passengers. It appeared that because I had a long surname that was difficult to spell and flew first class, I was often flagged by the thrown-together TSA check-in process for a body and luggage search. It was particularly frustrating since a faculty colleague from Cincinnati whose last name was Hendricks frequently flew on the same flight and sailed through the screening process. Being singled out for a personal search on almost every flight, I was always anxious approaching the check-in person and couldn't relax until I boarded the plane and heard the customary "Have a good flight."

My well-established schedule brought a semblance of order to my life, living alone in those early months, something I hadn't done since my first year in medical school. It was over twenty-two years prior, a generation of time. Waking up by myself in my quiet apartment and unfamiliar surroundings was strange. All the sounds and the physical landmarks of living in the family home were gone. I missed having my son around, even though he spent most of his time in the house on the computer or in his room. My daughter was in college, hundreds of miles away.

The evenings after work were especially difficult for me, more so as winter set in. For the first time in my life, the background noise of the television became a regular companion to dispel the quiet and loneliness of living by myself. Profound sadness would hit me when I turned out the lights and went to bed. My insomnia worsened, with trouble falling asleep, while the repeated awakenings in the early hours of the morning continued as before. As I lay there waiting for sleep to take me away from the reality of my life, I would quietly start crying, every night questioning how I could make it through the profound sadness of feeling alone to a place where I felt loved and was happy. The soulful music of Alison Krauss became a nighttime companion as several of her melodies echoed my internal pain and helped quiet the noise in my head, allowing me to fall into some sort of slumber.

I was alone, insecure, and vulnerable, often feeling that I had made a mistake in thinking that I could live on my own and start down a new path. After I moved out of the family home, thoughts of suicide became even more intrusive. There was an ongoing battle between a voice in my left ear telling me that I could make it, while a different voice in my right ear told me to just go ahead and end my suffering by killing myself. *Do it. All the pain will be over. But what about my children if I kill myself? Don't do it. You can make it through this.* This tug-of-war between thoughts of living versus ending my life was a daily battle. When would it stop?

As I eased into my new life, I wasn't looking for love when I reached out to a long-standing colleague two or three months after I started counseling. She and I had always had a good working relationship but didn't know each other at a personal level. When we talked, she admitted to being unhappy in her marriage as well. It was my desire that our relationship stay platonic, but mutual physical attraction and need for comfort led to sexual intimacy, and before I realized what had happened, I was involved. Our relationship didn't survive the combined turmoil of our lives and ended within six months when I admitted to myself that I wasn't ready to be involved with another person, causing a lot of damage to both of us.

Bewildering contradictory thoughts and desires accompanied every relationship. Feelings of desire might be quickly replaced by a sense of fear and dread if physical intimacy began. In these situations, I froze and found myself doing and saying nothing as a woman started to unbutton my shirt in an embrace. It was impossible to think clearly when that happened, almost like upcoming sex was rendering me speechless and unable to express myself. During a sexual encounter, my mind often drifted to places that were safe for me, such as walking through the woods, swimming in the ocean, or to a liaison from my happier times in college, anywhere but the present. Afterward, I felt ashamed, dirty, and disgusted with myself for not saying no to someone's advances. These feelings were confusing to me, since they had not happened in the years with my wife.

Compatibility in a relationship was not easy to assess quickly, as everyone puts on their best face when dating. Ultimately, I saw it as the most important aspect of deciding whether to continue going out with someone. If I had recognized how important it was or had been advised by my psychiatrist to do so, I could have avoided the anguish I created for myself and the women I dated. Dr. Dan's philosophy was that I needed to live my own life and deal with the bad decisions as well as the good ones. His views on these matters were often difficult to accept; there were times when I was dating that I desperately needed him to at least point me in the right direction to get out of the forest, since I was often lost and stumbling over the path on my own.

At times, I had no idea what I was doing, nor did I have control over what I was thinking or feeling. If a woman glanced my way for more than a second, I might misread it as an indication she was interested in me, while not recognizing that another person I'd met might be the better choice for me. As I moved forward in meeting others, I was embarrassed by my early dating behavior and wished that I had not been the tornado that caused so much damage in several women's lives.

In January 2003, Beth and I stood in front of the magistrate for the final divorce agreement. She was still wearing her wedding ring, while I had stopped wearing mine months before. It was a sad day for both of us. The marriage had not worked out the way we had hoped when we spoke the words "for better or worse, until death do us part." My emotions took me by surprise as I choked up and held back tears when the magistrate in his black robe looked up from the divorce agreement we had both already signed and asked me, as so many others had, whether I was sure this was what I wanted. When I said, "Yes, Your Honor, I'm sure," it ended twenty-three years of marriage, and we walked our separate ways to our cars. There were no hugs exchanged or handshakes, just goodbye and indications that we'd talk later.

Although there were a handful of conflicts between us, mostly in the first six months after the divorce, Beth and I for the most part were able to focus on the needs of the children, actually communicating more effectively and calmly than when we were married. She was flexible about my time with my son when I had to go out of town for a speaking engagement, which I greatly appreciated. We arranged for each of the children to have their own cars, and didn't argue over vacation time or holidays.

The termination of my relationship with Beth's parents, whom I loved and regarded with profound respect, added to the pain of the divorce. I missed seeing them, chatting about sports with my ex father-in-law or landscaping design options with Beth's mother. My former father-in-law and I had played tennis together, went to Pittsburgh Penguins hockey games, and formed a special bond early in our relationship when I helped guide his medical care after a misdiagnosis and a life-threatening illness.

Over the years, there were occasions when I spoke with my ex-mother-in-law on the phone or said hello face to face when I picked up the children from her house near Pittsburgh. However, Beth's father would pass me off quickly if he happened to answer the phone when I called on Christmas Day or Thanksgiving to speak to my children, and he stayed inside if I was picking up the kids from his house. I never saw him again, one of the few men in my life I loved and respected. Even though I had expected a reaction to the divorce, considering how strong our relationship had been and how much we cared for each other over the years, it was still very painful and hurtful to be cut off completely from them when both knew that I was under treatment for depression and trauma from my childhood.

Dr. Dan had made adjustments in my medications over my first eighteen months of counseling. The change to a higher dose of a different antidepressant had helped my depression considerably. My moods were better, with fewer thoughts of suicide. Although I still had nightmares waking me up around 2:30 a.m. on a regular basis, they were less gruesome and didn't linger over me like a dense fog throughout the day.

Since I was feeling better and not as afraid of leaving the safety of my apartment, I started connecting with women through an online dating site. Typically, after several email exchanges, we would talk on the phone as a next step before meeting, allowing each of us to judge if we had enough things in common to continue. If so, meeting for coffee or a glass of wine during happy hour was safe for me as I dipped my foot into the dating pond. Early on, I met a woman at a bar, where I ordered a glass of wine and she requested a vodka tonic and then another and within an hour was clearly intoxicated. The evening ended when I called a cab to take her home since she was so inebriated. With my father's history of alcohol abuse looming so large in my consciousness, I should have ignored her phone call the next day when she apologized for her behavior and asked if she could see me again. Although I was vulnerable and craving attention, I should have moved on, but I didn't. The next time I saw her she drank only tonic water with lemon, and we had an enjoyable time. However, her alcohol abuse couldn't be hidden, and after two dates we went our separate ways. Although I had made a poor decision initially, I was able to climb out of the hole on my own without Dr. Dan or anyone else having to throw me a rope. It was a big step for me.

As I dated, though, there was an ill-defined undercurrent that came out frequently in my dreams regarding relationships and sex. Instead of war images with decapitated bodies and blood everywhere in my nightmares, there were now scenes of me having sex with women in a public place and other scenarios that were horrifying and embarrassing. Despite these dreams being so disturbing, I had found them too disconcerting to share with Dr. Dan, but the most recent one was different.

As I approached my next session, my mood was heavy and I was in a dark place. It had been a difficult week at work and it was already dark at five o'clock, which I hated. It was early winter with overcast skies and a cold rain, making even the short walk from the coffee shop to Dr. Dan's office miserable. As I entered the waiting room and took off my winter coat, I was already dreading finally bringing up one of the disturbing sexually oriented dreams that I'd had earlier in the week.

When Dr. Dan walked down the steps and signaled that he was ready, I slogged up the stairs to his office, hung up my dripping wet overcoat on the rack, plopped myself into the chair, and sighed deeply as I took a long drink of my coffee to warm myself from the bitter cold outside.

Since it was obvious to him that something was different, he quietly asked, "Are you OK? You don't seem yourself today."

"I'm not. A very disturbing dream the other night rattled me to my core and sent me spiraling into a very dark place." I thought, *Finally. I've told him.*

He asked, "Do you want to talk about it?"

As I sat there, I struggled, trying to decide if I was able to open this box further, afraid of where it might lead.

Finally convinced that I couldn't put it off any longer, I said "Yes" and provided him with the details of the disgusting dream. Just saying the words aloud made my skin crawl. When I finished, I said, "Why would I have this type of dream? What does this mean? What is wrong with me?" There was no relief as I shared this with him, only shame.

Time seemed to stand still as he started to ask me the question, which echoed in my head. As he uttered the words, my brain heard them spoken in slow motion.

"Have you ever considered that you had been sexually abused by your father when you were a child?"

CHAPTER 26

Solving the Puzzle

Stunned by his question, I couldn't breathe, let alone respond. I felt like I had been pushed off the edge of a steep cliff and was free-falling to the rocks below. It's said that your life flashes before your eyes when facing death. Dozens of memories came to me in those few seconds, but the movie reel contained only the dreadful and traumatic events of my life.

Then I landed, back to reality, sitting in the chair. In an instant, I was crying and sobbing over the reality of the trauma that had just been unlocked. Somewhere deep in my brain the reality of my father sexually abusing me was hidden behind layers of protection. It had taken almost two years of counseling before I was able to open the door to this horrible abuse.

I still couldn't breathe amid my choking tears for what seemed to last for minutes, the way a baby holds its breath for an eternity before letting out a long wail. Finally, I was able to inhale a gulp of air, but the tears and crying continued. All the while, Dr. Dan sat there quietly, handing me tissue after tissue until I could talk in a halting manner, repeating, "Oh my God. Oh my God," while slightly rocking back and forth in my chair trying to grasp what was happening.

The puzzle pieces of my life now fit. The childhood dream of burying a body in the woods made sense, while the bizarre image of my dysmorphic arm and hand hovering over me as a child as I went to sleep was likely my father holding my mouth shut to silence me and threatening me harm if I told anyone. The images of being in the bathtub with my father, crying and yelling and someone coming to my rescue, had come from his abuse. How I was repulsed when my father made me rub his temples when he had a headache. It was now clear why I hated my father so much as a child that I hid when he was approaching the school while walking home from the beer joint. The disgust I felt from certain smells—body odor, beer, vodka, urine—were all linked to my father. It explained the intrusive thoughts of my father from my past when I was having sex as an adult. It all fit.

After calming down, I wasn't sure how to respond. Despite what had likely been obvious to Dr. Dan at the beginning of my counseling, I had never truly considered that sexual abuse by my father was at the root of so many of my issues. But I was confused about why the disturbing dream I'd had opened the door to the truth of my childhood.

I asked, "But why did this finally come out now?"

Dr. Dan replied, "The abuse occurred when you were young, and this secret was buried very deep in your mind. Your marriage and sexual relationship with Beth were safe enough for you to keep the abuse hidden. Now, since you're divorced, you're more exposed, more vulnerable, and these emotions have chipped away at the wall you had built up to protect yourself."

I had not been able to tell him about other memories, the disturbing dreams, the repulsion I felt being around my father, or, as an adult, having sex with intrusive childhood memories of my father floating in and out of my mind. Somewhere I finally found the courage to tell him more of the story.

I continued, "I have shared some of the memories and dreams from my childhood, but I haven't told you the entire story." There were images from my childhood that had always stuck with me.

"In this one, I'm likely four years old and sitting in the tub as it was filling with water, when my father walks toward me. He's naked and standing two feet away and my eyes are focused on his genitals, and then the scene ends, like the rest of the film had been edited out and discarded. There's no sound, just the video. No matter how often I have tried over the years to find the rest of the film in my head and splice it back, it wasn't there.

"Then, there was another bathroom scene, again when I was little, when someone—I don't know if it was my mother or one of my siblings—quickly lifted me out of the bathtub. I was naked and screaming but others were yelling at the same time. I was crying and cold. I'm then wrapped in a towel and quickly taken out of the bathroom. There was more commotion, then the memory ends. The rest of the film is gone again."

Dr. Dan paused for a second, then asked, "Do you remember any other similar episodes?"

"No. Just those two bathroom scenes. I don't remember ever taking a bath with my father again nor with any of my siblings. I do remember bathing alone and then hollering to my mother when I was finished, and she would come in to wash and rinse my hair. Although I sat there naked, with my privates covered by a washcloth, I never felt uncomfortable when she did that.

"Also, I didn't have any issues when I was ten years old and my cousin and I would take a shower together in his parents' bathroom when I stayed overnight in their house. Taking a shower after a high school practice or a game with dozens of other guys never bothered me. Yet, when I worked in the steel mill the summer after high school graduation, I was too nervous to wash off in the group shower with dozens of older men at the end of shift, even if I was covered in dirt, grease, and sweat. Although I wouldn't say the words aloud, the fear of being raped by one of the men was overwhelming. The same fear of being sexually abused by other inmates fed the fear about prisons and what would happen to me if I was ever placed in jail. Even driving past a prison, like the one on my drive to Portsmouth, triggered the same fear."

By this point in the session, I was no longer crying. I looked at the clock and saw that I didn't have enough time to discuss what was still on my mind.

It was difficult telling him about the intrusive images and memories I had of my father during sexual encounters with women and how confusing and disgusting they were. It might be the bath scene, my father's body odor, sleeping in the same bed with him as a child, or having to rub lotion on his back or his feet. Sometimes I felt squeamish when these images came back to me in the middle of an embrace or sexual intimacy. How could I have physical pleasure with a woman and emotional disgust at the same time? On numerous occasions when lying in bed with a girlfriend, I would drift away for a few seconds, traveling back to the past, prompting a question, "Where did you go?" Brought back to the present, I'd smile and say, "Nowhere. I'm fine," never being able to tell the truth of what was going on in my head at that moment.

Dr. Dan looked at the clock, indicating we were getting close to the end of the session. My mood had shifted. The shock and sadness were still there, but I started feeling angry and frustrated, with a touch of ire directed at Dr. Dan for failing to have considered this earlier in my counseling.

I asked him, "So, you must have suspected at times that I

had been sexually abused as a child. When did you start thinking that it was a possibility?"

He replied, "There were parts of your history that were
suggestive. Your early hatred for your father and wishing him
dead as an incredibly young child was consistent with something very traumatic, likely beyond physical abuse and neglect.
I became more suspicious when you related the experience
of this large hand hovering over your face while feeling that
someone might harm you or kill you. Those hallucinations
likely came from your father holding your mouth closed so
that you couldn't cry out while he likely threatened you with
harm if you spoke about his abuse."

I was angry when I asked, "If you suspected sexual abuse,
why didn't you bring it up earlier?"

He replied, "It's a complicated issue. Counselors in the field
may raise the possibility if a client presents mainly with sexual
abuse–related problems. In your situation, you had boxes of issues from your past, so one train hid the sound of another one
running along the tracks. It was your secret to let out in your
own time if you were able and wanted to approach the subject.
Survivors of child abuse often don't want to open the door to
that possibility. You weren't ready to discuss this until now."

His explanation made sense and eased my frustration and
anger. He was right. In our previous sessions, I couldn't talk
about the memories that I had just shared with him.

I asked, "So where do we go from here?"

"This is a big shock to you. It's going to take time for you to
process this. It won't be easy, I'm afraid."

As I left his office and walked down the stairs, I had never
felt so alone in the world. There wasn't a friend sitting in the
waiting room who would ask me how the session went, someone I could confide in, someone who would say that everything
would be OK. Just like in my childhood, I was on my own.

I don't remember sitting in my car crying like I had on

other occasions after a counseling session. Neither do I have any memory of driving back to my apartment, nor can I recall what went on that evening. But I did have an unopened bottle of wine, which I turned to, to ease my pain. I started drinking heavily in the evenings to drown out the noise in my head that wouldn't go away when I was alone. Although my friends at work had been supportive, I couldn't talk to them about being sexually abused. Even if a couple of the guys I knew hadn't walked away from me after my divorce with Beth, it's unlikely that I would've told them either. I was too ashamed and embarrassed, as if I should have been able to prevent the abuse from my father. I kept questioning, *Why, why me, why did all this happen to me?* Questions that never got an answer.

Was sexual abuse the one big question my brother Bob had wanted my father to answer when he moved back home? Had my old man sexually abused my three brothers, or my niece and nephews, or Mary Ellen? If he had abused only the males, it might help explain why all four of us had mental health problems. I remember the additional shock to the family when Stas revealed his own history of depression and anxiety not long after Tom was hospitalized, making me concerned that I would eventually develop some mental health disorder.

Before long, the remaining questions I had didn't matter. I wouldn't get answers to them since Tom was dead, I hadn't seen Bob in over ten years, and I had been estranged from my brother Stas for years.

Whatever progress I had made in previous counseling sessions was washed away by a torrent of new pain and hopelessness. I was drowning in the storm and had fallen back into a deep depression. Dr. Dan's words in the upcoming counseling sessions did little to ease my misery. He'd say repeatedly, "You were a little child. Try to think of how small you were at that age compared to your father, a grown man."

It didn't matter. My father had taken away my childhood

and affected my life in so many ways. As an adult, most of my close friends were women, since I didn't trust most men—now I knew why. The fear of being molested in the men's locker room at the city's pool caused me to scan the room quickly to see who was in there and if it was safe to change into my swimsuit. Sometimes, I even wore my swim trunks under my pants so that I wouldn't have to get naked.

The weeks and months following this horrendous revelation were a blur. I continued working in the office, seeing patients. My office staff may have noticed that I was sullen and more depressed, but it was the winter, always a depressing time of the year when living in the Midwest. The days were gloomy and gray, and the darkness of the night lasted forever. In the months afterward, I flew to multiple cities across the country to give lectures, stayed in pleasant hotels, and went out to dinner at great restaurants with my colleagues, where conversations were always superficial and wine flowed like a stream, but I don't remember any details of the trips.

During the local evening lectures, I trudged my way through presentations without the enthusiasm or passion that had been my hallmark. As I drove back to my apartment, I was often in a mental fog of depression and sadness, likely worsened by the depressive effects of drinking two or three glasses of wine in the two hours I was at the venue. Part of me hoped that I might fall asleep at the wheel and go off the road and be another traffic fatality. At home, a bottle of wine nightly became my solace as I tried to drown my sorrows with alcohol.

Although I don't recall the details of my life in the weeks after the session in which my world came crashing down, the overwhelming despair was ever-present. The revelation of sexual abuse as a child stacked another layer of PTSD on top of the pile of trauma Dr. Dan and I had already covered. Counseling sessions were no longer helpful in climbing out of the dark hole I had fallen back into. I better understood why victims of abuse might never want to open that part of their past; this was more painful than I would ever have imagined. In addition, the changes Dr. Dan made in my medication regimen did little to improve my feelings of hopelessness.

Staying alive for my children's sake was no longer the powerful deterrent it had been when I first considered suicide as the way to end my pain. Even though my sessions with Dr. Dan continued weekly as before, I had given up on being saved. I was hopeless, a battle-fatigued survivor of physical abuse, neglect, Tom's illness, the horrendous night when he wanted to do me harm, and my recent divorce. The scars and wounds from these battles had not fully healed when another bomb was dropped on me, draining the last ounce of strength I had left. I just couldn't take it anymore and wanted to lie there on the battlefield and die. Not seeing a path with counseling and medication, I felt suicide was the only way to end my pain.

In the past, although constant and troublesome, thoughts of how to end my life had been vague, with no real plan. Things were different now as I became methodical in developing a plan. My mind had transitioned from *should I do it* to how. I had to devise a means whereby my ex-wife would receive the life insurance payout, so it couldn't look like suicide, and it had to be as painless as possible, so crashing my car into a concrete column on the interstate wasn't an option. As a physician, I had access to samples of dozens of medications stored in locked cabinets and our refrigerator, as well as supplies of multiple drugs in our emergency crash cart for dealing with life-and-death situations in my office.

After hours one day when everyone had left, I walked a few feet from my office to the storage room. As I surveyed the medications, I hesitated, since taking the next action was the equivalent of purchasing a gun as a first step to ending my life in my apartment. After selecting the medications to take with me, I quickly wrapped them in a plastic bag, walked back to

my office, and then put the package in my well-worn briefcase. I turned off the lights in the office and walked to my car,
scared, nervous, and sad that my life had come to this point.

A week later, I was scheduled to give a lecture at a popular
steak house in Centerville, two miles south of Kettering. The
reception started at 6:30 p.m. with the lecture scheduled to
begin at 7:00 p.m. As the physicians and their staff registered
and started eating the shrimp cocktail hors d'oeuvres, I went
through my usual two glasses of wine and a third that I sipped
as I gave the lecture.

As I prepared to leave, everyone was having an enjoyable
time, laughing at jokes or talking about their children. The
pharmaceutical representatives were individuals I had worked
with for years, while my colleagues had attended my lectures
for decades and regularly referred their patients to me. As I
said my goodbyes, none of the people sitting around a table
suspected they would never see me again. How would they
react on hearing the news the next day that I had died in my
sleep? Would they care? The sadness of what was in front of
me that night brought me to tears as I left the restaurant and
drove fifty miles back to my apartment. Once inside, I looked
over the medications I had placed on my kitchen counter, so
out of place next to the coffeepot, the toaster, and a loaf of
bread. I wanted it to be over, no more agonizing over whether I
should or shouldn't do it.

I changed from my suit and tie into more casual clothes.
After pouring myself another large glass of wine, I sat down
on the sofa and started crying, thinking mostly about my
children and the effect my death would have on them. The
heaviness in my heart and the darkness in my mind worsened. I thought, *Is this going to be the night?* Alcohol would
help me cross the line of no return, so I drank the entire
bottle of wine in thirty minutes. It wasn't long before I was
drunk, crying and arguing both sides of what to do. *Should I*

call Dr. Dan? The room was spinning from the large amount of alcohol I had consumed, and I could barely move in my stuporous state. My sobbing became uncontrollable, accompanied by loud cries of hopelessness, much like I had reacted to the revelation of sexual abuse from my father. Even with all the wine I had drank, the dark dogs of death were still there, chasing me.

Suicidal thoughts propelled me down the track, like an out-of-control train gaining speed and approaching a dangerous curve. *What do I do? Is there anyone who can help me?* The alcohol and my state of mind had made me delirious and disoriented, like I had a temperature of 104 and prayed the fever would break. Except the fever wasn't breaking. Panicked, I couldn't decide what to do, as I went back and forth on taking the overdose or not. Who else was there to help me? There was only one person in my life that I could call who might understand my pain and desperation. That person was my sister Mary Ellen.

When I had informed her at the onset of my counseling that I was seeing a psychiatrist, she was supportive. We had talked every few months afterward, but I had not yet divulged the sexual abuse. I picked up the phone to call but hesitated to dial the number since I hated pulling her into this. Another brother on the edge.

Finally, I dialed her number. She answered the phone quickly. "Hello."

When I heard her voice, I didn't say anything, thinking, *Hang up. Don't do this to her. Don't involve her.* No words came out of my mouth as I waited, almost holding my breath. She said again, "Hello, this is Mary Ellen. Who is this?" I'm sure she heard me crying.

Between the sobs, I was able to finally say, "Mary Ellen, this is Larry." Hesitation, more sobs. "I'm not doing well."

Just hearing her voice brought comfort to me, but it also

triggered memories of the times when the two of us were whipped by our father or beaten by our mother with the wooden spoon.

The alarm and concern in her voice was intense when she asked, "Larry, what's wrong? You're scaring me. Are you OK? What's going on?"

Tears were running down my cheeks when I said, "I can't take it. I don't want to live anymore. Oh God! I'm so sorry to bring you into this." My words were slurred from the alcohol; the room was spinning as the debate raged in my head. *Why did I involve her? Shit. Don't do it. What about your kids? Just do it. Get it over with.*

She started to cry. "Oh my God. Please don't. Don't. It can't be that bad." She pleaded with me, "Please don't. It'll be all right." I wanted to believe her.

"It won't be OK. In my counseling, it became clear that I had been sexually abused when I was young. The past month has been horrible. This has to end. I just want the pain to be gone. It hurts so much." I was sobbing even louder and emotionally out of control.

Her tone changed as she asked, "Who did this to you? Was it one of the older boys in the neighborhood?" Two families from outside of Steubenville with teenage boys had moved into our neighborhood when I was seven or eight. Everyone stayed away from them when we were young because there were rumors that one of the teenagers had served time in a juvenile detention center for molesting a five-year-old boy.

It was difficult saying the words aloud, knowing that I would be letting out the dark secret from my childhood. "No, it wasn't one of the boys. It was Dad."

I could hear the shock in her reaction. She began crying harder as she said, "Oh God. I'm so sorry. I don't know what to say. I didn't know."

Between sobs, I asked her if he had ever molested her.

She replied, "No, he didn't. I don't know what to say. Please don't do this. I can't manage losing another brother. I can't lose you. I love you. Please don't do anything." Her pleas made their way through the noise in my head. Her tears were real.

She was now crying harder and grasping at a way to help me. "Please don't do anything. Please. Is there anyone you can call? Have you called your psychiatrist?"

I hadn't expected her emotional reaction. She was crying. She listened to me and believed me. She said she loved me, words that I had never heard from my parents and desperately needed to hear from someone. Her love for me pierced the darkness and was slowly bringing me back to reality. How would my children react to the news? Would my suicide scar them for life? Maybe they really did love me also but couldn't say it. My crying slowed as I said, "No, I haven't called him."

She asked, "Is there anyone that I can call for you? Do you want me to call Beth?"

"No, please don't call her. She doesn't care about me."

She said in a calmer voice, "I'm sure she does, and I'm sure both of your kids love you. Is there anyone else I can call to help you? Any of your friends from work who can drive down?" After a few seconds of hesitation, questioning whether I wanted to also bring her into this crisis, I gave her Anne's phone number, someone I had dated but had remained friends with after we broke up.

Mary Ellen pleaded with me, "Please don't do anything. I'll give her a call and see if she can drive down so you're not alone. Can you promise me that you won't do anything?"

I said, "I promise. I don't know what I would have done if you weren't home when I called. Thank you. I love you."

Both of us were still crying. She said, "I love you too. I'm glad you called me. I'll call Anne once I get off the phone and give you a call tomorrow evening to check on you. Is that OK?"

I had stopped crying by then and said, "Yes. I'll talk to you tomorrow. Thank you. Love you." As I hung up the phone, I realized my older sister had walked me away from the edge of the cliff. I was ready to jump and would have. Hearing her words and believing that she loved me and would miss me terribly ended the crisis.

After hanging up, I sat back on the sofa, contemplating what had just happened, moved by my sister's love and concern. With her help, the crisis had passed. I chose living over death.

CHAPTER 27

Moving Forward

After the phone call with Mary Ellen, I had been exhausted and had drifted off to sleep on the sofa when I was awakened from my slumber by a knock on the door. Dazed in my alcohol-induced state, I wondered who could be here so late, quickly realizing that it must be Anne. It was, and I let her in.

As I stood at the entrance to my apartment, she looked past me to where the empty bottle of wine was lying on the floor and the empty glass was tipped over on the coffee table.

I said, "Thank you for dropping everything and coming so quickly. I'm sorry to have brought you into this, but I'm glad Mary Ellen was able to reach you. I was in a terrible place. Come on in."

She laid her purse and a small overnight bag on the floor, gave me a hug, and asked, "Are you OK? Your sister was so scared and worried that I wouldn't get here in time. I'm so glad she called me."

Responding, I said, "I'm better but exhausted and

emotionally drained. Did Mary Ellen tell you what went on? And about my father?" Rehashing everything that had happened that evening would have to wait since I was too tired and too drunk to explain. She took a seat on the sofa while I sat on the chair opposite her.

"She did. You had told me about the issues from your childhood, but I never could have thought this was part of it."

I couldn't talk about the sexual abuse with her. It was too difficult and confusing in my head to let anyone else in on the deep dark secret that had affected my life and relationships, including the one with her. Fortunately, we were able to remain friendly after we broke up, but I needed to maintain the boundary between us.

I replied, "Neither did I. It was a terrible shock."

As she started to ask more questions about the abuse, I began to panic; I didn't want to talk anymore about my father. I couldn't, not yet. I said, "It's too difficult to talk about. I really am exhausted and need to sleep. Are you planning to stay overnight?" I had mixed feelings about this. I didn't want to be alone, but I was also vulnerable and didn't want to give her any signals that would rekindle a relationship.

To my relief, she said, "If it's OK with you, I'd like to stay. I can sleep out here on the sofa. But first, where are the medicines you planned to use?"

The abruptness of her question brought the reality of what I had considered doing in full focus as I sheepishly pointed to the package sitting on the kitchen counter. I had come close to ending my life. If Mary Ellen hadn't answered the phone, I wasn't sure what would've happened. Anne grabbed the package of medications and put it in her overnight bag to dispose of later. After I showed her where the linens were in the guest bathroom, I said good night.

In contrast to hundreds of other nights, I fell asleep in seconds and probably had the best eight hours of sleep in over a year. In the morning, I awoke with a pounding headache as I got dressed and took two ibuprofen along with my usual morning meds. The aroma of coffee brewing filled my small apartment as I opened my bedroom door and saw that Anne was dressed, the linens were folded on the sofa, and the coffee-pot was gurgling along. She had to leave early for an appointment back in Dayton and was waiting for me to wake up before departing.

She was a single mom with two young children and had asked her parents to cover for her overnight. Trying to put words to my gratitude, I said, "I can't thank you enough for dropping everything and driving down to help me. For the first time in months, I felt safe here and was able to sleep well because you stayed. You and Mary Ellen helped save my life. I will always be grateful to you." We both held back tears as I gave her a hug. "I'll call you in the next few days."

She asked, "Are you sure you'll be OK if I leave?"

At that moment, I wasn't sure how my life would move forward, but I didn't want her to worry. I said, "I'm OK, and I'm not going to try anything again."

Before she stepped out of the apartment, she asked, "Will you promise me that you'll call your psychiatrist and let him know what happened last night?"

I hadn't gotten that far in my mind, but she was right. I needed to talk to him. "Yes, I promise. I'll call him after having a cup of coffee." She smiled and said goodbye.

Locking the door after her, I walked into the kitchen to pour my morning mug of java, able to think more clearly about the events of the past twelve hours since I was sober. The crisis had ended, and I was alive. As I sat at my kitchen table, the world that morning felt different, as if a great weight had been lifted off my shoulders. The puzzle pieces of my life now fit together, and although the picture wasn't pretty, it was complete. In the days and weeks after, the support from Mary Ellen and

Anne helped me see that I did mean a lot to others and that my life was worth living.

Calling Dr. Dan's office after I finished my coffee, I left a message for him to call me back as soon as possible, since it was an emergency. When he called back within the hour, I was ashamed to tell him the events of the previous night. Although he sounded startled when I finished talking, there was no reprimand as I had feared. Rather, he said, "I'm glad you're all right. I can see you today at four o'clock. Will that work for you?"

Since it was a Friday with no patients scheduled, I told him I'd be there. Wanting to keep myself occupied, I drove up to Kettering to complete paperwork at my office and then drove back to Dr. Dan's office for the appointment.

Replaying the events of the previous evening time after time, I needed to get past the shame of wanting to end my life and the feeling that I was a failure, but I knew that wouldn't be easy. When I arrived in Mount Lookout and got another cup of coffee, I felt much better than earlier in the day. The sunny day and nice weather helped my mood. My headache was gone, and my thoughts were clearer. Repeatedly, I reminded myself that my father's sexual abuse wasn't my fault and there was nothing I could have done to stop him.

Dr. Dan had worked me into his busy schedule, so I had to wait a bit, which gave me time to reflect. Sitting there in the familiar waiting room drinking my coffee, I was more hopeful about getting better than I had been in weeks. In about five minutes, Dr. Dan came to the landing and said that he was ready.

Seated there across from one another, both of us waited for the other to start. I didn't know how to begin, avoiding his gaze and looking away, like I would when called to the principal's office in grade school. Dr. Dan finally asked, "How are you doing? Can we go over what happened?"

As I had been in my earliest sessions with him, I was nervous, and my mouth was dry. I took a sip of coffee.

I replied, "You remember how I have described my depression and thoughts of suicide as being chased by a pack of black dogs in the darkness of the night. They caught up to me last night. I just didn't have the strength to outrun them. I wanted the pain to go away."

He asked, "Did anything new happen since our last session? I know it's been difficult for you ever since your sexual abuse surfaced."

"No, nothing new happened. I had been working on a plan for some time." I told him what I had intended to do.

A light bulb seemingly went on in his head, and he then said, "So that's why you made casual references about these medications you have available in your office. You were throwing out hints in our previous sessions that you were developing a suicide plan. Is that true?"

Although relieved that he wasn't angry or frustrated with me, I was still guarded when I replied, "You're right. I was hoping that you'd figure out what I was thinking and say something, almost like I was hoping you'd figure it out and thwart my plan."

He replied, "You're exceptionally good at putting up a facade. I didn't catch the meaning of your references to medications, probably since you're a physician. So, why didn't you call me last night?"

I knew he would ask, but it was difficult to know why I hadn't. There were so many confusing feelings going through my head as I quickly downed the bottle of wine in my apartment. "I wanted the pain to end, and I didn't want you to intervene. Plus, I didn't want to disappoint you and feel even more like a failure. I know that sounds weird." I felt ashamed of my actions, knowing that I should have called him.

He said, "You're not a failure, and you don't disappoint

me. I've said this before. Counseling is not about me, it's all about you. I'm sorry for what happened yesterday, but I'm glad you reached out to your sister and she was able to be there for you."

As we talked more about the emotions that drove me to the edge of the cliff, I felt better about the conversation and knew he was correct. My patients would say the same thing to me about not wanting to disappoint me as I took care of them and their diabetes or heart disease.

I asked, "So where do I go from here?" This was all new to me, and I had no idea if he would recommend in-hospital treatment.

He replied, "Well, I can see that you're not in a crisis mode anymore and seem to be doing better, so I don't think you need to be hospitalized. I just recently adjusted your medications, so they still need time to kick in. You know that alcohol is a de- pressant and will only make you sadder. I'd like to see you cut back, but ideally you shouldn't be drinking at all with the med- icines you're taking." I knew he was right. I had never been a heavy drinker, even in college living in a frat house, so I didn't think it would be difficult to cut back.

He continued, "I'm sure you're aware of the no-suicide contract between a therapist and a patient. They have been shown to be effective. I don't believe we need to put some- thing in writing, but I'd like you to promise that you will call me if you find yourself going there in your head. Can you do that?"

In my own practice, I had used such an agreement several times after starting a depressed patient on an antidepressant medication while they were waiting for the first visit with a psychiatrist. I could do that for myself.

"I promise." I looked over at the clock. It was time to go, since my session was only for thirty minutes because he had added me on. We both stood up and shook hands on our agreement. Without thinking, I couldn't stop myself from say-ing, "I promise I won't disappoint you," quickly adding, "Sorry. It's a habit. I'll try not say that anymore."

I moved forward in my life, knowing that sexual abuse by my father helped explain why I had certain feelings and emo-tions. If intrusive thoughts came to me during sexual intimacy, I no longer was confused about their source. It was easier to push them back to the recesses of my mind so that pleasure from sex wasn't always followed by a sense of disgust.

Regarding my abusive father, I thought of ways to make him disappear from my mind by dehumanizing him. The first thing I did was to stop referring to him in conversations as my father, instead calling him Skinny, my mother's husband, or my sperm donor, remarks that elicited raised eyebrows from oth-ers and a need for a quick explanation from me. For a while, I saw myself as a victim, but over time I chose to wear the badge of being a survivor. Ongoing counseling with Dr. Dan helped immensely in that process, as did reading books on the subject by psychologists and multiple first-person accounts of adults who were sexually abused as children. As Dr. Dan had said repeatedly, the effect sexual abuse had on me was typical, but I did not want it to define me.

To my surprise, when I told my sisters Joanne and Patricia about the sexual abuse, Joanne genuinely seemed shocked that he had done this, assuring me that she didn't know about it. I believed her, since she was out of the home when the abuse started when I was around four years old. Patricia's response, on the other hand, was muted, not necessarily saying outright that I was lying but also not expressing outrage. She was still living in the house when I was little; in fact, I had been the ring bearer in her wedding when I was four or five years old. Was she the person in my dream who lifted me out of the bathtub when I was screaming while taking a bath with my father? Or did she suspect what was happening and just chose to say or do nothing? Or was she blameless, unaware of the actions of my sick father?

I kept the knowledge of my sexual abuse from my children for over a year, still holding on to a sense of shame and questioning what they would think of me. It had taken at least six months before I could talk about it to others as I tried to understand how the abuse had affected who I was and how I reacted to life. I doubted that my children would understand why my yelling at them was learned behavior from my childhood. As I discussed what to say to my kids at various times in my sessions, Dr. Dan had made the point that I should be relieved my children wouldn't fully understand, as only survivors of abuse or trauma can comprehend the pain carried throughout our respective lives.

Before talking to them, I spoke to Beth so she didn't hear it from my son or daughter, with no expectation on my part that this revelation might change her view of me and our past marriage. She responded with a sympathetic ear, expressing regret that this had happened to me.

My daughter was in college and my son was still in high school when I told them about their grandfather's sexual abuse. On occasions in the past, I had mentioned repeated physical abuse from my parents, my father's alcohol problems, and lack of food. My dad had died when my children were young, and my daughter had only a vague memory of him and the family home. Both of them were nonjudgmental and supportive, but as Dr. Dan had prepared me for, my issues weren't priorities in their lives.

At that stage, my sessions transitioned from the traumatic effects of sexual and physical abuse, neglect, and fear that someone was going to kill me, to counseling about relationships with men and women. Lingering after a lecture and chatting with pharmaceutical reps was once again back in my life, enabling me to reconnect with other men in Dayton

I had hung around with. Another single male physician and I began to get together once a week after work for a whiskey or two at a local bar, "shooting the shit" as we used to say in the Steubenville and Pittsburgh area. Instead of golfing by myself, I began accepting invitations to join others for a round and lunch afterward.

Unfortunately, I was still making unhealthy decisions in my dating relationships when I met Tracey. I was scheduled to chair a weekend meeting in Chicago and was seated next to her on the flight from Cincinnati. She was outgoing, attractive, had an interesting job with a large international corporation, and traveled often on business trips. I was drinking a glass of wine and noticed she was drinking coffee. Seeing that I had glanced over at her beverage, she said, "I don't drink anymore since I joined AA ten years ago." Even though she had been sober for a decade, my instinctive reaction was to stay away from dating someone for whom alcohol had been a major problem in their life. Unfortunately, as before, I overrode the warning and carried on with our conversation as we chatted about our lives, sitting in the plane on the tarmac waiting for a thunderstorm to clear the area.

Before landing, we exchanged business cards, both agreeing to see how a long-distance relationship might turn out. Initially, dating went well and was free of drama. Over time, I discovered that her life was not as idyllic as she had described on the plane. In addition, her flirtatious behavior with other men was difficult to accept. Her need to be at the center of attention became readily apparent when we were at dinner one evening with a group of her friends. She dominated the conversation at the table by fawning over a close friend's new boyfriend the entire time, and then questioned why this woman was so upset with her the next day.

There were dozens of times when I couldn't reach Tracey for days, with her not returning my texts or phone calls and then acting like nothing had happened or, more commonly, criticizing me for being too possessive. I grew weary of this behavior, which had always been a deal-breaker for me, and had gone through three or four breakups when it happened. When she was unreachable, I had suspicions that she was involved with another man; why else would you turn your cell phone off for an entire evening?

Our relationship came to an end when I was awakened around midnight one evening by a phone call from her closest friend. My initial reaction in my groggy state was to ask what time it was and why she was calling me. She called to inform me that Tracey had resumed an affair with a married man with whom she had previously been involved. It had been going on for months. Although angry over Tracey's deceit, the truth confirmed my feelings that she was seeing someone behind my back, based on how often I couldn't reach her and how she frequently walked out of earshot when answering a phone call on the weekends. Besides feeling betrayed, I also was angry that I had allowed myself to be taken advantage of and ended the relationship, swearing to myself that I would listen to my gut feelings and not make the same mistake in ignoring red flags.

CHAPTER 28

Homecoming

With the end of that relationship, the daily drama went away, my life became calmer, and I was in a much better place. The private practice was going well. I continued to give lectures locally, while my national speaking engagements took me out of town two weekends a month. Working out almost daily in the complex's exercise room became part of my routine, enabling me to put on nearly thirty pounds of muscle while eventually being able to run a six-minute mile on the treadmill. I started golfing again, by myself or paired up with other men at the course adjacent to the apartments. Venturing out to the nearby mall for a cup of coffee and a muffin, a minor excursion I had been afraid to do, was now a way to break up the long Saturday afternoons I spent alone on my free weekends.

Late in the second year after my divorce, my financial picture had improved to the point of being able to purchase a two-story historic home in Lebanon, Ohio, a lovely small town halfway between Cincinnati and my office in Kettering. It was a short walk from my house to the small downtown area for pancakes in the morning at The Breakfast Club or drinks and dinner at The Golden Lamb, a two-hundred-year-old inn with a wonderful year-round traditional turkey dinner. My ex and I had taken the children there frequently over the years, allowing each of them to buy a small gift in the shop downstairs before driving back home, creating dozens of happy memories. By moving there, a crossroads village from the 1700s where Charles Dickens and seven presidents had stayed overnight, I saw myself fitting in like a country gentleman, living alone in a home that had a large yard with two fifty-year-old native Ohio apple trees, providing plenty of fruit to make my homemade pies.

The fear of living alone was gone, replaced by the confidence that my future would be fulfilling even if I remained unmarried. Although I resumed meeting women online, the connections went by the wayside after two or three dates as I began to understand the hallmarks of a healthy relationship more clearly. There was no hurry in finding the right partner. Whenever I was still dating someone after a month or so, I would discuss her with Dr. Dan, asking for his advice. "What do you think?" I wanted his perspective. Dr. Dan became my wingman of sorts as I went down the path of dating, learning more about myself and learning how to say no and communicate what I wanted. I also had to learn how to trust my instincts about women I met and whether they were being honest with me.

He always replied, "I'm not going to tell you exactly what to do. It's best if you figure these things out on your own." I got it but didn't want to make another big mistake in dating someone like I had just done. I would have appreciated his counsel. Even though he never gave any specific guidance on my dating, he remained my sounding board as I met others. It became easier for me to understand the women I met and not to be blinded by their attractiveness. Instead of lurching forward with my eyes closed and ignoring red flags, I was now able to see the potential obstacles after meeting someone, and discuss the issues with Dr. Dan. On my journey, I once connected with a woman I liked and looked forward to getting to know her better. After just a few dates, however, I surmised that she must have PTSD, based on the constant hypervigilance she demonstrated one evening. It was the summer of 2004, and we were sitting outside on a bench in Hyde Park Square, one of the safest places in Cincinnati, enjoying our ice cream cones. As we sat there, I noticed her constantly fidgeting on the bench, looking up and down the street. After ten minutes, I asked if she didn't feel safe sitting there and whether she wanted to leave. She initially hesitated to tell me but then shared her terrifying experience with a man who threatened her with a knife and how she escaped. After I told her about my own trauma from my brother Tom, we agreed it was best not to continue seeing each other.

Later that summer, I agreed to a blind date with a close friend of one of my patients. Although it was clear we had significant differences between us on politics and attitudes on a handful of other subjects, I agreed to have a dinner date over the weekend. Jumping into a sexual relationship was one of the red flags in dating someone, an issue I had spent hours of counseling on. Unfortunately, once again, my inability to say no to sex set the tone throughout our time together. There were other red flags, such as her rude treatment of her housekeeper, the obsession with purchasing clothes she didn't need such as having five assorted styles of red leather jackets, and the conflicted ties with her parents and siblings who lived in the immediate area. The drama was at times worse than what I had lived with.

After two months of dating, her need to be at the center of my attention came into a clear view when she was upset over my focus on my son after a high school play. It was ridiculous, and I broke it off with her. I was proud of myself for finally doing what was best for me and moved on quickly with no regrets. A month later, she called, asking if I would be willing to meet her for a drink, which I agreed to since I felt confident that I would not fall prey again to the person I had dated for those months. When we met, I saw a different woman, one who apologized for her childish behavior, was more attentive, and voiced a commitment to change. Since she seemed genuine, I agreed to resume dating, which led to an engagement in six months and a marriage six months later.

The earliest of the differences between us was where to live. She dreaded the idea of moving into my house in Lebanon, while I thought her small ranch home in Kettering wouldn't accommodate my children when they visited. As a compromise, we sold our respective properties and bought a larger home in a different part of Kettering that was close to work for both of us. Unfortunately, there was little to bind us together. As the months progressed, we argued almost daily over basic household issues like who would shop for groceries or prepare meals, finances, and my expectations of shared responsibilities in our marriage. The conflicts escalated, and we began talking about divorce within six months of our marriage. This time, I had not fallen but had jumped into a different deep hole in the sidewalk of my own accord. Fortunately, through the years of counseling, I had acquired the skills needed to climb out on my own.

In the fall of 2005, while still married, I received an unexpected phone call. Although I didn't recognize the number, I answered the call instead of letting it go to voicemail, as I usually did. "Hello."

The voice on the other end sounded familiar. "Larry, this is your brother Bob." He was alive! Barely able to breathe from the joy, I said excitingly, "Bob, oh my God, it's so good to hear your voice. Where are you? What's going on?" There were a hundred questions I wanted to ask. He sounded the same as when I last talked to him fifteen years prior.

He explained that he had been committed to the state mental hospital in Weston, West Virginia, a month prior. The news didn't surprise me, and I was relieved that he was finally under a doctor's care, even if it had been forced on him through a court order. From my experience in talking to Bob after my father's death, I knew not to pester him with too many questions for fear he'd feel panicked and hang up.

I asked, "Where were you living when this happened? How did you end up getting committed to the hospital?" Images and memories of Tom's confinements in the Cambridge mental hospital floated by as we talked, and I hoped that Bob wasn't in the same type of place.

He replied, "I'd been homeless in Wheeling but was sleeping most nights in a Salvation Army shelter. I don't remember much of what happened from that day, since I was drunk, and I got into a fight at the Greyhound terminal. The police were called, and I fought back when they tried to handcuff me. I was then taken to Wheeling Hospital. Because of my behavior, the doctors thought I may have been high on PCP or meth, which I hadn't been using. They put me on a three-day hold in the psych unit, but then the hospital transferred me here."

Stumbling at first to find the words to continue, I was careful not to push him too much by throwing a barrage of questions his way. He had moved to Wheeling about three years prior when he heard the city was a good place to live if you were homeless. When I questioned him about why he didn't stay in the family home, he said that the house was in terrible condition since he had not been able to keep up the maintenance or pay for the utilities. He had lived in the family home, 815 Pekruhn Court, for years with candles providing light, burning logs in the living room fireplace for heat.

Without utilities, he had no running water, so I wondered how he lived with that and where he bathed. It was difficult to hear his response.

I asked, "If the house was in such bad condition, where did you live?" He was embarrassed when he admitted that he had been sleeping in an old broken-down minivan parked up the street, even in the winter. I felt so bad that his life had come to that point and that he had been unable to reach out to me, Mary Ellen, or one of our cousins for help.

I asked, "So, how did you actually get to Wheeling? It's a long way from home."

He replied, "I walked and hitchhiked thirty miles. I gathered some of my clothes and belongings in a trash bag and carried it with me, leaving everything else in the house. Most of my clothes smelled terrible anyways from the racoons that had gotten into the house. Once they made their way into the house from the hole in the roof, I started sleeping in the van."

I thought, *How did the house get a hole in the roof?* I couldn't imagine the house now being in such disrepair and being overrun by animals. Talking about the house triggered awful memories and how living there caused hundreds of nightmares that had ruined my sleep throughout my life. Needing to change the subject, I pivoted and asked, "Are you in the hospital for alcohol detox?" If so, that meant he would be discharged soon.

He admitted, "They're treating me for bipolar disorder. The docs here think I must have had a psychotic episode when I got into the fight, since I don't remember much of it. I must've hit one of them hard and broke his nose." I thought, *Just like Tom had kicked an attendant and broke his ribs.*

I wasn't surprised by Bob's diagnosis, since mental illness ran in the family, with Tom having schizophrenia, Stas with his depression and anxiety, a first cousin with bipolar disorder, and another first cousin who had been hospitalized for major depression in high school. It wasn't good news, of course, since Bob's mental health problems would be chronic and wouldn't go away, unlike if he had been on PCP or meth. He sounded surprisingly lucid and like himself from the days when he worked for the IRS. I asked, "How are you feeling? You sound great, like your old self."

He quickly replied in his usual cadence of speaking, "I'm feeling pretty good."

I asked, "What meds do they have you on?"

The medications he was taking were a standard treatment regimen for bipolar disease; the doctors had also placed him on treatment for high blood pressure and high cholesterol, similar to the regimen I was on.

After just talking to him for minutes, a sense of relief replaced my years-old dread of hearing that he was dead. The way he described the hospital, it sounded like he was in a good facility. I asked if it was all right for me to drive down to visit him in the hospital once I checked my calendar, thinking it was possible that I could make the trip the following Saturday. He said, "That'll be great. I haven't seen you for so long." I told him that I would talk to the nurse in his unit to discuss the details of a visit, knowing that each mental hospital had different protocols. Since Bob had mentioned that he had a roommate there, I figured he had been transferred out of an isolation unit to a general ward.

When I hung up, I was holding back tears. I couldn't believe that Bob was alive and that I had just spoken to him. After not hearing anything for years, I had thought he was gone forever. Hearing his voice was overwhelming, like he was Lazarus returning from the dead. The angst and sadness from the past disappeared and turned to joy and an eagerness to see him again.

After hanging up, I immediately called Mary Ellen to share the good news. Although she was excited and relieved to hear that he was alive, on medication and doing well, she was guarded in making any commitment to help, which was understandable. She still had deep unresolved emotional pain from dealing with both Bob and Tom and didn't want to get hurt again. I told her to expect a call from me once I returned home from the visit.

The week after talking to Bob, I had an appointment with Dr. Dan and was very excited to share the news about my brother. Our estrangement and the uncertainty whether he was dead or alive had weighed heavily on me over the fifteen years since I had last seen him and had consumed many hours of my counseling.

Sitting in the waiting room, I was anxious to share the great news about Bob, one of the few times that I had something happy to discuss, instead of bringing my usual litany of problems. Hope for the future, for both Bob and me, had returned. I questioned whether Bob's return would be a turning point in my therapy.

Sitting down in my chair in his office, I had a rare smile on my face. Dr. Dan read it easily, saying, "You seem to be in a good place. What's going on?"

Elated that I had this huge surprise to tell him, I blurted out quickly, "My brother Bob came back from the dead. Unexpectedly, he called me last week. He's been in the state mental hospital in Weston, West Virginia, for the past two weeks. I'll be driving down this weekend to visit him."

He was clearly surprised by the news and replied, "Really! Tell me what happened." I recapped the details of the conversation I had with Bob. Dr. Dan cautioned me about having high expectations about his treatment since he was in West Virginia. He explained that because of low reimbursement for services in the state's Medicaid program, continuity of care for patients with mental illness was affected by a constant turnover in counselors and doctors. Plus, the formulary, a list of medications available for patients in the state, was very restricted. It wasn't a surprise to hear, since Ohio's support for Medicaid patients in my practice was abysmal.

Finding a place for Bob to live was the highest priority of the next steps. I admitted to Dr. Dan that I was nervous taking on this role.

I added, "Over the past week, I've felt more positive than I have been for years, as it feels like a fifteen-year blanket of darkness has been lifted off me by just talking to Bob, one of the few people who loved me and supported me."

It would be a long five-hour drive from Kettering to Weston, located in the middle of West Virginia, near the Appalachian Mountains. I made a call to the hospital and spoke with the nurse manager of Bob's unit in the hospital and told her that I would be arriving early afternoon on Saturday. Sounding like a caring person over the phone, she was happy to hear that I was coming, as Bob had not had any visitors in the weeks since he had been there.

Starting out early in the morning with a large cup of coffee to sip along the way, I was happy and excited to see him, although a bit nervous. It had been a long time since I had any contact with him. What would we talk about? What would he look like? Had he gained weight? I was thirty-four years old when Bob cut off contact with me fifteen years prior. There were so many memories and so many things I wanted to tell him about my life and children. My daughter was twenty-one years old and in college. Bob was godfather to my son, who was eighteen and in his first year of university. Since they had been young children when he last saw them, I brought dozens of pictures of them spanning the years he had been absent from their lives.

The ride to the hospital went by quickly. It was a beautiful fall day with the trees along the drive beginning to display their fall colors. Approaching Weston's downtown, I slowed down to take in the quaintness of this mountain town. Driving farther down Main Street, I was startled to see an ominous, large, four-story stone building two blocks ahead on my right. When I saw a sign stating a hospital was up ahead, I was alarmed to think that Bob might be hospitalized there. Getting closer, I could see that it was unoccupied, with many of the windows boarded up and no lights on, and iron bars covering some of the windows. It was horrifying to see a facility looking like a scene out of a Stephen King novel. Glimpsing it brought back terrible memories of the Cambridge, Ohio, mental hospital and Tom's hospitalizations there. After my return home, I read that the Weston Lunatic Asylum was opened in 1864 and housed patients until the facility was closed in 1994 once the Sharpe Hospital, the new state mental health facility, opened. I couldn't imagine what it was like inside that prisonlike structure, shuddering at the thought that my brother Bob might have been sent there in the past.

As I drove through town, I was relieved to see a sign pointing the way to the new hospital. Winding up a steep hill to the parking lot, I saw that the complex resembled a sprawling new high school rather than a hospital for patients suffering from mental illness. Trees dotted the well-kept grounds of the facility, which had been built in the middle of a forest. Parking the car near the entrance, I was nervous as I walked in and registered as a guest and then took a seat in the empty waiting area.

It wasn't long before a nurse opened the locked doors and came out to greet me. I stood up as she said, "You must be Dr. Mieczkowski, Bob's brother. You two do look alike."

It had been so long since I had seen Bob that I had forgotten the comparison others made about us. When I married Beth, he was my best man, and when we walked out together at the front of the church, attendees said after the ceremony that they had mistaken Bob for me.

I replied, "Just call me Larry. I'm not too formal about being called a doctor. And yes, people often thought we looked alike. But I always said that I was the better-looking one."

Laughing a bit, she said, "Follow me. I'll take you to where Bob's waiting. He's always talked about you and is excited to see you."

The interaction with the nurse eased my nervousness. I noted the brightly painted walls with murals and scenes of the forest as I walked with her. Numbered corridors designating different patient care units came off the main walkway. There was another set of locked doors she opened with her security card. She said, "C'mon in. Bob's in this unit." The doors shut quickly behind us, and I saw a semicircle of patient rooms surrounding a main area bathed in sunlight, with lounge chairs and a TV mounted on the wall blaring with the sounds of a game show. There must've been a dozen men of all ages mingling about. Even though it had been fifteen years, I recognized Bob immediately. He was sitting in a chair watching TV, wearing his usual baseball cap. I chuckled to myself, knowing he was wearing it to hide his hair loss.

The nurse stopped, smiled, and said to me, "He's over there. Enjoy your visit." Then she walked away.

I was filled with happiness, relief that he was alive and well, but also sad that his life had put him in this place and that his dreams had turned into horrible nightmares. It broke my heart when he said that he had been homeless, in contrast to the comfortable bed I slept in at our house. There we were, only ten feet separating me from the brother I loved and hadn't seen for all those years. Savoring the moment before calling his name, I said, "Bob." He heard me, stood up, and walked toward me. As he got closer, I saw that he was sizing me up since I had physically changed over the years. My hair was thinner and showing signs of gray. I was heavier than when he had last seen me. Working out in the gym had paid off. I had put on nearly thirty pounds of muscle. With a big smile on his face, he said, "Hey," then paused. "When did you get so big?"

I laughed as I went to give him a hug and replied, "When did you get so old?" I lingered over the first embrace in decades from my former best friend and brother. Whatever nervousness I had felt was gone, replaced by the love I had for him and a sense of disbelief that this was really happening.

Since it was noisy in the main area, he suggested we sit outside, it being such a beautiful day with blue skies and a nip of fall in the air. He led me through unlocked doors to the bench area with a view of the forest in the distance and a high chain-link fence enclosing the unsecured area, but not topped with barbed wire like what was in place at the Cambridge mental hospital.

I sat across from him for a moment, just soaking in the reality of being together. When you haven't seen someone for fifteen years, it's hard to know how to start. There's so much that had happened in both of our lives since 1990. He wasn't wearing his glasses, which he had worn since he was kid. When I asked about them, he said they were broken in the fight with the police and he hadn't been able to get them replaced. He was clearly nervous as we talked, looking like he needed a smoke to calm his nerves. He had a pack of Swisher Sweets cigars folded in the sleeve of his T-shirt.

"Hey. It's OK if you want to smoke. It won't bother me." I could tell he was relieved, and he immediately lit one of his favorite mini-cigars and took a deep drag, which helped quickly once the nicotine took hold.

We talked about his life in Wheeling, his routine of eating meals at church pantries, spending his days in the public library or in the Greyhound bus terminal, and then waiting in line for hours to get a bed to sleep on in the Salvation Army shelter. By policy, he would have to leave in the morning and repeat the cycle every day, carrying his belongings with him in a black trash bag. He admitted to occasionally having to sleep under an overpass with other homeless men if the shelter filled up early. Inside, my heart was breaking as I took in the sad reality of his life.

I had cared for dozens of patients in my hospital work who were in similar circumstances as Bob, but it's vastly different when that homeless person is your brother. How had he gone from working at the Pentagon with a high security clearance and a generous salary to being homeless with no money? It was difficult not to think about him wearing a starched white shirt and tie under a Brooks Brothers suit as he went to work. Those days were long gone, and I doubted they would ever return. I had always questioned what had led to his mental breakdown. Was the stress of losing his business on top of my father's death the cause? Or had he also been sexually abused by our father?

As I filled him in on the details of my life over the prior decade, I minimized the successes in my career to not draw a comparison to his own business, shattered by the stock market crash in October 1987. He was interested in hearing about my children and was grateful that I had brought the pictures depicting their lives over the past decade. He couldn't believe how they had grown since he last saw them.

I had intended to tell him about my depression and the counseling with Dr. Dan, but I waited until he and I had a chance to catch up. I hadn't planned to say anything about the suicide attempt or the sexual abuse by our father. Although I wondered whether he had sexually abused Bob as well, I knew that I might never be able to ask him about it.

He was surprised to hear of my depression, seeing a psychiatrist, and taking multiple medications. He said, "Wow. I'm sorry to hear that. I just assumed you'd be living a great life. You know, being a doctor, being married with kids. So, what happened?" I couldn't tell him the entire story, so I focused on the trauma from the physical abuse, neglect, and issues with Tom.

The time flew by as we talked, trying to condense fifteen years of life into the time that had passed with us sitting outside on the bench. Although we could have continued, it was time to head back home, since I had a five-hour drive in front of me. After we walked back inside, he showed me his room, which was furnished more like a hotel than a hospital room. It had wooden nightstands, a reading chair, brightly painted walls bathed in the sunlight from a row of secure windows, and a standard door with no locks. It was reassuring that he was in such a comfortable environment. We went over to the nurses' station so that I could talk to the charge nurse and Bob's social worker. The most pressing matter was where he would be staying when he was discharged. The social worker said that the Wheeling Salvation Army shelter was willing to guarantee a place for Bob to stay after discharge until other arrangements could be made. I agreed to be next of kin for all notifications and needs, wanting to help him as much as I could, as he had done for me over the years.

I said my goodbyes and gave him a hug, telling him for the first time ever aloud that I loved him and would see him back in Wheeling when he was discharged. As I started the drive back to Kettering, I was happy and relieved to have seen him looking so well, since I really had no idea what to expect, based on my experiences with Tom in his schizophrenic state almost twenty years prior. Based on how Bob looked, and seeing the support systems that were in place, I hoped that he would be able to have a good life if he stayed on his medications and didn't stop them like Tom had repeatedly done. There was a list of people to call in Wheeling the next week to discuss what steps were required to get Bob long-term housing, get him on disability, apply for state Medicaid insurance, and other issues. I looked forward to seeing him when he would be discharged.

When I returned home, I called Mary Ellen and told her how the visit had gone and what steps would follow. I assured her that I was happy to take the lead on helping Bob, secretly hoping that she might be able to reconcile with him once he was in Wheeling and doing well. Since they hadn't helped Bob in the past when he lived by himself in the old family house, I didn't expect that Joanne and her husband, Ang, or my brother Stas would offer their help.

Over the ensuing months, I helped Bob make his way through the bureaucracy of trying to get on Social Security disability and state Medicaid for health insurance and to pursue more permanent housing in a federally subsidized Section 8 apartment. In the meantime, he had been helping the Salvation Army with various chores and projects and was thrilled when they rewarded him with his own room. Bob had always had an excellent work ethic, so I wasn't surprised by the news. This meant that he no longer had to leave the facility in the morning or worry about securing a place to sleep. He could make a cup of coffee for himself and watch TV in his room.

My brother was back. The medications he was taking had restored the chemical imbalance in his brain with few side effects. Bob was stable, compliant with taking his medicines, and seemed content.

I visited as frequently as I could, although I couldn't muster the strength to stay overnight in a local hotel. I was still struggling with nighttime fears when in a strange place that felt dangerous. So, I made the four-hour drive to Wheeling and back to Kettering the same day. When the weather was nice, we drove the short distance to Pittsburgh, visited places he hadn't seen since his younger years, and might have lunch at the Original Hotdog House located near Carnegie Mellon University or at other favorite food places in the strip district of Pittsburgh. On other visits, we simply took walks in Wheeling as we had done in Steubenville, stopping at a favorite coffee shop first, and then casually took a stroll to the new casino and racetrack, giving ourselves time to become reacquainted. He and I often spent time simply walking together like when we were kids, on our way to the baseball field, fishing in the river, or seeing a movie downtown.

Even though we were children at the time, he and I did the grocery shopping for the family at the A&P, over a mile away. We meandered our way through the aisles together—two children, six years apart—deciding on whether to buy a can of green beans or a can of corn all the while having to consider that we had a limited amount of money to spend and had to carry the groceries home, regardless of the weather. Picture two young boys grappling with four or five paper bags full of groceries, walking a mile home, then often having to listen to our mother criticize our choice of margarine, fruits, and vegetables. Although I joined him in complaining to our mother about always being the ones who had to grocery shop, I quietly enjoyed any time I could spend with Bob.

As he and I reconnected, I slowly felt better about myself and my own life. Bob had not stopped caring about me. The unmistakable love we had for each other hadn't been severed. I realized that I would never feel alone anymore, even if something happened to Bob. It was an epiphany in my healing process.

Except for a handful he had returned unopened, he acknowledged that he had read the letters and cards I had sent, not discarding them as I thought, and admitted to wishing that he had listened to my advice about seeing a counselor. Sharing his thoughts about the early years of our estrangement must have been difficult for him, and I was happy he felt comfortable talking about it. Both of us were hurting when we parted ways, but that pain had gone away once I saw him again. It was like the old days, walking alongside him.

On one of our longer walks, I mentioned the issues from

my childhood that were safe to discuss, the beatings and neglect from our parents, how I suffered the pain of a badly broken arm for over twenty-four hours because of fear of punishment, and my conflict with Tom, hoping that I might be able to approach the issue of our father and what he had done to me. Probably fifteen minutes into the conversation, I cautiously mentioned how Dad had really messed my head up, keeping it vague and open for interpretation. He interrupted me quickly, saying, "Larry, I don't want to talk about it," making it clear to me I had touched a nerve. I respected his need for privacy and didn't bring up the subject again.

CHAPTER 29

815 Pekruhn Court

A major obstacle in Bob's effort to get a low-income subsidized apartment was being the owner of the family home in Steubenville. Since the property was deeded under his name, he technically had a place to live, whether it was a livable habitat or not. I spoke with several different agencies about how to get it removed from his name and explained to Bob that I would have to drive up to Steubenville and confirm the condition of the house, and then the City of Steubenville would sign off on it being condemned and unsuitable for habitation. After this had been done, he would be free of having a financial asset under his name and could move forward on getting subsidized housing. Because Bob had warned us that he had set booby traps on the doors, I was apprehensive about going into the house and getting blown up. When I said as much to him, he reassured me that the threats were simply words; he just hadn't wanted anyone to bother him.

Opening the many boxes of trauma in my counseling sessions allowed me to exorcise the demons from my past, the physical abuse, neglect, verbal and emotional abuse, horrific nightmares, constant fear, Tom, sexual abuse, and so many other matters. The last dark place I had avoided for over fifteen years was now in front of me, the family home. Knowing that I would be alone in the belly of the beast, I wasn't sure that I could do it, and the prospect overwhelmed me with dread and anxiety.

At the start of my weekly session, Dr. Dan asked, "What's new about Bob?"

I replied, "He's doing well and staying on his medications. But to be eligible for a subsidized apartment unit, he can't have any property in his name, because they consider it as an asset and potential habitat, meaning that he won't quality for assistance, even though he has no income. Either the house gets sold or it's declared condemned and gets torn down. Wrestling with these issues has kept me awake at night."

He asked, "Have you been inside of the house in the past few years?"

"No, I haven't since my father died in 1988 but I have driven past it on occasion. The paint is peeling, there are slate shingles missing from the front of the roof, and the lower-floor windows are covered with plywood. If it's as bad as Bob says, no one will buy it. I know what I'd like to do with it." Memories of living there had been with me for weeks, invading my dreams on a nightly basis. There wasn't a single corner in the house where I was protected from my parents' anger or where I could hide and not hear them fighting and cursing each other with words and phrases that I'd had to listen to a thousand times.

Dr. Dan looked at me with concern on his face. "What would you like to do with it?"

"I'd like to burn the damn house down," I said angrily. "It would be easy to do, and no one would know how it happened.

I'd love to see it go up in flames and get rid of it forever, taking all the memories with it."

Dr. Dan saw and heard that I was seriously thinking about doing it. He voiced his concerns. "Look, you can't do that."

I interrupted him. "Why the hell not? Burning it to the ground renders the house clearly uninhabitable, and it would be taken off the city records."

He said again, "You can't do it, you shouldn't, and you know why. I understand your feelings and respect them. But you can cleanse the house of its sins by lighting candles and burning incense on the front porch."

I looked at him, somewhat dismayed that he really thought that lighting candles and burning incense could do away with the evil that permeated every two-by-four, the bedrooms, the bathtub, the kitchen where I was beaten with a wooden spoon hundreds of times, and every inch of the place. I didn't really want to argue this point with him anymore. "Well, the alternative to burning it down means that I would have to break into the house and take pictures demonstrating the poor condition it's in. I'm not sure I can do that, or whether I even want to go inside." My cousins and I had started dozens of bonfires in our teenage years next to the remnants of the pond in the woods. A little kerosene and half a dozen flammable hair spray canisters that would explode in sixty minutes, placed in three or four locations inside of the house, would do the trick. I'd have enough time to get out of the house before it erupted in flames.

Dr. Dan asked, "When are you planning to drive up to Steubenville?"

"This upcoming Saturday." Just three days away.

He said, "My final plea is to please not do it. Setting the house on fire is only going to pair a lifetime of horrible events with another horrible act. I don't think setting the house on fire will free you of your memories and pain."

Since it was at the end of our session, we both stood. I said,

"I've not made up my mind what to do, but I have time to think about it. I always appreciate your thoughts." Then I walked out of his room. Leaving the office, I realized this had been the only time in my years of counseling that he ever voiced a strong opinion on my actions or thoughts. My next appointment with him was a week away, if I didn't end up in jail in my hometown.

CHAPTER 30

The Final Act

Even though I had been seeing Dr. Dan for years and was on antidepressants and other medications to help me sleep, my nightmares continued unabated, centered around my father and the house with a frequency and intensity that withstood my best efforts to banish them from my dreams. Decades ago, I had naively thought that the deaths of my mother, father, and Tom would somehow eliminate the chaos in my head during the day and the torturous nightmares at night. Eventually, several years after his death, Tom no longer appeared in my dreams coming down the steps and entering the kitchen with a smirk on his face, telling me that he was still alive after I saw him and screamed out, "You're supposed to be dead!" Dreams involving my mother and her neglect continued, but they weren't as disturbing as those surrounding my father and the house.

He and the family home still remained the central figures in my dreams. How could I free myself of the nightmares and fear that continued to plague me? The rage and anger that I had carried with me since I was a child fed the desire to burn the house down, with little consideration of the consequences. Would tearing the house down with a bulldozer really be any different than burning it to the ground? Both would serve the same purpose in removing any physical remains of the evil that had taken place there and hopefully free me from the nightmares that still held me captive at night. The harsh reality of being caught in the act, arrested, and jailed for torching the house would only compound my problems and brought me to the sober acceptance that I would leave the destruction of the house to the city. I didn't need any more misery added to my life.

I let Mary Ellen and Joanne know that I was driving up and planned to break into the house through the back door with a crowbar and sledgehammer, hopeful there were mementos to salvage for them. For myself, I would be happy if I could find the three albums full of photos I took with my old Kodak Instamatic camera when I was twelve years old. Since there were no keys to unlock the front or back doors, Bob had said that he entered the house through the small cellar door, but it was padlocked from the outside and he had lost that key, too. Mary Ellen had offered to join me, but I declined her help since I didn't want her to see the condition the house was in and be upset with Bob. She let Joanne know, and we planned to meet up afterward at Mary Ellen's house in Mingo Junction.

Throughout my life, I have learned to avoid dangerous and scary places. Breaking into the house was the opposite of everything my instincts were screaming at me—*don't go.* Would my breaking into the house to salvage mementos of the past be a fool's errand? I hoped that I would be able to overcome my fears once I arrived, as I was a nervous wreck on the four-hour drive.

Once again, I was driving north on Route 7 with the Ohio River on my right, passing the rusted steel mills in Martins

Ferry, Tiltonsville, and Mingo Junction to find myself on the fringes of Steubenville. It was a beautiful, cloudless day, the kind that occurs a few times a month, when you could see five miles up the river. I got off the highway and drove up Washington Street to make my way to Polish Hill. The local Kroger store near our house was still open, but the other businesses in the strip mall were closed. The two houses where the teenagers lived who had harassed my father on his way to work were boarded up. As I drove past another street, there were at least half a dozen empty lots covered with weeds poking through the gravel where houses had once stood.

Turning onto Highland Avenue, I parked the car in the old church lot, also overgrown by weeds, and got my box of supplies out of the trunk. Our house was one of the few structures still standing on Pekruhn Court. The exterior paint had almost completely peeled off, the front window on the first floor looking out to the concrete porch was boarded up, the roof above the front porch was partially collapsed, and trash was strewn about the lot. The exterior of the house was much worse than I had imagined. Empty lots where houses had stood were all that remained of a hundred-year-old neighborhood where Polish American families once lived in well-kept houses with flower beds full of roses and where any available outdoor space was used for a vegetable garden. My grandfather's house across the street from ours had been torn down years ago. The Szydlowski's house, catty-corner to us, the place where I had found my mother watching TV with her friend after I woke up alone in our house as a six-year-old, was still standing and occupied.

There weren't any sounds of children playing in the streets; no food-delivery trucks parked in front of the local grocery store with their diesel motors running, spewing black exhaust. It was deserted. I didn't see a single person as I walked up to the house. All so different from when I was a kid.

The house next to ours on the right, where my childhood friend had lived, was intact and occupied, based on a dog chained in the front yard and a vegetable garden wilting in the hot sun. The two-story apartment building on the other side of our home needed a coat of paint but otherwise looked the same as it did fifteen years prior. Hearing music and TV sounds coming out of the upper-floor units brought back the frightful memory of running up the back stairs of the building where my sister Joanne lived and hiding after I flew through the windowpane of our front door over forty years ago. It seemed like it had happened yesterday.

I walked to the back of our house, past the boarded-up first-floor family and dining room windows. The wooden gutters were pulling away from the roof, letting rainwater running off the roof worm its way into the house.

Before I tried getting in through the back door, I looked over to our small backyard, where a lilac tree had once stood. In the spring each year, hundreds of pale lavender-colored blooms would open, filling the kitchen with fragrance when the wind blew. My father had tried to destroy it to spite my mother in one of his drunken rages. It had finally died, leaving a few dead branches emerging from the ground. My mother loved having the tree there, and I remembered how devastated she was when he used lighter fluid to burn it down.

As expected, the wooden storm door was locked. After three or four hard whacks with the sledgehammer, I realized that getting inside was going to be more difficult than expected. If the door hadn't been opened for years, it likely was sealed tightly shut, warped by the effects of the weather and the seasons.

I resumed the pounding, trying to create a split where I could then use the crowbar. It was a warm day, and I started sweating. The sound of pounding with the sledgehammer against an unyielding door reverberated around the neighborhood, likely drawing attention from neighbors. Within five minutes, a man living in the house behind ours walked up to the nearly torn down picket fence separating his property and ours. I had seen him approach out of the corner of my eye and had laid down the hammer. He asked in a non-threatening tone, "Hey, what's going on? What are you doing breaking into the house?"

I wasn't too nervous since I didn't look like a typical drug addict breaking into a home to steal the copper tubing and then selling it as scrap metal to support their habit. Walking to him, I explained who I was and why I was there. After, he relaxed and said, "So you're the doctor from Cincinnati. Bob frequently talked about you and was proud of what you had accomplished. How's he doing, and where is he? I haven't seen him for at least three years."

He and I chatted for another ten minutes about what had happened to my brother over the previous three or four years. As he was leaving, he said, "Tell him that Red said hi and hopes he's doing OK. Try to make sure you board it back up. I don't want any druggies stripping the house of the copper pipe."

It took two or three more swings of the sledgehammer to break the door handle and lock. When I used the crowbar to pry open the door a crack, a loud whoosh of humid, putrid-smelling air immediately whipped past my head, making me feel a bit nauseous. I got the storm door wide open and walked in.

It was dark in the house, so it took time for my eyes to adjust. I had forgotten that the house didn't get much direct sunlight since it sat in the shadows of the adjacent buildings, and I hadn't brought a flashlight. The foul smell was over-whelming, while the air made me cough as soon as I stepped in. From the kitchen, I could see the blue sky through a gaping hole in the ceiling all the way through Mary Ellen's bedroom floor and ceiling up to the roof. I couldn't help but sneer a bit, remembering my father's complaints about the roof and my uncle's poor workmanship. With the heat of the day, I felt like I was walking in a sauna. As I looked around in the kitchen, I remembered the hundreds of times as a child I was beaten by my mother with that wooden spoon.

Going from room to room on the first floor, I saw that few things could be salvaged. The furniture had been sitting there for years in the undisturbed humid air fed by rainwater pouring into the house. With the windows and doors shut, the house and its contents were rotting from the inside. Mold grows quickly in this type of humid environment, and it covered the carpet and the furniture on the first floor.

The quiet in the living room was the opposite of when, as a kid, the TV blasted the entire day and was deafening. My mother had died there on the sofa. It's where I had been forced to rub my father's temples when he had a headache as he lay there passed out on the floor. The living room sofa where I had sat as my aunt kept slapping my face to force the truth out of me was covered in black soot from the fireplace Bob had used for heat. The images of my running through the house and flying through the glass windowpane were vivid. I thought, *My God. How did I not get shredded by the broken glass?*

My photo albums were in a sideboard in the dining room, and although they had some water damage, the hundreds of photographs in them, most of which I had taken when I was a young teenager, preserved images of my young self. The dining room table that I had hidden under when my mother locked my father out was now covered with dust, weathered yellow newspapers, and other household debris.

I stepped onto the landing leading up to the second floor and paused, remembering the night after my college graduation nearly thirty years prior when I had stood there filled with fear as I saw Tom with his army shovel. There was only quiet now in the dark room where I had thought I would be killed by my psychotic brother.

The steps creaked like before when I walked up the stairs. I went down the hallway to look at the hole in the roof and the floor of the bedroom over the kitchen. It was hard to believe how such a nice bedroom could be destroyed by time and water. Staying in the doorway, I investigated the bathroom. Too many memories of the past came flooding back. I couldn't go in.

When I entered the boys' room where I had slept, I found boxes of Bob's business records in addition to almost a hundred limited-edition decorative plates he had purchased in the eighties for investment purposes. I was sure he would want them since most of the plates were in the original boxes and had never been opened. Opening the closet door, I saw it was packed tightly with Bob's starched button-up shirts still covered in dry-cleaning plastic, his Brooks Brothers suits, and multiple pairs of dress shoes. Bob and I had not talked about whether he wanted me to retrieve these items, so I decided that I would take a handful of clothing items with me and let him decide later.

My parents' bedroom was next. The bed was still in the middle of the room. It was brighter in this room than the others since the windows had not been boarded up, and the room faced west and was bathed in sunlight. The brightness of the space enabled me to push aside the horrible memories from the past and enter the room. The cedar chest was there and shut tightly, where I hoped to find mementos that had not been damaged by mold or water. Although my class photos and sport teams' group pictures were gone, there was a treasure trove of other articles. My mother's mink stole was there on the top and in pristine condition. Joanne would be thrilled. Dozens of homemade doilies and tablecloths from Poland were there in excellent condition, to be divided among us. Plus, my parents' wedding photos were in decent shape. Newspapers and food rations from the World War II years had been saved. Why my mother kept the coupons for gas, butter, sugar, and other items wasn't clear. Because they did preserve a slice of history my family had to contend with, I placed a dozen of them in an envelope along with other smaller mementos.

After loading my SUV with what I had collected, I went back into the house, wanting to head down into the cellar. Although as a child I feared being down there alone when I was washing my clothes, I hadn't remembered anything horrible happening to me. My father spent hours in the unused coal bin, which served as his workshop. He would sneak downstairs when we were occupied watching TV in the evenings to his work area to drink more of the vodka he had hidden. I was on edge walking over to the basement door. I opened it and stepped onto the landing. Jackets were still hanging on a rack covering the small space where I hid as a young boy and contemplated pushing my father down the steep stairs to land headfirst on the cold concrete cellar floor. Suddenly a chill came over me and I froze, standing rigid with fear, unable to take a step down the stairs. My heart was pounding, and a shiver spread like lightning through my entire body. I couldn't go into the cellar, and I didn't have to. Horrible things must've happened to me down there when I was a child, and I must've completely blocked them out, as many survivors of abuse do.

I was finished, having accomplished a feat I never thought I could do. Since the back door I had left ajar had swelled in the hour or so while I was inside, I was unable to pull it shut, so I nailed it closed instead, not just to keep people out but also to keep the evil inside that had damaged so many lives. Walking to my vehicle, emotionally and physically drained by the experience, I was proud that I had overcome my fears. Before pulling out of the parking lot, I took one last long look at 815

Pekruhn Court, my family's home since 1940, where all seven of us children had lived. It seemed incomprehensible that so much harm had come from living there. The house would only be a memory once it was torn down and not be a permanent reminder of my family's collective pain and suffering.

My thoughts were all over the place as I drove the short distance to my sister Mary Ellen's house, where she and Joanne were waiting. As I pulled up to the house, they came out before I even finished parking, clearly anxious to hear what I found and retrieved. Both asked almost at once, "How'd it go? What did you find?"

I had deliberated over what to say to them on the drive down. Choosing my words carefully, I said, "What Bob said about the condition of the house was accurate. It's not livable. It'll have to be torn down." I saw the look of shock on their faces.

"How can that be?"

When I described the large hole in the roof extending down through Mary Ellen's bedroom ceiling and floor, with water dripping into the kitchen, I saw that this was hard to digest. Like me, they had not been in the house for over a decade. I continued, "There was a lot of water damage to the furniture, the carpet, and just about everything on the first floor."

One of them said, "Even the TV and dining room furniture?"

I replied, "Yes. None of the furniture can be salvaged. I did make my way upstairs and found boxes of the plates Bob bought back then, most unopened." I gave each of them a plate from open boxes, expecting to give Bob the rest once he had a place where he could store things.

Joanne anxiously asked, "Was the cedar chest there? What did you find?"

Instead of answering, I popped the trunk open and lifted the box holding the contents of the cedar chest. The mink stole was on top. Joanne was thrilled and immediately draped it over her shoulders, saying how much she had loved the fur piece my father had bought for our mother on their twenty-fifth wedding anniversary. Then, I took out the tablecloths, lace doilies, and other items from Poland, which reminded us of our mother and grandmother. Mary Ellen and Joanne made their selections from the pile. I kept a couple of lace doilies, a decorative hand-stitched tablecloth for a side table, and the photographs.

Tired and anxious to get started on my drive back to Kettering, I said my goodbyes. They both thanked me for what I had done and acknowledged my bravery in breaking into the house. Bob's warnings of the house being booby-trapped had scared everyone away.

On returning home, I didn't waste any time in contacting the housing authorities of Steubenville and describing the condition of the property. When I spoke with the person overseeing the city's procedure for condemning homes and explained the circumstances, he was sympathetic and said that he would move the process along quickly. A few days after we talked, he called and gave me the news that the house was placed on the demolition list. However, he cautioned that it might be months before the house was actually torn down because of the backlog of over two hundred houses. Explaining the urgency to arrange housing for my brother Bob, I pleaded with him to move the demolition date up as soon as he could. He said that he would do whatever he could to help.

It was only a few days later when he called and left a message on my phone with the exact date when the house would be torn down. As I listened to the recording, I found myself wrestling with mixed emotions about the upcoming destruction of our family home. Despite hating the place and not having been in it for fifteen years, there was something about the finality of it all that made me sad. Why would I be grieving the loss of the family home when it had been the location of so much pain and suffering?

As the day for tearing down the house got closer, my feelings continued to baffle me. Since this was all new to me and I had not known anyone who'd lived through the experience of having their family home torn down, I needed to talk to Dr. Dan about it at my next visit and hoped he could help me sort out my feelings.

Once we sat down, he started the session like always. "How are you doing?" He even smiled when he said, "I see you're not in jail."

I chuckled as I responded, "No, I'm not. I came to accept that tearing the house down with a bulldozer would have the same effect as burning it to the ground, plus I didn't want to create any more problems for myself, as you had advised. I was able to break into the house and go through it and retrieve two or three boxes of items before it gets demolished."

"So, it really was in bad shape as Bob had said."

I replied, "Yes, but it was much worse than I had imagined. No one had been inside for nearly four years, and it felt like I was breaking into an ancient tomb that had been sealed shut for a millennium. It was rotting from the inside out, and almost everything on the first floor was covered in soot and mold. It was dark and so quiet inside. Going from room to room brought back all the horrible and terrifying things that happened to me. When I opened the door to the basement, I froze, unable to take one step down the stair as paralyzing fear spread through me like lightning."

He responded, "You've never mentioned the cellar before as a concern, right? Do you have any memories that this triggered?"

I shook my head. "No. It's a blank. I went into the basement to wash my own clothes when I was a kid and to hang up my wet clothes after sled riding. My father always snuck down to his work area to drink more of his vodka in the evenings. But nothing horrible that I could remember."

He said, "You should trust your reaction. It's likely things happened to you there as a child, scary enough that you froze and had a fight-or-flight response when you stepped on the landing. As you know, often individuals who are survivors of abuse don't remember any of the details of what happened to them. You were very brave in doing what you did."

"I had to. I needed closure on this so that I could move on. I was proud of myself, as I wasn't sure that I would have the courage to do it."

He said, "You should be. So, what's happening with the house itself? Will it be torn down?"

I again nodded. "Yes. The man in the housing office in Steubenville moved it along quickly, and the house is scheduled to be torn down next Thursday."

He said, "Wow. That was fast. How are you feeling about this? It may be hard for you to see it torn down. Were you planning to be there?"

"No," I said. "I have a busy schedule that day, and I can't afford to cancel all the appointments. I'm confused that I'm feeling sad about these final steps, like I am grieving the upcoming loss. I could understand feeling that way if it had been a warm, welcoming home, but it wasn't that. It was a place of hell for me."

He replied, "I don't think it's unusual for you to feel the way you do. I'm sure you had some good times in the house. You talked about the family get-togethers around the holidays and how much you enjoyed your cousins being in the house. It also sounded like you and your friends had fun playing baseball and hiking in the hills. This is not to minimize what you went through there, but it was your home, where you lived with Bob and Mary Ellen, both of whom loved you. It's OK to have mixed feelings." When he put it that way, it all made sense.

We moved on to other issues that were of concern. At the end of the session, we agreed that I would follow up with him in six weeks, sooner if I needed it.

When the day of the demolition came, I couldn't stop thinking about it as I was seeing patients. The sadness that had confused me was gone, replaced by an acceptance of what needed to happen. A week or so later, I received the formal paperwork certifying the house was gone. It was done.

The following spring, it had been over six months since the house was torn down. I was finally ready to visit the site, went alone, and parked in the same church lot. This time, as I got out of the car, there wasn't a dilapidated and abandoned two-story house standing in a line of occupied aging structures. After walking through the weed-covered parking lot, I stood on the narrow street in front of what had been our family home. The lot was narrower and smaller than I remembered, since in my mind's eye I still had the image of the old house looming over me as a kid. My family home was gone. All the debris—the rotting furniture, the kitchen counters, the cedar chest, and all physical reminders of the family home—had been carried away by dump trucks, to be buried in one of the city's landfills. The hole in the ground that was once our cellar was now filled with coarse gravel and dirt. Weeds and wild grasses were already emerging from the ground. I imagined that over time grasses and trees would cover the empty lot as nature reclaimed what had been hers for thousands of years before Polish immigrants built their homes in Polish Hill.

I was happy to see that nature had begun burying the sins of the past. As I looked around at the other empty lots, I saw they were also covered with grasses and a scattering of small locust and maple trees emerging out of the ground. Would the entire neighborhood be returned to the earth in fifty or a hundred years?

Standing on the empty lot, I said a few silent prayers and

blessed myself with the sign of the cross. I realized I was no longer that child praying for God to take me to heaven. Back then I always questioned why my prayers were never heard, but there was clearly a different path for me. I finally accepted that if my life had ended when I was young, thousands of lives would have been different, and not just whether my children would have existed. Children had been born to dozens of women in my practice who had miscarriage after miscarriage until I placed them on thyroid replacement that other doctors said wasn't needed. I had too many patients to count with extensive heart disease who had been told that they wouldn't live beyond a year but were still alive and doing well decades later because of my care. Plus, the privilege of lecturing on managing diabetes and other heart risk factors had reached thousands of doctors across the country, having a ripple effect for their patients.

I turned and walked away from where my home had once stood. I drove off, never to return. Life would move on.

Epilogue

Once I successfully dealt with the housing issues, Bob moved from the Salvation Army shelter into a comfortable studio apartment in one of the federally subsidized high-rise buildings in Wheeling. Conveniently located only a few blocks from the hospital and physician offices where he went for outpatient care, it was also in walking distance to a grocery store, the library, and the core business district. Since he only had a mattress on the floor to sleep on and a folding chair of his own, I purchased several furniture items from IKEA for his apartment. When he saw the cartons in the back of my van, he was surprised that a complete bed-frame set came packed in one box and was even more impressed that I had the drill and other tools needed for assembly. He good-naturedly teased me, asking, "When did you become so handy?"

Considering he had been out of touch with the rapidly changing world for years, everything was new to him. Cell phone technology was a revolutionary change in communication as I led him through the nuances of texting, like my son had done for me years prior. Computers and the internet were equally unfamiliar.

Life went well for both of us over the next six months.

We saw each other every two or three weeks and talked on the Sundays when I had not driven up to Wheeling. Then one Sunday, he didn't call, interrupting our well-established routine. When I tried to reach him later in the evening, he didn't pick up, and I was unable to leave a message since the voicemail was full. Typically, in the past, if he couldn't reach me at home, he would call the toll-free number at my office during the workweek. Not hearing from him was concerning, so I planned to drive to Wheeling on the upcoming weekend to check up on him. Then, on Friday I received a phone call from a nurse on the psych unit at Wheeling Hospital letting me know that Bob had been admitted through the emergency department. He had stopped his medications and was taken to the ER by the sheriff when his behavior became erratic in his apartment building. My heart went out to him, but I dreaded the thought of repeating the cycle of another brother going off his medications and repeating the chaos like Tom had for nearly a decade.

Driving up on the weekend to visit, I was more apprehensive than I had been for over a year. Wheeling Hospital's psych unit was decades old, dingy, and depressing. When I saw Bob, he had been back on his medications and wasn't psychotic or threatening like Tom had been. Instead, he was quite lucid and pleasant, behaving like he had been over the past year. He openly talked about why he had stopped the medications, saying that he had been feeling so well he thought that he didn't need them, a common occurrence in all fields of medicine but particularly a problem in treating patients with mental health disorders. Although he said he had learned his lesson, I was skeptical, having heard that before from Tom and hundreds of my patients throughout my career.

When I asked why he didn't answer my phone calls, he replied that having a cell phone in his unit proved to be more of a liability than a benefit because other residents pressured

Bob to let them use it, mostly for buying drugs. So he stopped using the phone. Since he didn't want to deal with these issues anymore, we agreed that he could reach me weekly on my toll-free office number from the public pay phone in his building. I gave my phone numbers to the nurse and social worker in case one of them needed to contact me. The nurse said that he would most likely be discharged within the next three days, so I expected to hear from him afterward.

None of that went as I had hoped. When I didn't hear from Bob the following week, I called the hospital unit and was told that he had been discharged. To my disappointment, he had reneged on our agreement that I would continue as his next of kin. As a result of his decision, the nurse was restricted from telling me how he was doing and who would be his contact person. Bob didn't return any of the calls I made to the building manager to check on him. After weeks of trying to reach him, I had no choice but to accept that he had once again cut me out of his life. Why had he done this? For years after Bob and I became estranged, I couldn't stop blaming myself for being partially responsible for the split. But I had done everything I could to support him once he called me from the state mental hospital in Weston. He was the one who chose to stop his medication, despite my insistence and his doctors' that he needed to take them for the rest of his life. On a deeper level, I believed that our reconnecting had brought back too many painful memories from his past, issues that he wanted to keep buried and hidden from me. I doubt that I'll ever get the answers to my questions.

Bob and I haven't talked since the day I saw him in the hospital eighteen years ago. His absence from my life is still hard, and I miss him very much, but it doesn't haunt me as it did before we reconnected. I'm grateful that I had the unexpected joy of my brother being back in my life for that year. There isn't a day when I don't think of him fondly. Two of my nephews are still in contact with him and report that he's doing well. He's living in a nice apartment, taking his medications, has enough food to eat, and hopefully is able to deal with whatever demons may still be chasing him.

Reconnecting with Bob back then and arranging for the family home to be torn down were pivotal events in my healing process, as was finally having the strength to sever ties with my sister Joanne. For most of my adult life, I dreaded picking up the phone and hearing "Hello, Larry, this is Joanne" as much as I hated hearing my father's voice when he would call on some Sundays to check in after my mother died. Although Joanne claimed not to have been aware of the sexual abuse, she was fully cognizant of the physical beatings and neglect I had suffered from my parents. I couldn't forgive her for standing on the sidelines and not trying to stop the abuse. As for Mary Ellen, she's happy in her own life, still married and now with a grandchild. Fortunately, she remembers very little of her childhood and the beatings and trauma we both experienced. We may see each other only once or twice a year, but my love and bond with my sister has only grown since the night she helped save my life.

Dr. Dan had said at the onset of my counseling that the pain and memories would never completely go away. He was accurate in this regard. However, a goal of the hundreds of hours spent in therapy was acquiring the skills needed to cope with my tortured childhood and the trauma that I had experienced and to move forward without the fear that had plagued me. Without the hard work and pain of the seven years of counseling, I would not have been able to connect with my current wife, Joey, (nickname for Joanne), in the summer of 2008. Nor would I have been healthy enough to marry her four years later and build a loving and peaceful life together.

Over twenty years have passed by since I first crossed the

threshold into counseling with Dr. Dan. Many of the sessions are as vivid as the days I shared my life with him in that room on the right. The hard work and dark places my therapy took me enabled me to break down the walls that I had put up to protect myself from real and perceived threats. Slowly over the years, I garnered the ability to accept what had happened to me, finally reaching a life without anger, resentment, or angst. Sure, there are triggers, even today, that bring back the past, such as Sundays at five o'clock, the day and time that my father always returned home from his fishing weekends. I'm a stronger man now, confident, and not seeing myself as a victim but as a person able to speak freely about the abuse and trauma in my life, a huge transition from the embarrassment and shame I kept inside for decades. I had not initially accepted how difficult and lengthy the process would be, despite Dr. Dan telling me it would take years.

I have frequently been asked, after telling someone about my childhood, whether I have forgiven my parents for what they did to me. There's not a black or white answer. Forgiveness is a complicated issue for me, especially since I was raised Catholic and had "Honor thy father and thy mother" beaten into me by the nuns. Some say that there can be no forgiveness unless the offending individuals offer words of repentance, which didn't happen. I learned, however, that the best way I could fully banish the anger toward them in my heart and make room for forgiveness was to follow the philosophy that "Living well is the best revenge." In that context, I have forgiven them.

I've always seen my story as one of survival, no less daunting than making it safely out of the harsh wilderness or coping with a cancer diagnosis and years of chemotherapy. I've learned much throughout my journey and hope that this narrative of my life will be a positive voice for others who are survivors of abuse, those who struggle with PTSD, or those who have friends or relatives with mental illness. There are lots of us out there, all trying to find our way through the dark memories of the past.

ACKNOWLEDGMENTS

To Joey, my loving and supportive wife, who listened to my whole story shortly after we met and accepts me for who I am, past and present. For her confidence that I had the ability to tell my story, and for being a sounding board in all aspects of putting my thoughts and emotions on paper, helping me to become a better writer. I couldn't have done this without her by my side. My heartfelt gratitude goes to my sister Mary Ellen, who has loved me unconditionally my entire life and has remained steadfast in her support for me—from those early years when she stood up to the older boys who bullied me to one of my darkest moments. To my brother Bob, whose love and support helped me to believe in myself and become the man I am. Bob, Mary Ellen, and I will always be comrades in arms. To my daughter, Alexandra, who has stood with me as we worked on our relationship over the years. Her support helped me to keep writing when I shared some of the difficult events in my life during our weekly phone calls. Also, major thanks to Joey's brother, Jeff Chrzczon. After reading several chapters and finding my story compelling, Jeff connected me with Kevin Anderson & Associates (KAA) in New York. I am grateful to David Cashion, my editor at KAA, for his critique, analysis, and encouragement. David's wit, sense of humor, and heartfelt comments were deeply appreciated. Thanks to Mark Weinstein for his guidance in navigating the development of the manuscript and support in connecting me to my publisher,

Girl Friday Productions (GFP). To the entire Girl Friday team, you're the best! From my early discussions with Karen Upson, sales director, I felt confident that my memoir was in the right hands. I would like to thank Adria Batt for her support in marketing and oversight of the website design. Much appreciated. Abi Pollokoff, by far you are the best project manager I have ever worked with in my career, bar none. I don't know how you kept all the plates spinning in the air, but I am grateful for your support and deep understanding of the difficult issues I brought to our discussions while helping me walk the path of creating a book out of words on a piece of paper. Thank you to Alyssa Brillinger and all the others working behind the scenes—I couldn't be happier with the finished products. To my two best guy friends, Joe D'Amico and Danny Ingersoll, for their support as I shared my story at numerous breakfasts and lunches over the years and for providing feedback at various stages of the book's development. Thanks to my high school teachers Eileen Mascio Krisak, Sister Martha Kunesh, and a few others along the way who challenged me to seek excellence in my academic work. To my stepdaughters Lauren, Emily, and Julia, for welcoming me into their lives over the past sixteen years. There are times, places, and people that alter the course of a person's life. The real Dr. Kirkendoll came into my life at the right time and place, helping me to climb out of that deep hole no matter how many times I slipped and fell back to the bottom. I will be eternally grateful he was the one who walked down those creaking stairs and welcomed me into his office, *The Room on the Right.*

ABOUT THE AUTHOR

LAWRENCE MIECZKOWSKI, MD, (Dr. Mitch) is an award-winning physician, speaker, and author. Growing up in the gritty rust belt town of Steubenville, Ohio, he made his way through many obstacles to become recognized for his academic and leadership skills, including being rewarded with a full scholarship to Carnegie Mellon University (CMU). Through high school and college, his life experiences were broadened through working weekends and holidays as a nurse's aide in the local hospital and working summers in a steel mill or as an iron worker in a chemical plant.

After graduating from CMU in 1978, he completed medical school at the University of Cincinnati before pursuing an internal medicine residency and additional research in heart disease prevention. Since 1988, when he was selected by the National Institutes of Health for a leadership role educating other physicians, Dr. Mitch became a sought-after speaker on a variety of medical topics in the US, Canada, Kuwait, United Arab Emirates, and other lower Gulf nations. He is the author or coauthor of numerous scientific articles and op-eds, including a viral *HuffPost* piece that recounted his own near-death experience in the healthcare system. He lives with his wife in Ohio.

www.ingramcontent.com/pod-product-compliance
Lightning Source LLC
Chambersburg PA
CBHW030407130626
46549CB00004B/1666